Of Men and Manners: The Englishman and His World

Of Men and Manners:
The Englishman
and His
World

Essays compiled by Katherine Feldberg

UNIVERSITY OF MIAMI PRESS
Coral Gables, Florida

Originally published as *Wie der Engländer sich und die Welt sieht*
1965 Nymphenburger Verlagshandlung GmbH., Munich

This edition Copyright © 1970 by
University of Miami Press

Library of Congress Catalog Card Number 73-81619

ISBN 0-87024-122-2

Designed by Mary Lipson

Manufactured in the United States of America

Contents

ix Preface
xiii Acknowledgments
Harold Nicolson xv On Writing an Essay

England and the English

Dorothy Sayers 3 The Gulf Stream and the Channel
A. L. Rowse 11 The Rhythm of English History
John Alfred Spender 17 On Liberty
G. K. Chesterton 22 Paying for Patriotism
Hilaire Belloc 24 Fortitude
Gerald Gould 27 Refuge from Nightmare
Graham Greene 30 At Home
George Sampson 34 Humane Education
Charles Prestwich Scott 36 Newspaper Ideals

From Moses to Churchill

Winston Churchill 43 Moses, the Leader of a People
Eden Phillpotts 53 Confucius
Leonard Woolf 56 A Civilised Man
G. M. Trevelyan 59 John Woolman, the Quaker
Lytton Strachey 65 A Sidelight on Frederick the Great
Anonymous 70 Terror and Virtue
G. P. Gooch 72 Bismarck's Legacy
Richard Church 77 Winston S. Churchill

Literature and Art

Graham Greene 81 The Lost Childhood
T. S. Eliot 86 Hamlet
Hilaire Belloc 91 King Lear
Robert Lynd 94 Robinson Crusoe
Virginia Woolf 98 The Novels of Turgenev
D. H. Lawrence 105 The Grand Inquisitor
John Lehmann 114 The Life of the Prodigal Son
Ford Madox Ford 126 The Apotheosis of John Galsworthy
Cyril Connolly 129 Thomas Mann
Edward Charles Sackville-West 134 The Legacy of Germany in Music and Literature
J. B. Priestley 140 Orchestras Tuning Up
Neville Cardus 141 Mozart, the Unparalleled
George Bernard Shaw 145 Beethoven's Centenary
Aldous Huxley 150 Popular Music
Neville Cardus 154 The Closed Mind
Peter Quennell 157 Epilogue, from *The Sign of the Fish*
Aldous Huxley 162 The Best Picture

Kaleidoscope

Charles Morgan 171 The Enduring Italy
D. H. Lawrence 175 Flowery Tuscany
E. M. Forster 184 The Solitary Place
Freya Stark 188 The Pagan Gown
John Galsworthy 193 Burning Leaves
Llewelyn Powys 195 The First Fall of Snow
Ronald Duncan 198 Three Peach Stones
Joseph Conrad 200 A Preface to *A Handbook of Cookery*, by Jessie Conrad
A. A. Milne 203 Love and Marriage
C. E. Montague 206 The Blessings of Adam
Alice Meynell 212 The Foot
W. Somerset Maugham 215 The Fragment
J. B. Priestley 218 Youth in Disguise
Rose Macaulay 222 Flower Shop in the Night

About the Authors

223

Preface

*What governs the Englishman is his inner
atmosphere, the weather in his soul.*

Santayana

This collection of modern English essays endeavours to introduce the American reader to a kind of literature which is typically English. Next to poetry, the essay has been and still is the most congenial form of literary expression for the English writer. The "voluntary restriction in space" which the essay form imposes offers a challenge congenial to his temperament. This in itself reveals much of the English character. The essay is in constant use in English schools, universities, and newspapers, and this has furthered the clear and pithy form of expression we often find in the every-day speech of English people.

Of the earlier "classical" English essays many anthologies have been published, but excellent essays are still being written to-day. Yet, widely scattered in books, journals, and newspapers, they are not always easily accessible to the non-British reader. The 49 essays in this volume were written during the last fifty years. One might question the "modernity" of some of these essays but for the purpose of this book it does not really matter whether an essay was written in 1930 or 1960 because England is not "modern" in the American or Continental sense; everything refers back to traditions, opinions, judgements, etc., which are buried in its history and the subconscious of its people.

The collection was made with the non-British reader in mind, and in fact first published in a German translation. The essays were chosen for what, to the editor, seemed characteristic English attitudes of mind. tolerance in public and private life, a gift for compromise, the attraction of anything expressive of personality and individuality and an inherent streak of non-conformity—attitudes that explain the sometimes puzzling British approaches to every-day life, to literature, to political problems, and to history—and are favourable to good essay writing. Englishmen view not only with tolerance and patience their own pecularities but apply the same yardstick to non-English personalities, though there are certain limits when tolerance and patience are replaced by unequivocal opposition.

Philological, historical, or political considerations had no influence on the selection; no essay was included merely because it might be "representative" for one or the other writer. The collection nevertheless contains many well known names—which goes to prove Belloc's contention that the work of a good writer reproduces "not only in its sentiment, but in its very rhythm, the stuff and colour of the nation".

The reader will perceive how preoccupied, also in this form of their literature, English writers are with nature. Dorothy Sayers attributes much of the erratic English temperament which sets the foreigner so many incomprehensible puzzles, to the weather and climate of this "skew-wiff" island, i.e., to the influences of Gulf Stream and Channel by which "everything that appears remarkable in the temperament of the British can be sensibly and satisfactorily accounted for". The almost lyrical, but never sentimental, descriptions of landscape in the essays by E. M. Forster and D. H. Lawrence would scarcely have been written if the authors could not have counted on interested and appreciative English readers. Hilaire Belloc characterises King Lear as the best example to represent England to "an alien intelligence" not because of the problems with which the play is concerned but because "King Lear has something about him which seems the product of English landscape and English weather". Much of what is enduring in English writing and poetry is owed to this awareness and preoccupation with nature in all her manifestations in and around the island. And J. B. Priestley has expressed this interaction of landscape and art to perfection:

> Our fields and woods and hills are more often than not covered
> with mists so light that they are nothing but a haze, in which hard

edges are rubbed away and colours are softened and blended; the fields will suddenly be silvered, the woods will be full of golden smoke, the hills will take on the bloom of ripe damsons, and the sky will be a wash of delicate colouring as if some water-colourist were for ever at work there; and this is the sensitive, the misty-eyed and faintly flushing face of England that is at once the despair and the delight of her artists. The English mind is like this landscape of hers. There, too, is a haze, rubbing away the hard edges of ideas, softening and blending the hues of passion. . . . Let the sunlight disappear, and everything is grey and very soon seems heavy and sodden. Let the mist be completely banished and the land lie naked and quivering in the sunlight, and there is an end to this enchantment. This, then, is the English mind, where mirth and melancholy play like light and shadow, sunshine and mist; a mind that, once robbed of its bloom and golden haze, is utterly without charm, giving us the leaden-eyed Englishman of the satirists. Fortunately that bloom and that golden haze are there for ever in the long splendour of English literature [J. B. Priestley, "The English Character" from *Four in Hand,* W. Heinemann, London, 1934].

It is gratifying that University of Miami Press thinks this volume might be of interest to American readers. If the book, which has been a labour of love, should help to acquaint them with the spirit of this island it will have achieved what the editor set out to do.

K. F.

Acknowledgments

We are grateful to the following persons and publishers for permission to reprint copyright material in this volume: A. D. Peters & Co. Ltd., London, for "Fortitude" and "King Lear" by Hilaire Belloc; William Collins Sons & Co. Ltd., London, for "Mozart, the Unparalleled" by Neville Cardus; Sir Neville Cardus and *The Guardian* for "The Closed Mind" by Neville Cardus; A. P. Watt & Son, London, and Mr. Chesterton's Executrix for "Paying for Patriotism" by G. K. Chesterton; Laurence Pollinger Ltd., London, for "Winston S. Churchill" by Richard Church; The Hamlyn Group, Meltham, Middlesex, England, for "Moses, The Leader of a People" by Winston Churchill; Cyril Connolly for permission to reprint his essay "Thomas Mann"; J. M. Dent & Sons Ltd., London, for "Preface" to *A Handbook of Cookery* by Jessie Conrad; David Higham Associates Ltd., London, for "Three Peach Stones" by Donald Duncan; Harcourt, Brace & World, Inc., New York, for "Hamlet" by T. S. Eliot; David Higham Associates Ltd., London, for "The Apotheosis of John Galsworthy" by Ford Madox Ford; Random House, Inc., New York, for The Solitary Place" by E. M. Forster; The Society of Authors, London, for "Burning Leaves" by John Galsworthy; The Shoe String Press, Inc., Hamden, Connecticut, for "Bismarck's Legacy" by G. P. Gooch; Associated Book Publishers (International) Ltd., London, for "Refuge from Nightmare" by Gerald Gould; Viking Press, Inc., New York, for "The Lost Childhood" and "At Home" by Graham Greene; Harper & Row, Publishers, New York, for "Popular Music" and "The Best Picture" by Aldous Huxley; Viking Press, Inc., New York, for "Flowery Tuscany" and "The Grand

Inquisitor" by D. H. Lawrence; David Higham Associates Ltd., London, for "The Life of the Prodigal Son" by John Lehmann; J. M. Dent & Sons Ltd., London, for "Robinson Crusoe" by Robert Lynd; A. D. Peters & Co. Ltd., London, for "Flower Shop in the Night" by Rose Macaulay; Doubleday & Co., Inc., Garden City, N.Y., for "The Fragment" by W. Somerset Maugham; The Executors of Alice Meynell and Burns & Oates Ltd., London, for "The Foot" by Alice Meynell; Curtis Brown Ltd., London, for "Love and Marriage" by A. A. Milne; Mrs. Rose Elton and Chatto & Windus Ltd., London, for "The Blessings of Adam" by C. E. Montague; *The Spectator,* where this essay first appeared, for "The Enduring Italy" by Charles Morgan; *The Observer* Ltd., London, for "On Writing an Essay" by Harold Nicolson; Hutchinson Publishing Group Ltd., London, for "Confucius" by Eden Phillpotts; Laurence Pollinger Ltd., London, and Malcolm Elwin, Literary Executor to the Llewelyn Powys Estate, for "The First Fall of Snow"; A. D. Peters & Co. Ltd., London, for "Orchestras Tuning Up" and "Youth in Disguise" by J. B. Priestley; William Collins Sons & Co. Ltd., London, for "Epilogue" by Peter Quennell; Macmillan & Co. Ltd., London, for "The Rhythm of English History" by A. L. Rowse; Curtis Brown Ltd., London, for "The Legacy of Germany in Music and Literature" by Edward Charles Sackville-West; Cambridge University Press, London, for "Human Education" by George Sampson; A. Watkins, Inc., New York, for "The Gulf Stream and the Channel" by Dorothy Sayers; The Editor of *The Guardian,* London, for "Newspaper Ideals" and "Robespierre" by Charles Prestwich Scott; The Society of Authors, London, for "Beethoven's Centenary" by George Bernard Shaw; A. P. Watt & Son, London, and Mr. John C. Spender for "On Liberty" by John Alfred Spender; Beacon Press, Boston, for "The Pagan Gown" by Freya Stark; Mrs. A. S. Strachey and Harcourt, Brace & World, Inc., New York, for "A Sidelight on Frederick the Great" by Lytton Strachey; Longmans, Green & Co. Ltd., London, for "John Woolman, the Quaker" by G. M. Trevelyan; Mrs. I. M. Parsons and The Hogarth Press Ltd., London, for "A Civilised Man" by Leonard Woolf; and Harcourt, Brace & World, Inc., New York, for "The Novels of Turgenev" by Virginia Woolf.

Harold Nicolson

On Writing an Essay

The Observer, I hear, has set an essay competition on the theme of "eyes". It is hoped that many youths and maidens, many business men and naval officers, many opticians and oculists, will take part in this contest of sensibility and style. The theme is excellently chosen, since it allows the widest latitude for individual invention. It may not, however, be out of place to make some interim suggestions as to what an essay really is.

The nature of this coy branch of letters has been obscured by the perpetual misuse of its name. Montaigne first used the term *essai* to designate a literary experiment: Bacon, seventeen years later, adopted the word as a title for the compact condensations of his own commonplace books. Thereafter the term appears to have got completely out of hand.

Locke used it for his formidable treatise on human understanding: Dryden used it for his dialogue on English dramatic theory: Pope used it both for his didactic poem on criticism and for his four philosophic epistles addressed to Bolingbroke: Macaulay used it for his elaborate articles on literary, historical and political themes: Matthew Arnold used it for his eulogies of sweetness and light: and Mark Pattison and Jowett used it to expound, with some acerbity, the broad Church point of view. To apply this gay title to philosophical, didactic or polemical themes was as inappropriate as to tie a pink ribbon on a demolition bomb.

An essay is not intended by nature to expound a doctrine, to clinch an argument, or to convey information; it should avoid all direct discussion of current controversies or topical conditions, as it should eschew, as Bacon and Burton did not eschew, the too overt display of erudition. It should be equable, humane and placid, reflecting, in the pool of a given temperament, the surrounding landscape and figures, the lesser lights and shadows of the ways of men. Its purpose is to teach nothing, but to illumine much. Essentially it is a conversation, conducted by a writer with readers of different characters and experience: it should remain amicable, tentative, modest and companionable: good manners should be preserved.

The writer of a book or treatise is as a man embarking on a voyage. He arranges his affairs, he selects and packs his luggage, and thereafter follow months or years of effort, exhilaration and distress. The essayist is as a man taking a short stroll in his own garden; he should be in a eupeptic condition, appreciative of the sights and sounds around him, and anxious to communicate to others the pleasure that he feels.

He must return to his desk in a mood of leisurely and amused compassion. It is essential that he should, when he begins to write, have no idea at all what he intends to say: he should be as purposeless as a magnolia blossom, intent only on receiving *l'idee au vol pur:* he must strive to feel spontaneous. Nor should he, ever, for one instant, forget the apophthegm of Dr. Johnson that an essay is "a loose sally of the mind": he should cultivate the loose and dawdling mood.

I do not wish to suggest that an essay can be undertaken in a spurt of carelessness. There are many positive qualities that the essayist must possess. He will find that long and wide experience of men and manners is of advantage to him, and that it is useful to be familiar with at least one literature other than his own. He must possess urbanity, originality, humour, sympathy, curiosity, and a certain fastidiousness.

Above all, perhaps, he should remember that although the ideas and opinions he expresses may be allowed to vary, and even to conflict, his central mood, the reflection of his own temperament, must be consistent and even constant. He must communicate his own personality to the reader, and his tone therefore should be confiding without falsity, intimate without causing embarrassment.

Modesty should prohibit him from exposing his profounder thoughts and emotions; but his momentary impressions and sentiments should be displayed without false shame. His greatest temptation will be to communicate charm by indulging in self-dispraise or whimsicality: even the greatest of our essayists have tumbled down that stair. A residue of reticence and dignity must be retained.

The style adopted by an essayist must be personal to himself; it is a mistake to imitate the manner of Bacon or Cowley, of Chesterton or Beerbohm, of Leigh Hunt or Lamb. The form given to his essay should not be rigid, but should reflect his own floating mood. "I profess not method," wrote Sir William Cornwallis, one of the early pioneers, "neither will I chain myself to the head of my chapter."

Certainly an essay should possess shape and design; but its contours should be neither too deliberate nor too obvious. An essay, I repeat, should resemble an amicable conversation, carefully, but not too carefully, conducted and composed. The essayist, moreover, should care very much for words.

So now you all know how to write about eyes.

From *The Observer*, October 18, 1952.

England and the English

Dorothy Sayers

The Gulf Stream and the Channel

"When Britain first, at Heaven's command, / Arose from out the azure main . . ." her guardian angels did not content themselves with merely singing a strain or so to celebrate the occasion. They took practical measures—or at any rate they perpetrated two practical jokes—whereby they ensured that Britain and her inhabitants should remain a sort of standing practical joke to the end of time. Everybody—even the British themselves—must have noticed the effect produced by this country upon the more staid and serious peoples of the European continent— and, indeed, of any continent: it is precisely that mixture of startled recoil, affronted dignity, nervous irritation, reluctant amusement, and apprehension about what is going to happen next which characterises the person who has walked through a harmless-looking door and received a bucket of water on his head. There is something about the British which is felt to be unwelcoming, freakish, and irresponsible; they are solemn on the outside and frivolous at heart, and behind their most decorous appearances there lurks a schoolboy grin; they are not unsuccessful in statesmanship, trade, or warfare, yet about their politics, economics and military organisation there is always an air of improvisation, as though they did not take the future seriously; above all, you never know where to have them, they do not fit handily into any pigeon-hole, they display an almost morbid reluctance to be *gleichgeschaltet*—a thing offensive to any tidy mind. Of the three nations which make up Great Britain all share these characteristics to some extent, but the English are the worst.

When Neptune shouldered Britain out of the sea, he did not make a neat engineering job of it. Characteristically, Britain came up skew-whiff, with one edge thick and hard and the other soft and thin, like a slice of wedding cake. The guardian angels, observing that her more vulnerable side was precisely that which lay nearer to Europe and was consequently the more open to attack, did their best to square matters up. They arranged that the twenty-two miles separating the Kentish coast from the mainland should be filled with a stretch of water so disagreeable that, without very weighty reasons indeed, nobody in his senses would have any stomach for crossing it. So far, so good; a sensible, but dull precaution. If nobody even attempted to cross the Narrow Seas, where would be the fun? The island must be made desirable—then indeed the joke of making it so near yet so inaccessible would acquire a rich flavour. With coal and iron it was already well stocked; but make it also fertile, and there it would hang, a veritable fruit of Tantalus, bobbing at the mouth of hungry adventurers. The latitude in which the place stood was unfavourable; but the resources of celestial plumbing were not exhausted. The guardian angels, with a chuckle, turned on the hot-water tap off the distant shores of Panama and released the Gulf Stream into the English Channel. By those two geographical jokes—the Gulf Stream and the Channel—everything that appears remarkable in the temperament and history of the British can be sensibly and satisfactorily accounted for.

The effect of the Channel, first and foremost, is to make it difficult and unpleasant to get into this country, and equally difficult and unpleasant to get out. Consequently, Britain has never been a pleasure resort. The only people who cross the Channel in large numbers for pleasure are the British themselves, who, having no other road by which to go anywhere, have in desperation hardened themselves to the idea, and have even come to take a perverse pride and pleasure in the asperities of the Dover-Calais passage. In Tudor times, sturdy Englishmen were actually known to undertake the ordeal as a medicinal measure 'to scour the stomach', as prudent persons will from time to time take a treatment or a course of liver pills. But foreigners have never taken kindly to the idea of rattling backwards and forwards across the Narrow Seas for the sake of the trip. When foreigners came to England, they were apt to stay. The whole history of Britain up to and including the Conquest is a history of invasions. Roman, Phoenician, Angle, Saxon, Dane, one after another they faced the water-jump—gritting their teeth at the prospect, but lured by the promise of tin, or oysters, or fertile territory—arriving green in the face, and determined that, whatever happened, they would not go back. The men of Norway, whose passage was colder and longer, but on the whole less nauseating, alone preferred raiding to settling; but even they sometimes found it more convenient to stay than to go. With each fresh invasion, the older inhabitants were pushed back towards the north and west; and with each fresh invasion, the southern and eastern parts of Britain became steadily more mongrel and polyglot. Lastly came William the Norman, and, like a catalyst, precipitated the unstable mixture that was the south-eastern portion of Britain into that solid and rock-like deposit which we call England. A score of Celtic and Nordic dialects fused with the Romance languages to make the English tongue. A new England, looking with new eyes at the Channel which she had seen all her life, suddenly discovered what it was for. There were no more invasions.

From the moment that England became Channel-conscious she became Channel-minded, and has remained so ever since. Bedded in her historic memory is the recollection of her first duty: to keep herself to herself. The phrase itself is characteristic of her people; I think I have never met an English working man or woman who did not boast of keeping the neighbours at arm's length; to be ignorant of other people's affairs and to cast a veil of impenetrable secrecy about one's own is, to the average English person, the primary mark of respectability. The boast is usually quite unjustified, but that is not the point: what we like to think ourselves is often more revealing than what we actually are. The immediate reaction of all English people to a foreign invader or a foreign idea is to make access as difficult as possible. The Celtic fringes sometimes claim to be more open-minded than the English and better mixers; that is because of the many centuries during which they had little occasion to stare apprehensively across the Straits of Dover.

For anyone of English blood there is no more agreeable pastime than to watch the people of cosmopolitan mind trying to induce the British people to toe the line of simplification and standardisation. They are always so naive, earnest and plausible, and they invariably use all the wrong arguments. At one time it was the Channel Tunnel, which would make it so much easier for foreigners to get to England. At another time it is a proposal to establish casinos in all the South Coast towns so as to attract foreign money. Periodically it is suggested that we should abolish an old-fashioned coinage and a chaotic system of weights and measures, so that foreigners need no longer waste time and energy and qualify for the madhouse by attempting to work out half-crowns in terms of centimes, or reduce square yards (by bundles of 30.1/4) to perches, roods and square miles and thence to square kilometres. And from time to time persons with much feeling for business facilities and none for literary history, implore us to get rid of our English spelling in favour of something which it would be easier for foreigners to understand and remember. The British listen politely to all the arguments and do nothing about anything, and the cosmopolitan cries out in despair against their lack of logic. To no purpose. The British are not so illogical as all that. They understand perfectly that these reforms would make things easier all round. But they do not want things made easier; they want, instinctively and passionately and inarticulately want, everything to be kept difficult. Behind the barrier of the rod, pole, or perch, and the barbed entanglement of the letters OUGH they retire as into a fortress. To make things too easy is to ask for an invasion, even if it is only an invasion of privacy. It is useless to tell the Briton that if the serried ranks of iron railings were removed, his house and grounds, to say nothing of his public parks, would look nicer and be more get-at-able; the very idea of being 'got at' makes him uncomfortable. The only thing that will inspire him to tear up his railings is the conviction that they are needed to defend his moat against a still more serious invasion. Unconsciously in peace, consciously in war, the Channel is the magnetic axis about which the British mind rotates.

Now, if the Channel had been filled with the stuff you would expect from its position on the map, the English national temperament, thus conditioned by its chilly environment, would probably have been rigid, narrow, morose, repulsive (in Jane Austen's, if not in the modern sense of the word) and monomaniac. The more engaging and exasperating absurdities of the British arise from the circumstance that the waters which run through the Channel are those of the Gulf Stream and no other. Because of the Gulf Stream the invaders came; because of the Channel they stayed here and turned into Englishmen. The British, even now, do not really object to the arrival of foreigners, provided they come in assimilable numbers and turn into islanders. What is disliked is the inquisitiveness of the tripper and acquisitiveness of the conqueror. So long as the intention is not hostile, and the new arrivals do not, cuckoo-like, oust the established inhabitants from the nest, the more the merrier. It all adds to the rich confusion of the English language and the glorious jumble of racial types which give flavour to the national hodge-podge. Variety, individuality, peculiarity, eccentricity and indeed crankiness are agreeable to the British mind; they make life more interesting. It is a failure to understand this passion for variety which reduces to despair the people who want to introduce uniform systems of education and neat plans for laying out model townships—or other things, as witness the testimony of the author of *A Canuck in England:*

> Being invited to people's bathrooms is a popular idea, for you really get to know people when you have used their bathrooms a few times. Not the least of the factors which contribute to intimacy is the fact that English plumbing is still worked by a chain. Every chain has its own little idiosyncrasies. Many of them simply defy the uninitiated to manage them properly. Consequently, dignified hostesses, when showing you where the bathroom is and which towel is for you, have also to give a lesson in managing the chain.

Quite so. The British do not at all mind their institutions being so inconvenient and even inefficient, provided they are all as different as possible. You have only to look at a hundred specimens of British handwriting selected at random and compare them with a hundred specimens from Germany or France or Italy. The general impression you gather is that all the foreigners have used, not only the same copybook, but the same pen. And you would be quite right. It is the pen that the British keep in post offices. It is kept in post offices precisely because it is the only pen the British can be relied on not to take a predatory fancy to; it is the pen that makes all handwriting alike. Even if you try to make all British schoolchildren write the same hand (and baffled educators have almost abandoned the attempt) before they have reached man's estate their calligraphy will rebelliously break away and blossom into a rank luxuriance of individualism—the bold, the squinny, the flourishy, the curly, the microscopic, the spidery, the cramped, the sprawling, and, above all, the hieroglyphic, the cryptic, and the triumphantly illegible. And note: that of the whole document the most indecipherable hieroglyph will be the signature. That is the one part which can be made secure even from random guesswork. With the secretiveness of a savage who fears that to give away his name is to assign a magic power over his person, the British correspondent spins an inky cocoon of protection about his identity. Thus Gulf Stream and Channel co-operate—the one to produce an entertaining variety, and the other to make things difficult—in the formation of the British character.

Wherever you turn in this island, you meet the same phenomenon—a proliferating diversity which, impenetrable as a lush jungle, impedes the advance of the foreign explorer. A fine example is the English Common Law, which has no code and scarcely any statutes. It is all case law, an intricate cat's cradle of precedents. It appears to know nothing of right and wrong, but only of rights and wrongs established by long custom, and to base its authority on no general principle, but only upon an endless series of improvisations—such-and-such a decision, made by a particular judge in a particular year between two particular men about a particular goose, insult or party wall. Learned foreigners come and watch British Law in operation; they observe that it works; they even admire its justice; but the trick of it is not communicable. Reforming zealots look at it with the eye of an irritated housewife confronted with the spidery chaos of a scholar's den; they long to take dustpan and broom to it—clear out the old junk and reduce it to a spring-cleaned order. But that would not do; the magic is in the disorder—clear it up, destroy the bewildering old documents, codify the result and set it out neatly upon the shelves as in a public library, and we should find that we could no longer lay hand on those things that we call our liberties: for the easier you make the law, the more readily can you drive a coach and horses through it. Oppression strides over code law as an invading army marches down an arterial road, but the Common Law of England is a maze, baffling and secure; to march through it you would have to hew it down and root it up completely.

Or consider the Church of England. And having considered it in all its rich ambiguity, consider how you would explain it to an intelligent Latin, who supposes that in matters of faith you must be *either* a Catholic, a Protestant or an atheist, and must hold your particular view with a fierce and rational passion which hews chasms of partisan cleavage through your entire political and social outlook. Then you will suddenly see why the foreigner, struggling to make himself at home in the Englishman's castle, feels as though he had been enticed into an exceptionally well-made apple-pie bed—a bed filled with a surprising assortment of inappropriate things and bristling with difficulties. And when at last you have deciphered British handwriting, interpreted the

Common Law, and explained the Church of England, you will perhaps be in a position to make clear to others why the British Empire holds together without visible means of support, and how it is that in the British mind the word 'Empire' is understood to be a synonym for 'liberty'. For the Empire too is a collection of individual decisions, improvised together into a constitution which is both highly idiosyncratic and altogether inscrutable.

But perhaps it is not really necessary to undertake all these specialised studies. Life is short; and for the ordinary observer the quickest and surest way to an understanding of British peculiarities is to purchase a mackintosh and a sunbathing outfit, come to Britain, and there experience the practical jocularity of the Channel and the Gulf Stream in its most intimate and pervasive form.

It has, I believe, been said that Britain possesses no climate, only weather. The weather of this country has been much abused—by foreigners, with some justice; by ourselves, with no justice at all, unless we are prepared to hate ourselves; for our weather is our character and has made us what we are.

All British institutions have an air of improvisation; and seem allergic to long-term planning. Indeed, what else can you expect in a country where it is impossible to predict, from one hour to another, whether it will be hot or cold, wet or dry, windy or still—where every arrangement for an outdoor sport or public function may have to be altered at the last minute owing to uncontrollable causes? 'Rain stopped play,' 'If wet, in the Parish Hall,' 'Weather permitting'—such phrases punctuate the whole rhythm of our communal life, and compel a general attitude to things which is at once sceptical, stoical, speculative and flexible in the last degree. You may plan an agricultural economy, for instance, with a reasonable certainty that any one season will be favourable for wheat *or* potatoes—but, without a miracle, not for both; yet the miracle may occur, like any other anomaly in this unaccountable country, so you must leave a corner of the mind open to miracle. You may have thunder in February, snow in May, hail in July, and a heat-wave in November; these conditions naturally discourage any tendency to fixed opinions and a doctrinaire outlook. The Briton is an incorrigible traveller: he will cheerfully pack up his things at short notice for a round trip to Honolulu and the Arctic Circle: why not? he need only to take much the same outfit that he requires for a week-end in Cornwall or Kirkcudbright. He can survive in Siberia, the Sahara, Tibet,

Calcutta, or the Gold Coast as readily as in Mexico, Mandalay, Alaska, or the island of Juan Fernandez; why not? he has been inoculated against every conceivable climate, as against so many diseases, by small protective doses of the appropriate weather; it is the Gulf Stream that built the Empire. The whole aim and object of British weather is to make everything difficult and nothing impossible; and if the Briton is too much in the habit of muddling through it is because he is meteorologically conditioned to the idea that he can reckon on absolutely nothing in his journey except his eventual arrival. For though he may be impeded by gales, floods, blizzards, fogs, snow-drifts, sun-strokes, land-slides, spring tides, or the Severn Bore, it is seldom indeed that he is bodily whirled away by a tidal wave, tornado, or cataract, frozen to death, struck lifeless by heat or thunder-bolts, smothered in sand-storms, buried by an earthquake or an avalanche or overwhelmed by the sudden eruption of a volcano.

I have dwelt upon all these things, not to make the Briton appear more lovable, for the Channel has taught him to expect—nay, to desire—astonishment rather than affection, but by way of explaining why it is so difficult to commit him to hard and fast plans for an improved and standardised society. Before you can make him behave like other people, you must fill up the Channel and divert the Gulf Stream; till then, he will always confront you with the impish incalculability of his own weather—a downpour to the west, bright sunshine to the east, and fog in the Straits of Dover.*

From *Unpopular Opinions*, Gollancz, London, 1946 (written in 1943)

*Editor's Note: The introduction of the decimal system in Britain does not invalidate Dorothy Sayer's argument, for the move is not popular with the man in the street.

A. L. Rowse

The Rhythm of English History

People are apt to think of the English State and polity, our institutions and their history, as a very conservative affair. This is a mistaken, or at least a very inadequate and one-sided, view. What makes the inner heart and rhythm of English society difficult to understand, and what is at the same time the clue to it, is the paradox of an outward conservatism with a continuing capacity for inner change and development. There is a saying that "you may change anything in England provided you don't change appearances", and there is a good deal in it. Its truth is lost upon less subtle observers, who are misled by the retention of older forms—monarchy, House of Lords, the Church of England, and what not—and fail to notice how these and other institutions have adapted themselves to changed circumstances, sometimes with a complete change of function.

Yet, think: English history has been as dynamic as that of any country in modern times. If it has not had the somewhat staccato rhythms of French or Spanish history in the nineteenth century, it has not been the less inwardly flexible and changing for that.

What is the explanation of this paradox that makes the inwardness of our history and polity more subtle and difficult to lay hold of than that, perhaps, of any other country?

There is no simple formula that one can give by way of answer. The explanation lies in our history itself, and in the nature of English society.

Modern England has emerged out of the experience of revolutionary changes just as much as the United States from those of 1776 onwards, or France from 1789, or Russia from 1917. All great countries, except perhaps Germany and Japan, have been through the experience of a real revolution. And England is no exception, only ours took place in the seventeenth century. The fact that it is further off in time does not make it any the less important in the development of modern society, for the experience and the ideas that were thrown up in the course of it, exerted a prodigious influence upon the Continent all through the next century, and had a considerable part in inspiring the ideas of freedom behind the American Revolution, until indeed the great Revolution of 1789 set a new model for the nations.

But no one can think that English history during that formative period from the mid-seventeenth to mid-eighteenth century was unexciting, or that the English were necessarily a placid or phlegmatic, a dull and uninteresting folk. At any rate their contemporaries abroad, respectable French, Italians, Spaniards, did not think so: they regarded us then as the most restless, turbulent, and changeable of peoples. And not without reason; for in the course of half a century we had had two revolutions, two civil wars and narrowly escaped another, executed one king and sent another packing, tried a Parliamentary Republic and a military Protectorate under Oliver Cromwell before arriving at a mixed constitution of our own making, after a pattern of our own, under which we settled down. After that record nobody need think of us a wholly conservative people with no talent for change.

What was it that emerged from all those changes and experiments? Well, in the first place, to take the most obvious, though not necessarily the most important: the English pattern of constitutional monarchy, which we have found to work satisfactorily ever since. It is a very convenient and useful form, and anything but rigid; as it has developed, the monarchy has this great advantage, that it provides us with a symbol to which we can all look, whether overseas or at home, the visible embodiment of the unity of our peoples and form of society—a head which is at the same time separate from the centre of real political power.

That is a great advantage; it is a very neat and practical division of function between the head of the State, with a very important social purpose to fulfil, and the political leadership whose job it is to carry on the work of government. It is an intolerable burden, in modern conditions, where one and the same man is expected to fulfil both functions. Only a superman can be expected even to attempt it—and the English do not much believe in supermen in politics. The monarchy serves the indispensable purpose of giving us continuity and at the same time flexibility: whatever the changes and chances of politics, there is a figure to which we can look, and that applies both at home and within the Commonwealth overseas. It is probable that no other constitutional form would fulfil that purpose anything like so well: it has shown a really remarkable flexibility and capacity for adaptation. In that sense the monarchy may be truly described as a democratic monarchy, an institution which is a help to the smooth and efficient working of democracy, and not a hindrance.

All this was implicit in the victory of the very moderate and English Revolution of 1688, though no one could be expected to have foretold it. What that cardinal event in our history meant, to put it in a sentence—and I do not think anyone has said it before—was a victory for constitutional flexibility and change; it kept the possibility of future development open. That was a great advantage compared with the rigid authoritarianism of Continental monarchies, of which the pattern was the oldest and greatest monarchy in Europe, the French *ancien régime*. When it became necessary in course of time to reform that, to bring it up to date, it needed a tempest with much uprooting of some things that were to be regretted, along with the dead wood. It would have been better for France if the old monarchy had had the capacity for change and self development within itself. It would have saved France a great deal of trouble and suffering in the nineteenth century, and actually it would have given her greater stability, a less fractionalising polity.

The flexibility of the English constitution which emerged from the Revolution of 1688 has a similar advantage over the rigidity which the Fathers of the Constitution imposed upon the young United States a hundred years later. No one knows better than the Presidents of the United States themselves the almost insuperable difficulties such a constitution puts in the way of governing the country and the shifts they have been put to in order to get round them.

The peculiarity of English constitutional development goes back then to the seventeenth century; it is there that you must look if you wish to understand the *difference* between our course and that which other nations took—the almost universal tendency on the Continent at that time was towards authoritarianism, monarchy on the model of Louis XIV, bureaucracy, centralisation, and the subjection of the individual to the State. We took a different turning and held on a course of our own with a system of Parliamentary government, of voluntary local administration, an emphasis upon freedom of speech and person, a deep note of individualism in our public life which was given full play.

Sometimes it had too much play; and there is no doubt that this course we took had some disadvantages and was more difficult to manage. We had to pay the price of political freedom in the hectic party conflicts of the reigns of Queen Anne and of George III. Foreign opinion—like that of Frederik the Great—often got the impression that you could not rely on Great Britain because of the conflicts between parties and the changes they involved. But that was a mistake: underneath these changes there was continuity of purpose and a deeper reliability. In the long struggles with Louis XIV and Napoleon no power was more constant or held more tenaciously to its purpose than Great Britain. And often the very flukes and alterations of party fortunes, in contributing flexibility, helped towards the success of the nation.

The Revolution of 1688 was not at all an idealistic affair; it issued no lofty-sounding (and disputable) Declaration of the Rights of Man. It was essentially a practical solution of difficulties in government, full of moderation and compromise. Common sense was its keynote, and Locke, the philosopher of common sense, its prophet. It was the beginning of our modern period of government by a mixed polity, in which the aristocracy, the gentry, the business classes ruled, with the emphasis as time went on from one to the other. But even in the heyday of the aristocratic age, the eighteenth century, they never ruled *against* the people; the whole art of governing was to retain the people's confidence and support. It was their success which exerted such a profound influence on political thinkers abroad, like Montesquieu and Voltaire, and later Guizot, Royer-Gollard, de Tocqueville.

The English political system proved its strength and flexibility in the course of the prolonged and double strain imposed upon it by the twenty years' struggle with Napoleon and by the Industrial Revolution. As the Industrial Revolution unfolded its tremendous developments, it created a new middle class which came in time to out-rival the older political classes in power; it called into being a new industrial working class; it altered the whole balance of forces in the English polity. It provided the greatest test the political system could possibly have. The whole question was—would it be sufficiently flexible to adapt itself to the new and changing balance of forces in the country, so as to guide and control them without a breach in continuity; or would there be an upheaval?

For a time in the 1830s, and again in the 1840s, the issue lay in doubt. On the Continent lesser strains produced many revolutions in those decades from 1830 to 1851. But in England, with the Reform Bill of 1832, the governing class decided upon the policy of concession: they deliberately chose to share power with the growing middle class, and as the century went on they constantly increased the area of their support with extensions of the franchise, by the Reform Bills of 1867 and 1884, ending up with universal suffrage in our time.

Government in England in the last century has had, then, a constantly extending basis of support—unlike the constitutional July monarchy in France, which, in many ways France's most promising constitutional experiment, was yet ruined by having far too narrow and exclusive a basis of support—virtually the *haute bourgeoisie* alone. The keynotes of English government in this period have been—keeping close contact with the people, concessions and a spirit of comprehension on the part of the governing classes instead of exclusiveness, flexibility, and a capacity for adaptation in institutions. Both parties, Conservative as well as Liberal, contributed to the work of adapting the institutions of the old aristocratic State to the circumstances; the grand figure in this achievement was Gladstone, who started as a Conservative and ended up as an advanced Radical looking to the twentieth century. It is this that makes him such a symbolic figure in the English nineteenth century—as against Germany's Bismarck; and this is the significance of the work he did for the State.

With the course of time—it is a long time since the seventeenth century—compromise, comprehensiveness, concession have come to be more than a policy; they have become a habit, deep instinctive impulses in English political life—and perhaps they answer to something in the character of our people, as it has developed in modern times. So much is this so, that in the twentieth century the development of an independent working-class movement in politics has not on the whole been met with obstruction, as in many countries abroad, notably Bismarck's Germany, but with the recognisable desire to comprehend it and bring it within the political system, brought up to date and renewed. The result is that the English Labour Movement, so far from being revolutionary, is deeply the reverse. It takes an integral part in the work of the English State; its part in guiding the country through the crisis of this war is far greater than its part in the last war; more responsibility is passing to it, and will continue to do so.

The response of the British people to this crisis in their fortunes has proved their essential soundness—which some in the outer world had begun to question in the decade since 1931. The Germans talked once more of the decadence and effeteness of the British people, in spite of their experience of us in 1914-1918. And that precisely because, like any civilised people, we preferred peace to war. Our marked preference for peace, in that decade of concessions, was yet another sign of the profound happiness of our people and their contentment in their own way, of the soundness of their impulses under the forms of government which they have evolved by the process of trial and error and by the method of compromise to suit their own circumstances and character.

Most thinking people realise that the end of the war and the social transition before us will provide another test of the combined strength and flexibility of our polity; but we all believe that it will prove equal to whatever test comes, after what we have been through.

From *The English Spirit: Essays in History and Literature,* Macmillan, London, 1944

John Alfred Spender

On Liberty

All definitions of liberty are unsatisfactory. The word has a glamour in our thoughts which fades when we try to define it. It is never without qualifications; it is always more than the absence of restraint which the dictionary declares it to be. Let us try to avoid all subtleties and think of liberty as embodied in a free country—a country in which the citizen voluntarily accepts the restrictions necessary to order and well-being, but in other respects is left the fullest possible scope for the development and expression of his individuality and character in word and in deed. Opinions differ even about this, but at all events we can start from the point that we have liberty to talk about liberty—an indulgence which in a large part of Europe would expose the talker to the rigours of prison cell and concentration camp.

Many of us, I expect, are a little weary of being reminded of Burke's saying that eternal vigilance is the price of liberty. It is, of course, true, but we need to know what we have to guard and whence the threat to it comes. The first thought that occurs to me is the very simple one that liberty is built on peace and can have no other foundation. Our free government, as we enjoy it, is the substitution of Law for Force, of argument for physical strife. It is an achievement of many centuries; it rests on the belief that free discussion is the likeliest way of doing justice and reaching sensible conclusions about policy. But it has rules of its own which must be observed. It requires tolerance and mutual forbearance. It requires that minorities shall submit for the time being, when they are outvoted in Parliament; and be content to work for a future in which they will have made their views prevail by reason and argument. If any of these assumptions fail, if our feelings become literally too strong for words, if minorities will not submit, and fly from words to blows, or if majorities so abuse their power as to drive minorities to physical resistance, then it is all up with liberty. Whichever party is physically the stronger will and must crush its opponents. The revolutionary inscribes Liberty on his banner, but if he succeeds he is bound to become a dictator.

Our own Parliament prides itself on being "Sovereign", and people are apt to think it can do anything; but all through its history it has been groping along the edge of the unmapped boundary which divides the things that can from the things that cannot be settled by argument and reason. Even so recently as the year 1914, it came near crossing this boundary in its disputes on the Irish question. Let it once be crossed, and we are outside the region in which discussion avails. The word is now the blow, and the question is simply which party is physically the stronger. We are no longer arguing with an opponent, we are seeking to crush him. No room for liberty here.

This is obvious when we are at war with another nation, but we are slower to recognize it in our domestic affairs. We hear people talking light-heartedly of class war, and yet claiming to be champions of liberty. This, if they mean anything by the word "war", or if they seriously contemplate suspending the forms of free government, is self-contradiction. No kind of war—class war or any other—can be reconciled with liberty. When we begin talking military language in our politics, put our political parties into uniforms, let them arm and drill or even pretend to arm and drill, then we should be aware that liberties are being taken with liberty.

All this is being illustrated for us in certain European countries. In these you have the frankly avowed dictatorship of a party which has got on top and has to keep itself on top. That it can only do by silencing its opponents and removing all the guarantees which in the free State the law offers for the life and liberty of the subjects. Its rule covers the whole of life; there is no stopping place between political and other liberties. Its doctrine must be declared infallible and imposed on the school, the home, the newspaper, the theatre, upon art, science and religion. The idea that political liberty can be sacrificed and other liberties kept proves under this test to be groundless.

This brings me to one of the most insidious arguments that is being used for the undermining of liberty. It is suggested that political liberty is of no value because we, or many of us, do not enjoy what is called "economic liberty". We must be prepared, or so we are told, to sacrifice political liberty in order that we may obtain economic liberty. Communist and Socialist writing abounds in this argument, and I should like for a moment to examine it.

It is, of course, true, that we are all, in a sense, slaves to our circumstances. There are a few idle rich at one end of the scale and a few tramps at the other who are so independent of circumstances that they can live, what they term, the free life—the life of the race course, let us say, or the life of the road. These are not generally thought to be the most admirable specimens of human kind. But the rest of us have to earn our living, keep regular hours, do a long day's work and have only short holidays, be careful not to offend against custom and prejudice, show deference to employers and a great many other people whom in our hearts we think to be our inferiors. The lot of some is undoubtedly much harder than that of others, and this inequality is one of the great social evils. Who can but sympathise with the poor man when he cries out that he is a wage slave? It is a cry which strikes a chord in a much wider circle than he sometimes seems to be aware of, for in a multitude of seemingly well-to-do homes there is the same sense of insecurity, the same sense of servitude, the same feeling of being involved in a round of meaningless toil for unappreciative masters.

To mend these conditions, so far as they can be mended, is precisely the aim of all good politics, indeed we may say of civilization itself, which has no other purpose than to release the spirit of man. But it is surely an extraordinary paradox to suggest that we shall further this object by surrendering our political liberty? Will the workman be better off if he is deprived of the right to strike, the right to vote, the right of voicing his grievances, or promoting his own political party? Is Government likely to do better for him or for any of us when the stream of criticism is cut off, and it is in a position to silence instead of answer its opponents? Is there anything in the condition of the countries which have sacrificed their political liberty to encourage the hope that economic liberty can be won that way? Are the workers better off, are they freer men, are their masters in the Communist or the Facist State less tyrannical, more considerate?

I cannot pretend to answer these questions. I can only plead that they should be very carefully considered before we conclude that the sacrifice of political liberty will open the road to economic liberty.

Broadly speaking, we have two types of society presented to us today—one the regimented, disciplined type in which the State undertakes to provide for us all on condition that we obey its rules, think its thoughts, accept what it offers us; the other our own free type which leaves us at liberty to go our own way, to rebel against its rules, to think our own thoughts, to say what we want, to make our private profit. It is customary nowadays to call private profit by rather opprobrious terms, but if you think it out, it plays a considerable, and I would even say a quite respectable, part in economic liberty. For if a man makes a profit by selling things to you and me, the presumption is that he is supplying things which you and I want, not things which he thinks we ought to want. To be able to pick and choose between the large variety of things which competing manufacturers and shop-keepers cater for the taste is the British housewife's prerogative. Let her go shopping where she has to wait in a queue for rationed supplies of things which the State thinks she ought to have, or which are the only things it produces, and she will discover the difference, and perhaps learn what a great part the free choice plays in her life.

Both these types of society are possible, and described on paper the regimented and disciplined type undoubtedly looks much tidier and neater. Indeed, if you assume that human beings can be treated like the inmates of a prison or a workhouse, whose wants can be measured from day to day, and who can be set to work at any task which their masters prescribe, and at any wage they think fair, there ought to be no great difficulty in catering for them. In such a community there need be no more unemployed than there are on Dartmoor, and it should—at all events on paper—be possible to make production and consumption meet without any of the miscalculations which attend supply and demand, and cause unemployment in the actual world. I say on paper, for there would still remain the possibility that the caterers would make a mistake in measuring their quantities, or that harvests would fail, in which case millions would perish who, if left free to cater for themselves, would have managed somehow to keep alive. All human enterprises, however, have their liabilities, and some may think the experiment worth the risk.

Over against this is the free society, of which ours is the type, looking at times very ragged and untidy, bearing on its back all the reproaches for what is wrong and lamentable in human effort and human nature, changing all the time, never perfectly conforming to its own rules, still less to its ideals. Its problem is to reconcile freedom with a more orderly arrangement of life, and some freedom it will have to sacrifice in the process. If I tried to suggest what its aim should be it would be something in these terms—a society in which all would be assured of a sufficient minimum but none prevented from adding to it by his own effort and enterprise subject always to the right of the State to take from his superfluity to increase the minimum. A society which relies on free speech, free criticism, free invention, to carry it forward, and which positively encourages the varieties and inequalities which result naturally from the differing capacities of men and women. It is, after all, these which give spice and flavour to life, and those who get in advance of their fellows show the way to the rest. Discourage the pace-makers and you slow down the whole movement.

Each generation is called upon to find its own balance between the contending principles of liberty and authority, but I believe it to be true that civilization progresses in so far as, on the whole, liberty gains on authority. We seem in these times to be in a phase of reaction from liberty. War has familiarized us with authority, and the far-spreading unrest which has followed has made us timid about social order. Liberty is assailed from the right and from the left; in the name of advanced thinking we are asked to embark upon courses which are as perilous to liberty as the frank and open assault on it of the opposite party. It is time to be on our guard. If in our zeal to build a new Jerusalem we allow ourselves to toy with military ideas in our domestic politics, talk lightheartedly of class war, think of crushing minorities, suspending Parliament, overriding law courts; or if alternatively we put our political parties into uniforms and train them to be violent if they don't get their way, we may say good-bye to liberty. Liberty will not live in this atmosphere of war. It demands peace, respect for opponents, and the acceptance of evolution, not revolution, as the method of political change.

I have tried to give some practical reasons why we should cherish liberty, but I think of it also as something which possesses what philosophers call absolute value for the human soul, something which no civilized man or woman can lose without loss of self-respect. It is this something which has inspired poets and orators and made millions of willing martyrs. We have inherited it—we especially in this country. Let us see that we guard it.

From *Last Essays,* Cassel, London, 1944 (given as a broadcast talk in 1937)

G. K. Chesterton

Paying for Patriotism

Somebody was recently remonstrating with me in connection with certain remarks I have made touching the history of English misgovernment in Ireland. The criticism, like many others, was to the effect that these are only old unhappy far-off things and battles long ago; that the present generation is not responsible for them; that there is, as the critic said, no way in which he or I could have assisted or prevented them; that if anyone was to blame, he had gone to his account; and we are not to blame at all. There was mingled with his protest, I think, a certain suggestion that an Englishman is lacking in patriotism when he resurrects such corpses in order to connect them with crime.

Now the queer thing is this: that I think that it is I who am standing up for the principle of patriotism; and I think it is he who is denying it. As a matter of fact, I am one of the few people left, of my own sort and calling, who do still believe in patriotism; just as I am among the few who do still believe in democracy. Both these ideas were exaggerated extravagantly and, what is worse, erroneously, or entirely in the wrong way, during the nineteenth century; but the reaction against them today is very strong, especially among the intellectuals. But I do believe that patriotism rests on a psychological truth; a social sympathy with those of our own sort, whereby we see our own potential acts in them; and understand their history from within. But if there truly be such a thing as a nation, that truth is a two-edged sword, and we must let it cut both ways.

Therefore I answer my critic thus. It is quite true that it was not I, G. K. Chesterton, who pulled the beard of an Irish chieftain by way of social introduction; it was John Plantagenet, afterwards King John; and I was not present. It was not I, but a much more distinguished literary gent, named Edmund Spenser, who concluded on the whole that the Irish had better be exterminated like vipers; nor did he even ask my advice on so vital a point. I never stuck a pike through an Irish lady for fun, after the siege of Drogheda, as did the God-fearing Puritan soldiers of Oliver Cromwell. Nobody can find anything in my handwriting that contributes to the original drafting of the Penal Laws; and it is a complete mistake to suppose that I was called to the Privy Council when it decided upon the treacherous breaking of the Treaty of Limerick. I never put a pitchcap on an Irish rebel in my life; and there was not a single one of the thousand floggings of '98 which I inflicted or even ordered. If that is what is meant, it is not very difficult to see that it is quite true.

But it is equally true that I did not ride with Chaucer to Canterbury, and give him a few intelligent hints for the best passages in The Canterbury Tales. It is equally true that there was a large and lamentable gap in the company seated at the Mermaid; that scarcely a word of Shakespeare's most poetical passages was actually contributed by me; that I did not whisper to him the word "incarnadine" when he was hesitating after "multitudinous seas"; that I entirely missed the opportunity of suggesting that Hamlet would be effectively ended by the stormy entrance of Fortinbras. Nay, aged and infirm as I am, it were vain for me to pretend that I lost a leg at the Battle of Trafalgar, or that I am old enough to have seen (as I should like to have seen), ablaze with stars upon the deck of death, the frail figure and the elvish face of the noblest sailor of history.

Yet I propose to go on being proud of Chaucer and Shakespeare and Nelson; to feel that the poets did indeed love the language that I love and that the sailor felt something of what we also feel for the sea. But if we accept this mystical corporate being, this larger self, we must accept it for good and ill. If we boast of our best, we must repent of our worst. Otherwise patriotism will be a very poor thing indeed.

From *The Common Man*, Sheed & Ward, London, 1950 (published posthumously)

Hilaire Belloc

Fortitude

In Périgueux, which is the capital of Périgord, in the hill districts of Central France, there is a strange building; strange, not for its history or for anything mysterious about it, but for two qualities; its incongruity and its strength without apparent purpose. This building is the cathedral of Périgueux and of Périgord.

It is incongruous because being of extremely ancient foundation it is wholly modern in construction, so that you might think on looking upon it from within or from without that it had been designed and accomplished all within some few years of the 19th century. It is incongruous as being something Eastern, though cut off by hundreds of miles from any Eastern thing. Its roof is in five cupolas (or seven if you count the smaller ones); they are not domes; they are essentially Oriental cupolas; they would not be astonishing near any of those Mediterranean shores which have been affected by the neighbourhood of Mahomedan things. But they are unique here in Périgord.

But that other quality of which I have just spoken; the quality of strength combined with newness and unsupported by anything but its own stark self is more remarkable even than the exotic lines of the building. It is built of huge blocks of stone almost without ornament: great slabs of wall from roof to ground; great drums of masonry from roof to ground; and that is nearly all. A man might feel, looking at those exactly squared, precisely sawn, unchiselled stones, that they would never weather. They suggest nothing of tradition. They are one of those French things which hardly even attempt beauty, or if they attempt it fail. Huge blocks, enormously solid, and apparently without story or legend, and almost without meaning. Yet their meaning is profound, and those huge stone blocks are connected with my theme, which is Fortitude.

Inside the cathedral, on a side altar of the northern transept, if I remember right, the undecorated solid bare transept of mere stone (but what stone!), the semi-circular arch, the absence of all detail and of nearly all colour, but the presence of Strength—there stands a mosaic. It is the mosaic of an elephant rather large as elephants are wont to be. It has a quiet eye and an immovable expression. Under it, also in mosaic, is the word "Fortitude". And there you are.

It has been remarked by men from the beginning of time that chance connections may determine thought: a chance tune heard in unexpected surroundings, a chance sentence not addressed perhaps to oneself and having no connection with the circumstances around, the chance sight of an unexpected building appearing round the corner of a road, the chance glance of an eye that will never meet our eyes again—any one of these things may establish a whole train of contemplation which takes root and inhabits the mind forever. So it was with me all those years ago in the matter of the elephant of Périgueux and his Fortitudo. Perhaps I remember it better because I was in the company of the wise when I thus came across it for the first and last time.

Fortitude (and her elephant) were here set up in a Christian church because fortitude is entitled one of the great virtues. Now what is fortitude? It is primarily Endurance: that character which we need the most in the dark business of life. But if fortitude be endurance, it is also creative endurance, and at the same time it involves some memory of better times and some expectation of their return. It involves, therefore, fidelity and hope; and without these two, fortitude would be of little use: but above all fortitude is endurance.

Fortitude is the virtue of the menaced , of the beleaguered. It is the virtue of those of them that man the wall, or that are called upon to last out. This thing, Fortitude, is the converse to and the opposite of aggressive flamboyant courage, yet it is the greater of the two, though it often lacks action. Fortitude wears armour and holds a sword, but it stands ready rather than thrusts forward. It demands no supplement; it is nourished not from without but from within. It is replenished of its own substance. Fortitude does not envisage new things; rather does it tenaciously preserve things known and tried. It builds, but builds unwittingly, not following an inspired plan nor a mere vision, but of necessity; and from stone to stone of daily conservative achievement.

Sometimes fortitude will earn fame, but not often. Always, however, it will earn reward; for even when the defensive fails at the end, if it has been of an efficient sort it makes an air and a name surrounding and enshrining itself. So have the great sieges of history done. So will our time of trial to-day, if we use it aright.

There was a time in the long story of Christendom (which is also Europe) when fortitude was everywhere and was known everywhere to be supreme. That time was the 9th to the 10th Century, from the death of Charlemagne to the awakening which began with Cluny, continued through the annealed, architectural, legislative Normans in the South as in the North, and rose in the flame of the Reconquista and the enormous march of the Crusades.

Between that darkening and that sunrise lay the night of Europe, wherein we nearly perished. Then indeed were we under the siege, from the murderous pirates of the northern seas, from anarchy within and the failure of law, from the Asiatic Mongol hordes riding to the Lech and their disastrous battle, even reaching the Saone for one moment at Tournus. The Mahomedan, our superior in seamanship and arms, had mastered all the Levant and Africa. In all the temper of that time was threat and the imminence of disaster. Destruction seemed native to it and the air of defeat: invincible opponents: desperate resistance against odds filled all that was left of our inheritance. There was no respite, no long truce, no relief; only continual battle. There was no support at all save in ourselves nor even any final confidence, and of prophecy hardly any save prophecy of evil and of the end.

Yet we rallied and we conquered. We baptised the pirates when we had tamed them; we recovered Spain; we marched 2000 miles until we had stormed Jerusalem. We re-established universities; we sat up triumphantly the Gothic of the pointed arch. The West rose up again in glory, having been saved by Fortitude.

From *The Silence of the Sea and Other Essays,* Cassel, London, 1941 (written in 1940)

Gerald Gould

Refuge from Nightmare

Some two months ago—it may have been more or less; I was never one to write by the calendar—I found myself walking up a little crooked hill in Buckinghamshire, and paused at the joint of the road's raised elbow to look back upon a peaceful scene. There was still the blackness of winter over the fields; in full sunlight, or even moonlight perhaps, an inquisitive eye might have found a few of those half-hidden, whole-hearted, idiotically optimistic flowerlets that come long before the swallow dares to pretend a summer, before the ash-buds are black in the front of March (they were black and solid this year before mid-February, as if nature had had a better hope than man). But in the dim beginning of evening, which was the occasion of my stroll, everything looked bare and wintry enough to remind one of northern history, and the patience of British peasantry and the British soil. The sky, closely regarded, yielded a pale star or two; but retreating daylight still held at bay the advancing and arrogant constellations. The smoke of farm fires reminded one of man's existence: it seemed a tolerable thing. Not an aeroplane, not a motor-car, not a telegraph-pole or a "wireless" wire broke the traditional passivity of the place. A horse was being led back to stable, a heavy horse of the quiet plough-wise kind. Not a building in sight could have been less than two hundred years old. Here was something, I thought suddenly, which usually has to be sought in remoter pastures: a piece of life with the dim and ancient quality of death, its counterpart and coeval: a picture unblurred by the generations: something that did not know about the Great War, or even the wars of Napoleon: that might conceivably go on, with little disturbance, if invasion or revolution or social or commercial collapse destroys the cities. Invention, save the most primitive, and adventure, save the inevitable business of birth and dying, and romance, save for the encouragement that darkening lanes lend to young lovers, were as far away as conflict and progress and retrogression. Experience, might, in this setting, be stripped, one felt, to its barest—and lose nothing. Time, the uneasy god, was here at ease. The evening predicted the morning, but no new thing.

Strange! There was I, in a shabby London suit, a mere hour's journey from printing-presses and stock markets, yet isolated from my kind! Well, not isolated: there was the horse, and the gradual man who led him: equally kindly, equally indifferent, equally of the soil and of the seasons. I am not one of your earth-bound sentimentalists to pretend I can discern more "reality" (whatever that may be) in country lanes than in city streets; I have no nostalgia of the loam; sentimentalities in plenty I might confess to, but not that one. All the same, it was strange! I said good-night to the man with the horse and he to me; the horse plunged by, with clanky, acquiescent footfall, enormous in the shadows. I needed reassurance; and perceiving that one of the old houses on my route was of the public kind, I went in and asked for a pint. An aged labourer, gnarled and withered into the likeness of a tree, a portion and parcel of his own countryside, greeted me, not wholly—I think—without contempt. He made me conscious again of my town clothes. He was eating bread and cheese, and I have, alas! no bread-and-cheese conversation. When I have said it is wonderful weather for the time of year, I am finished. He had a pint and I had a pint, and we sipped discreetly.

On the table lay a daily paper; and out of embarrassment, just to make my lack of small talk seem less discourteous—for I had read the stuff already in London—I picked the paper up and reviewed the headlines. I do not remember what they were. I know that they prefigured clearly enough, for anybody not politically imbecile, the yet more startling headlines of last week. The world came back upon me; and it was in essence and intention, a world of fear and quarrel.

Even the blameless pacific sentiments of the particular paper gave me small comfort. Talk about "reality"! What came real from the outside world except noise and pain? It seemed as though the human animal, divorced in his millions from the enabling contact of earth and ageless habit, had gone mad to the shrieks of his own inadequate machines. To tell the truth, the news of recent years comes together into a blur, a coagulation of vipers, a ball of woe, stinking and threatening, if one but does visualize it with the strength of feeling. For the mind, scrupulous and analytical, the picture is less terrible. One can discern tendencies. One can take comfort. One can nurse hope—there is reason in hope, and hope in reason. But the general unanalysed effect is of ugliness and screaming. Those who love peace and ensue it are confronted by the old dilemma, proved unrebutted through centuries of blood-shed, perhaps to remain unrebutted till men come with cleaner hands and calmer minds to the job of manhood—peace is good, it is good for the good, we must lay down our arms, we must pass resolutions, we must testify and memorialize: only, on the other hand, the cruel and the blind possess themselves of arms, ignore resolutions, laugh at easy and benevolent idealisms. So that to do what is right may be to hand over the world to those who do what is wrong—to hand over the world, and our children in it. I am not stating this dilemma for argument here. I am not thinking in terms of social expediency or ethical decision. I speak only of that queer sense of unreality, of impermanence, which comes upon a creature sharply confronted with the clamor of the countries and the peace of the countryside. Alone, or companioned only by the agents and materials of growth and tillage: alone under the sky, upon the road, between the fields, one could be sane and believe in sanity; but even that, only at the price of forgetfulness. Come into the inn, with the lights and the fire—and instead of the fiddler's old tune there is a multitudinous roar as from crazy orchestras, the tunes of the world's purposes are gone mad and bad, the noise of mankind at shrieking odds with itself rises up at one from a crumpled paper, the ancestral voices are everywhere prophesying war.

I drained my mug and went out again and walked a little way further up along the hill. The air was darker than before, and I thought it colder. But there were more stars.

From *Refuge from Nightmare and Other Essays,* Oxford University Press, London, 1936 (written in 1933)

Graham Greene

At Home

One gets used to anything; that is what one hears on many lips these days, though everybody, I suppose, remembers the sense of shock he felt at the first bombed house he saw. I think of one in Woburn Square neatly sliced in half. With its sideways exposure it looked like a Swiss chalet: there were a pair of ski-ing sticks hanging in the attic, and in another room a grand piano cocked one leg over the abyss. The combination of music and ski-ing made one think of the Sanger family and Constant Nymphs sighing pathetically of private sorrow to popular applause. In the bathroom the geyser looked odd and twisted seen from the wrong side, and the kitchen impossibly crowded with furniture until one realised one had been given a kind of mouse-eye view from behind the stove and the dresser—all the space where people used to move about with toast and tea-pots was out of sight. But after quite a short time one ceased to look twice at the intimate exposure of interior furnishings, and waking on a cement floor among strangers, one no longer thinks what an odd life this is. "One gets used to anytning"

But that, I think, is not really the explanation. There are things one never gets used to because they don't connect: sanctity and fidelity and the courage of human beings abandoned to free will: virtues like these belong with old college buildings and cathedrals, relics of a world with faith. Violence comes to us more easily because it was so long expected—not only by the political sense but by the moral sense. The world we lived in could not have ended any other way. The curious waste lands one sometimes saw from trains—the cratered grounds round Wolverhampton under a cindery sky with a few cottages grouped like stones among the rubbish: those acres of abandoned cars round Slough; the dingy fortune-teller's on the first-floor above the cheap permanent waves in a Brighton back street: they all demanded violence, like the rooms in a dream where one knows that something will presently happen—a door fly open or a window catch give and let the end in.

I think it was a sense of impatience because the violence was delayed—rather than a masochistic enjoyment of discomfort—that made many writers of recent years go abroad to try to meet it half way: some went to Spain and others to China. Less ideological, perhaps less courageous writers chose corners where the violence was more moderate; but the hint of it had to be there to satisfy that moral craving for the just and reasonable expression of human nature left without belief. The craving wasn't quite satisfied because we all bought two-way tickets. Like Henry James hearing a good story at a dinner-table we could say, "Stop. That's enough for our purpose", and take a train or a boat home. The moral sense was tickled: that was all. One came home and wrote a book, leaving the condemned behind in the backrooms of hotels where the heating was permanently off or eking out a miserable living in little tropical towns. We were sometimes—God forgive us—amusing at their expense, even though we guessed all the time that we should be joining them soon forever.

All the same—egotistical to the last—we can regard all those journeys as a useful rehearsal. Scraps of experience remain with one under the pavement. Lying on one's stomach while a bomb whines across, one is aware of how they join this life to the other, in the same way that a favourite toy may help a child by its secret appeal to adapt himself to a strange home. There are figures in our lives which strike us as legendary even when they are with us, seem to be preparing us like parents for the sort of life ahead. I find remembering in my basement black Colonel Davis, the dictator of Grand Bassa, whose men, according to a British Consul's report, had burned women alive in native huts and skewered children on their bayonets. He was a Scoutmaster and he talked emotionally about his old mother and got rather drunk on my whisky. He was bizarre and gullible and unaccountable: his atmosphere was that of deep forest, extreme poverty and an injustice as wayward as generosity. He connected like a poem with ordinary life (he was other people's ordinary life): but it was ordinary life expressed with vividness. Then there was General Cedillo, the dictator of San Luis Potosi (all my dictators, unlike Sir Nevile Henderson's, having been little ones). I

remember the bull-browed Indian rebel driving round his farm in the
hills followed by his chief gunman in another car, making plans for
crops which he never saw grow because the federal troops hunted him
down and finished him. He was loved by his peasants, who served him
without pay and stole everything he owned, and hated by the
townspeople whom he robbed of water for his land (so that you
couldn't even get a bath). His atmosphere was stupidity and courage
and kindliness and violence. Neither of these men were of vintage
growth, but they belonged to the same diseased erratic world as the
dictators and the millionaires. They started things in a small way while
the world waited for the big event. I think of them sometimes under
the pavement almost with a feeling of tenderness. They helped one to
wait, and now they help one to feel at home. Everybody else in the
shelter, I imagine, has memories of this kind too: or why should they
accept violence so happily, with so little surprise, impatience or
resentment? Perhaps a savage schoolmaster or the kind of female
guardian the young Kipling suffered from or some beast in himself has
prepared each man for his life.

   That, I think, is why one feels at home in London—or in Liverpool
or Bristol, or any of the bombed cities—because life there is what it
ought to be. If a cracked cup is put in boiling water it breaks, and an
old dog-toothed civilisation is breaking now. The nightly routine of
sirens, barrage, the probing raiders, the unmistakable engine (Where are
you? where are you? where are you?), the bomb-bursts moving nearer
and then moving away, hold one like a love-charm. We are not quite
happy when we take a few days off. There is something just a little
unsavoury about a safe area—as if a corpse were to keep alive in some of
its members, the fingers fumbling or the tongue seeking to taste. So we
go hurrying back to our shelter, to the nightly uneasiness and then the
"All Clear" sounding happily like New Year's bells, and the first dawn
look at the world to see what has gone: green glass strewn on the
pavement (all broken glass seems green) and sometimes flames like a
sticky coloured plate from the *Boy's Own Paper* lapping at the early
sky. As for the victims, if they have suffered pain it will be nearly over
by this time. Life has become just and poetic, and if we believe this is
the right end to the muddled thought, the sentimentality and
selfishness of generations, we can also believe that justice doesn't end
there. The innocent will be given their peace, and the unhappy will
know more happiness than they have ever dreamt about, and poor

muddled people will be given an answer they have to accept. We needn't feel pity for any of the innocent, and as for the guilty we know in our hearts that they will live just as long as we do and no longer.

From *Collected Essays,* Viking, New York, 1951 (written in 1940)

George Sampson

Humane Education

Humane education has no material end in view. It aims at making men, not machines; it aims at giving every human creature the fullest development possible to it. Its cardinal doctrine is "the right of every human soul to enter, unhindered except by the limitations of its own powers and desires, into the full spiritual heritage of the race". It aims at giving "the philosophic temper, the gentle judgement, the interest in knowledge and beauty for their own sake", that mark the harmoniously developed man. Humanism is a matter of life, not of a living. We pretend to believe this, but our practice betrays us; for the latest argument in defence of the "Greats" man is that certain business people prefer him to any other. Would the value of his education be less if they didn't? A whole book has been produced in America to prove that the classics are a sound business proposition. Well, we haven't got quite to that depth here, yet. Some of us still cling to the old belief that there are things in life immeasurable even in dollars. I have in earlier pages denounced the prevalent and pernicious doctrine that elementary education is the process of fitting children to become factory hands or domestic servants. I want to denounce with equal earnestness the prevalent and pernicious doctrine that education is the process of unfitting children to become factory hands or domestic servants. When teachers urge children to study for the sake of getting good positions, do they not realize how they are falsifying the currency of life? To suggest to boys that a clerk is something better than a carpenter, an insurance-agent better than a bricklayer is entirely wrong. It is not the extension of education to all that is socially dangerous, but the belief that education ought to mean a black-coated calling. Yet no people are more frequently guilty than teachers of suggesting that a boy is "too good" to go into a workshop and ought to go into an office. The County Councillor who recently urged that as ninety per cent of the elementary school children would have to go into manual labour they did not need a good education is not more dangerous to society than the teachers who openly or tacitly believe that if elementary school children receive a good education they ought not to go into manual labour. Surely the experience of the war should have taught us that it is not what a man has to do that degrades him, but what he is, in habit and association. We must get into our minds the vital truth that education is our contribution to the whole twenty-four hours of man, and not merely to the eight or six or five that he sells to an employer. Vocational or professional training, as we have said, may or may not be education; but into the early foundation stages of education the circumstances of occupation must never be allowed to enter. We want the educated boy to rise but we want him to rise above himself, not above somebody else. If we teach the village boy to read for himself and think for himself, if we give him, not merely instruction or information, but the ability to take a view of things and share in man's spiritual heritage, it is not because we want him to grow up into the village squire, but because we want him to walk "in glory and in joy / Following his plough, along the mountainside".

The beginning of a humane education here advocated will not involve a domestic revolution, or a rearrangement of the social system, or a new scale of moral values, or a preference of one sort of -ocracy or -ism or any other, or an upheaval of any sort. A humane education is a possession in which rich and poor can be equal without disturbance to their material possessions.

From *English for the English,* Cambridge University Press, London, 1921, 1970

Charles Prestwich Scott

Newspaper Ideals

A hundred years is a long time; it is a long time even in the life of a newspaper, and to look back on it is to take in not only a vast development in the thing itself, but a great slice in the life of the nation, in the progress and adjustment of the world. In the general development the newspaper, as an institution, has played its part, and no small part, and the particular newspaper with which I personally am concerned has also played its part, it is to be hoped, not without some usefulness. I have had my share in it for a little more than fifty years; I have been its responsible editor for only a few months short of its last half-century; I remember vividly its fiftieth birthday; I now have the happiness to share in the celebration of its hundredth. I can therefore speak of it with a certain intimacy of acquaintance. I have myself been part of it and entered into its inner courts. That is perhaps a reason why, on this occasion, I should write in my own name, as some sort of spectator, rather than in the name of the paper as a member of its working staff.

In all living things there must be a certain unity, a principle of vitality and growth. It is so with a newspaper, and the more complete and clear this unity the more vigorous and fruitful the growth. I ask myself what the paper stood for when first I knew it, what it has stood for since and stands for now. A newspaper has two sides to it. It is a business, like any other, and has to pay in the material sense in order to live. But it is much more than a business; it is an institution; it reflects and it influences the life of a whole community: it may affect even wider destinies. It is, in its way, an instrument of government. It plays on the minds and consciences of men. It may educate, stimulate, assist, or it may do the opposite. It has, therefore, a moral as well as a material existence, and its character and influence are in the main determined by the balance of these two forces. It may make profit or power its first object, or it may conceive itself as fulfilling a higher and more exacting function.

I think I may honestly say that, from the day of its foundation, there has not been much doubt as to which way the balance tipped so far as regards the conduct of the paper whose fine tradition I inherited and which I have had the honour to serve through all my working life. Had it not been so, personally, I could not have served it. Character is a subtle affair, and has many shades and sides to it. It is not a thing to be much talked about, but rather to be felt. It is the slow deposit of past actions and ideals. It is for each man his most precious possession, and so it is for that latest growth of our time the newspaper. Fundamentally it implies honesty, cleanness, courage, fairness, a sense of duty to the reader and the community. A newspaper is of necessity something of a monopoly, and its first duty is to shun the temptations of monopoly. Its primary office is the gathering of news. At the peril of its soul it must see that the supply is not tainted. Neither in what it gives, nor in what it does not give, nor in the mode of presentation must the unclouded face of truth suffer wrong. Comment is free, but facts are sacred. "Propaganda", so called, by this means is hateful. The voice of opponents no less than that of friends has a right to be heard. Comment also is justly subject to a self-imposed restraint. It is well to be frank; it is even better to be fair. This is an ideal. Achievement in such matters is hardly given to man. We can but try, ask pardon for shortcomings, and there leave the matter.

But, granted a sufficiency of grace, to what further conquests may we look, what purpose serve, what task envisage? It is a large question, and cannot be fully answered. We are faced with a new and enormous power and a growing one. Whither is the young giant tending? What gifts does he bring? How will he exercise his privilege and powers? What influence will he exercise on the minds of men and on our public life? It cannot be pretended that an assured and entirely satisfactory answer can be given to such questions. Experience is in some respects disquieting. The development has not been all in the direction which we should most desire.

One of the virtues, perhaps almost the chief virtue, of a newspaper is its independence. Whatever its position or character, at least it should have a soul of its own. But the tendency of newspapers, as of other businesses, in these days is towards amalgamation. In proportion, as the function of a newspaper has developed and its organisation expanded, so have its costs increased. The smaller newspapers have had a hard struggle; many of them have disappeared. In their place we have great organisations controlling a whole series of publications of various kinds and even of differing or opposing politics. The process may be inevitable, but clearly there are drawbacks. As organisation grows personality may tend to disappear. It is much to control one newspaper well; it is perhaps beyond the reach of any man, or any body of men, to control half a dozen with equal success. It is possible to exaggerate the danger, for the public is not undiscerning. It recognises the authentic voices of conscience and conviction when it finds them, and it has a shrewd intuition of what to accept and what to discount.

This is a matter which in the end must settle itself, and those who cherish the older ideal of a newspaper need not be dismayed. They have only to make their papers good enough in order to win, as well as to merit success, and the resources of a newspaper are not wholly measured in pounds, shillings, and pence. Of course the thing can only be done by competence all round, and by that spirit of co-operation right through the working staff which only a common ideal can inspire. There are people who think you can run a newspaper about as easily as you can poke a fire, and that knowledge, training, and aptitude are superfluous endowments. There have even been experiments on this assumption, and they have not met with success. There must be competence, to start with, on the business side, just as there must be in any large undertaking, but it is a mistake to suppose that the business side of a paper should dominate, as sometimes happens, not without distressing consequences. A newspaper, to be of value, should be a unity, and every part of it should equally understand and respond to the purposes and ideals which animate it. Between its two sides there should be a happy marriage, and editor and business manager should march hand in hand, the first, be it well understood, just an inch or two in advance. Of the staff much the same thing may be said. They should be a friendly company. They need not, of course, agree on every point, but they should share in the general purpose and inheritance. A paper is built up upon their common and successive labours, and their work should never be task work, never merely dictated. They should be like a racing boat's crew, pulling well together, each man doing his best because he likes it, and with a common and glorious goal.

That is the path of self-respect and pleasure; it is also the path of success. And what a work it is! What illimitable possibilities of achievement and of excellence! People talk of "journalese" as though a journalist were of necessity a pretentious and sloppy writer; he may be, on the contrary, and very often is, one of the best in the world. At least he should not be content to be much less. And then the developments. Every year, almost every day, may see growth and fresh accomplishment, and with a paper that is really alive, it not only may, but does. Let anyone take a file of this paper, or for that matter any one of half a dozen other papers, and compare its whole make-up and leading features to-day with what they were five years ago, ten years ago, twenty years ago, and he will realise how large has been the growth, how considerable the achievement. And this is what makes the work of a newspaper worthy and interesting. It has so many sides, it touches life at so many points, at every one there is such possibility of improvement and excellence. To the man, whatever his place on the paper, whether on the editorial or business, or even what may be regarded as the mechanical side—this also vitally important in its place—nothing should satisfy short of the best, and the best must always seem a little ahead of the actual. It is here that ability counts and that character counts, and it is on these that a newspaper, like every great undertaking, if it is to be worthy of its power and duty, must rely.

From *The Manchester Guardian,* May 5, 1921

From Moses to Churchill

Winston Churchill

Moses, the Leader of a People

"And there arose not a prophet since in Israel like unto Moses, whom the Lord knew face to face; in all the signs and wonders which the Lord sent him to do in the Land of Egypt, to Pharaoh, and to all his servants, and to all his land, and in all that mighty hand, and in all the great terror, which Moses shewed in the sight of all Israel".

These closing words of the Book of Deuteronomy are an apt expression of the esteem in which the great leader and liberator of the Hebrew people was held by the generations that succeeded him. He was the greatest of the prophets, who spoke in person to the God of Israel; he was the national hero who led the Chosen People out of the land of bondage, through the perils of the wilderness, and brought them to the very threshold of the Promised Land; he was the supreme law-giver, who received from God that remarkable code upon which the religious, moral and social life of the nation was so securely founded. Tradition lastly ascribed to him the authorship of the whole Pentateuch, and the mystery that surrounded his death added to his prestige.

Let us first retell the Bible story.

The days were gone when Joseph ruled in Egypt. A century had passed. A new Pharaoh had arisen who knew not Joseph. The nomadic tribes of Bedouins who, in the years of dearth preceding the Great Famine, had sought asylum by the ever-fertile banks of the Nile, had increased and multiplied. From being a band of strangers hospitably received into the wealth of a powerful kingdom, they had become a social, political and industrial problem. There they were in the "Land of Goshen", waxing exceedingly, and stretching out every day long arms and competent fingers into the whole life of Egypt. There must have arisen one of those movements with which the modern world is acquainted. A wave of anti-Semitism swept across the land. Gradually, year by year and inch by inch, the Children of Israel were reduced by the policy of the State and the prejudices of its citizens from guests to servants and from servants almost to slaves.

Building was the mania then, and here were strong, skilful, industrious builders. They were made to build. They built for Pharaoh by forced labour treasure cities or store cities, for the real treasure then was grain. Two such cities are mentioned in Exodus—Pithom and Rameses. The Egyptologist Naville has uncovered the city of Pithom, which was indeed built in the time of Rameses, and lies in that "Land of Goshen" on the north-east frontier, where the Children of Israel were settled. The fluctuations of the Nile could only be provided against by enormous granaries filled in good years. The possession of these granaries constituted the power of government. When a bad season came Pharaoh had the food and dealt it out to man and beast in return for plenary submission. By means of this hard leverage Egyptian civilisation rose. Grim times! We may imagine these cities built by the Israelites in the capacity of state serfs as enormous food-depots upon which the administration relied to preserve the obedience of the populace and the life of the nation.

The Israelites were serviceable folk. They paid their keep, and more. Nevertheless, their ceaseless multiplication became a growing embarrassment. There was a limit to the store depots that were required, and the available labourers soon exceeded the opportunities for their useful or economic employment. The Egyptian government fell back on birth control. By various measures which are bluntly described in the book of Exodus, they sought to arrest the increase of male Israelites. Finally they determined to have the male infants killed. There was evidently at this time a strong tension between the principle of Jewish life and the ruthless force of established Egyptian civilisation. It was at this moment that Moses was born.

The laws were hard, and pity played little part in them. But his mother loved her baby dearly, and resolved to evade the laws. With immense difficulty she concealed him till he was three months old. Then the intense will-to-live in the coming generation led her to a bold stratagem. It has its parallels in various ancient legends about great men. Sargon, the famous Sumerian King, was abandoned by his mother in a basket of reeds, and rescued and brought up by a peasant. There are similar stories about the infancies of Romulus and Cyrus. In this case the only chance for the child was that he should be planted upon the Court. Pharaoh's daughter, the Princess Royal, was accustomed to bathe in the Nile. The routine was studied. A little ark of bulrushes floated enticingly near the bank from which she took her morning swim. Servants were sent to retrieve it. Inside this floating cradle was a perfect baby ... "and the baby wept! " The heart of the Princess melted and she took the little boy in her arms, and vowed he should not perish while her father's writ ran along the Nile. But a little sister of the infant Moses judiciously posted beforehand now approached. "I know where a nurse can be found". So the nurse was sought, and the mother came. In the wide economy of an Imperial household a niche was thus found where the baby could be reared.

The years pass. The child is a man, nurtured in the palace or its purlieus, ranking, no doubt, with the many bastards or polygamous offsprings of Oriental thrones. But he is no Egyptian, no child of the sheltered progeny of the Nile valley. The wild blood of the desert, the potent blood of Beni Israel not yet mingled with the Hittite infusions, is in his veins. He walks abroad, he sees what is going on. He sees his own race exploited beyond all economic need or social justice. He sees them the drudge of Egypt, consuming their strong life and seed in the upholding of its grandeur, and even grudged the pittance which they earn. He sees them treated as a helot class; they, the free children of the wilderness who came as honoured guests and had worked every hour of their passage! Upon these general impressions he sees an Egyptian beating an Israelite; no doubt a common spectacle, an episode coming to be accepted as part of the daily social routine. But he has no doubts; not for a moment does he hesitate. He knows which side he is on, and the favours of the Court and the privileged attachments which he had with the ruling and possessing race vanish in a moment. The call of blood surges in him. He slays the Egyptian, amid the loud and continuing applause of the insurgents of the ages.

It was difficult to conceal the corpse; it was even more difficult to conceal the tale. No very lengthy interval seems to have elapsed before it was known throughout the palace that this somewhat nondescript and hitherto favoured denizen had bit the hand that fed him. How easily can we recreate their mood! The most cultured and civilised states and administrations of the present day would have felt with

Pharaoh that this was going altogether too far. Very likely Egyptian public opinion—and there is always public opinion where there is the slightest pretence of civilisation—fixed upon this act of violence as a final proof that the weakness of the government towards these overweening strangers and intruders had reached its limit. At any rate Pharoah—which is as good a name as any other for the governing classes in any country at any time under any system—acted. He decreed death upon the murderer. We really can not blame him; nor can we accuse the subsequent conduct of the slayer. His action also conformed to modern procedure. He fled.

In those days a little island of civilisation had grown up under the peculiar physical stimulus of the Nile flood and the Nile mud with all the granary system to grip it together—a tiny island in a vast ocean of bleak and blank starvation. Few and far between were the human beings who were able to support life beyond its shores. There were, indeed, other similar islands in other parts of the world, in Mesopotamia, in Crete, in Mycenae; but to Moses the choice of Egypt or the wilderness, all that was now open, was, in fact, virtually a choice between swift execution and the barest existence which can be conceived.

Moses fled into the Sinai Peninsula. These are the most awful deserts where human life in any form can be supported. There are others, like the vast expanses of the Sahara or the Polar ice, where human beings cannot exist at all. Still, always a very few people have been able to keep body and soul together amid the rigours of the Sinai Peninsula. There are nowadays a few hundred Bedouin inhabitants. But when an aeroplane makes a forced landing in the Sinai Peninsula the pilot nearly always perishes of thirst and starvation. In these dour recesses the fugitive Moses found a local chief and priest named Jethro. With him he took up his abode; he rendered him good service, married his daughter, Zipporah, and dwelt in extreme privation for many years. Every prophet has to come from civilisation, but every prophet has to go into the wilderness. He must have a strong impression of a complex society and all that it has to give, and then he must serve periods of isolation and meditation. This is the process by which psychic dynamite is made.

Moses watched the skinny flocks which browsed upon a starveling herbage, and lived a life almost as materially restricted as theirs. He communed within himself, and then one day when the sun rode fierce in the heavens, and the dust-devils and mirages danced and flickered amid the scrub, he saw the Burning Bush. It burned, yet it was not consumed. It was a prodigy. The more it burned the less it was consumed; it seemed to renew itself from its own self-consumption. Perhaps it was not a bush at all, but his own heart that was aflame with a fire never to be quenched while the earth supports human beings.

God spoke to Moses from the Burning Bush. He said to him in effect: "You cannot leave your fellow-countrymen in bondage. Death or Freedom! Better the wilderness than slavery. You must go back and bring them out. Let them live among this thorn-scrub, or die if they cannot live. But no more let them be chained in the house of bondage". God went a good deal further. He said from the Burning Bush, now surely inside the frame of Moses, "I will endow you with superhuman power. There is nothing that man cannot do, if he wills it with enough resolution. Man is the epitome of the universe. All moves and exists as a result of his invincible will, which is My Will".

Moses did not understand the bulk of this, and asked a great many questions and demanded all kinds of guarantees. God gave all the guarantees. Indeed, Moses persisted so much in his doubts and bargainings that we are told Jehovah (for that was the great new name of his God that spoke from the Burning Bush) became angry. However, in the end He made His contract with the man, and Moses got a fairly reasonable assurance in his own mind that he could work miracles. If he laid his staff upon the ground he was sure it would turn into a snake, and when he picked it up it would become a staff again. Moreover, he stipulated that he must have a spokesman. He was not himself eloquent; he could give the driving force, but he must have a competent orator, some man used to putting cases and dealing in high affairs, as his assistant. Otherwise how could he hold parley with Pharaoh and all the Ministers of the only known civilisation his world could show? God met all these requests. A competent politician and trained speaker in the shape of one Aaron would be provided. Moses now remembered his kinsman Aaron, with whom he had been good friends before he had to flee from Egypt. Thereupon action! Jethro is told that his son-in-law intends to start on a great adventure. He gives his full consent. The donkey is saddled; Zipporah, the two children, and the family property are placed upon its back, and through the dust clouds and blazing sunlight the smallest, most potent and most glorious of all the rescue forces of history starts upon its expedition.

Undue importance can easily be given to the records of the

protracted duel between Moses and Pharaoh. The plagues of Egypt are famous, and most of them were the kind of plagues from which Egypt has frequently suffered—pollution of the Nile and the consequent destruction of its fish; multiplication of frogs and their invasion of the land; flies beyond all bearing, lice abounding (but some authorities say they were gnats); the death of cattle; darkness over the face of the earth such as is produced by prolonged sandstorms; the prodigy of hail in the Nile Valley; finally the death of the first-born by pestilence. The local magicians, entering fully into the spirit of the contest, kept going until the third round, measure for measure and step by step. But when the dust turned into lice they admitted with professional awe that this was "the finger of God".

Great interest attaches to the behaviour of Pharaoh. Across the centuries we feel the modernity of his actions. At first he was curious, and open to conviction. Quite mild plagues brought him to reason. He was ready to let the Israelites depart into the wilderness and sacrifice to their potent God. This serious concession arrested all his building plans and caused considerable derangement in the economic life of the country. It was very like a general strike. It was no doubt represented to him that the loss to the national income from the cessation of labour would be disastrous to the State. So he hardened his heart and took back in the evening what he had promised in the dawn, and in the morning what he had promised the night before. The plagues continued; the magicians dropped out. It was a dead-lift struggle between Jehovah and Pharaoh. But Jehovah did not wish to win too easily. The liberation of the Children of Israel was only a part of His high Purpose. Their liberation had to be effected in such a manner as to convince them that they were the Chosen People, with the supreme forces of the universe enlisted in their special interest, should they show themselves faithful. So Jehovah laid on His plagues on the one hand, and hardened the heart of Pharaoh on the other.

It has often happened this way in later times. How often governments and peoples plunge into struggles most reluctantly, terrified of their small beginnings, but once swimming in the torrent go on desperately with immense unsuspected reserves and force in the hope of emerging triumphantly on the other shore. So Pharaoh and the Egyptian Government, once they had taken the plunge, got themselves into the mood that they would "see it through"; and this perhaps "hardens their hearts". However, the plagues continued and one misfortune after another fell upon the agonized State, until finally a collapse occurred. Pharaoh decided to "let the people go".

Amid the general confusion which followed this surrender the Chosen People spoiled the Egyptians. They begged, borrowed, and stole all they could lay their hands upon, and, gathering themselves together laden with treasure, equipment, and provender, launched out from the island of civilisation into the awful desert. Their best chance was to cross the isthmus which joins Africa with Asia and make for the regions we now call Palestine. But two reasons which could not be neglected weighed against this. First, the Philistines barred the road. This formidable people had already carried their military organisation to a high pitch. The Israelites after 150 years of domestic servitude in Egypt were in no condition to encounter the fierce warriors of the wilds. Secondly, and concurrently, Jehovah had told Moses he must lead the liberated tribe to the neighbourhood of Mount Sinai, where other revelations of the Divine Will would be made known to them.

They marched accordingly to the northern inlet of the Red Sea. There is much dispute as to their numbers. The Bible says they were 600,000 men, with women and children in addition. We may without impiety doubt the statistics. A clerical error may so easily have arisen. Even to-day a nought or two is sometimes misplaced. But more than two thousand years had yet to pass before the "nought" and all its conveniences was to be at the disposal of mankind. The earlier forms of notation were more liable to error than our own. Unless the climate was very different from the present it is difficult to see how even 6000 persons could have lived in the Sinai Peninsula without supernatural aid on a considerable and well-organised scale.

But now once again Pharaoh has changed his mind. No doubt the resentment aroused among the Egyptians by the wholesale pillage to which they had been subjected in their hour of panic, combined with the regrets of the government at the loss of so many capable labourers and subjects, constituted a kind of situation to which very few Parliaments of the present age would be insensible. The Egyptian army was mobilized; all the chariots set out in pursuit. The fugitive tribesmen, having reached the shore of a body of water called the "Yam Suph", at the extreme northern end of the Gulf of Akaba, were trapped between the sea and Pharaoh's overwhelming host. Their situation was forlorn, their only resource was flight, and flight was barred by salt water.

But Jehovah did not fail. A violent eruption occurred, of which the volcanic mountains of these regions still bear the traces. The waters of the sea divided, and the Children of Israel passed dryshod across the inlet. Pharaoh and his host, hotly following them, were swallowed up by the returning waters. Thereafter, guided by a pillar of smoke by day and of fire by night, the Israelites reached the neighbourhood of Mount Sinai. Here Moses received from Jehovah the tables of those fundamental laws which were henceforward to be followed, with occasional lapses, by the highest forms of human society.

We must, at this point, examine briefly the whole question of the miracles. Everyone knows that the pollution of rivers, the flies, frogs, lice, sandstorms, and pestilence among men and cattle, are the well known afflictions of the East. The most sceptical person can readily believe that they occurred with exceptional frequency at this juncture. The strong north wind which is said to have blown back the waters of the Red Sea may well have been assisted by a seismic and volcanic disturbance. Geologists tell us that the same fault in the earth's structure which cleft the depression of the Dead Sea in Palestine runs unbroken to the Rift Valley in what we now call the Kenya province of East Africa. The Sinai Peninsula was once volcanic, and the Bible descriptions of Mount Sinai both by day and by night are directly explicable by an eruption, which would have provided at once the pillar of cloud by daylight and of fire in the darkness. Flocks of quails frequently arrive exhausted in Egypt in their migrations, and some might well have alighted in the nick of time near the encampments of the Israelites. Renan has described the exudation by certain shrubs in the Sinai Peninsula of a white gummy substance which appears from time to time, and is undoubtedly capable of supplying a form of nourishment.

All these purely rationalistic and scientific explanations only prove the truth of the Bible story. It is silly to waste time arguing whether Jehovah broke His own natural laws to save His Chosen People, or whether He merely made them work in a favourable manner. At any rate there is no doubt about one miracle. This wandering tribe, in many respects indistinguishable from numberless nomadic communities, grasped and proclaimed an idea of which all the genius of Greece and all the power of Rome were incapable. There was to be only one God, a universal God, a God of Nations, a just God, a God who would punish in another world a wicked man dying rich and prosperous; a God from whose service the good of the humble and of the weak and poor was inseparable.

Books are written in many languages upon the question of how much of this was due to Moses. Devastating, inexorable modern study and criticism have proved that the Pentateuch constitutes a body of narrative and doctrine which came into being over at least the compass of several centuries. We reject, however, with scorn all those learned and laboured myths that Moses was but a legendary figure upon whom the priesthood and the people hung their essential social, moral, and religious ordinances. We believe that the most scientific view, the most up-to-date and rationalistic conception, will find its fullest satisfaction in taking the Bible story literally, and in identifying one of the greatest of human beings with the most decisive leap forward ever discernible in the human story. We remain unmoved by the tomes of Professor Gradgrind and Dr. Dryasdust. We may be sure that all these things happened just as they are set out according to Holy Writ. We may believe that they happened to people not so very different from ourselves, and that the impressions those people received were faithfully recorded and have been transmitted across the centuries with far more accuracy than many of the telegraphed accounts we read of the goings-on of to-day. In the words of a forgotten work of Mr. Gladstone, we rest with assurance upon "The impregnable rock of Holy Scripture".

Unluckily the stresses of the Exodus, the long forty years, or whatever the period may have been which was needed in the wilderness to sharpen the Children of Israel from a domesticated race into an armed force of conquering warriors, led them to make undue claims upon Jehovah. They forgot the older tradition which the Pentateuch enshrines. They forgot the enlightened monotheism which under the heretic Pharaoh Akhnaton had left its impression upon Egypt. They appropriated Jehovah to themselves. In Renan's words, they made Him revoltingly partial to the Chosen People. All Divine laws and ordinary equity were suspended or disallowed when they applied to a foreigner, especially to a foreigner whose land and property they required.

But these are the natural errors of the human heart under exceptional stresses. Many centuries were to pass before the God that spake in the Burning Bush was to manifest Himself in a new revelation, which nevertheless was the oldest of all the inspirations of the Hebrew people—as the God not only of Israel, but of all mankind who wished to serve Him; a God not only of justice, but of mercy; a God not only of self-preservation and survival, but of pity, self-sacrifice, and ineffable love.

Let the men of science and of learning expand their knowledge and probe with their researches every detail of the records which have been preserved to us from these dim ages. All they will do is to fortify the grand simplicity and essential accuracy of the recorded truths which have lighted so far the pilgrimage of man.

From *Thoughts and Adventures,* Macmillan, London, 1932

Eden Phillpotts

Confucius

One counts the majestic figure cf Confucius as among the first humanists in recorded history, for his creed arrested human thought and challenged mankind five hundred years before the dawn of Christianity, and many millions of us continue to be his followers. The high quality of the Chinese race owes no little to his teaching and I gaze with emotion upon the clash with the present ideology of their neighbour Russia and the peril that threatens China's older moralities. Pure reason formed the basis of what Confucius lived to teach. Against the difficult problems confronting his age, he declared that a rational, tolerant and patient attitude could best conform with human dignity, and he preached these virtues throughout the length and breadth of his wandering pilgrimages. He voiced the Golden Rule with evangelic fervour in a single Chinese word, which for us can best be translated by "Reciprocity". He never lost his faith in the value of this obligation, or his confidence that it lay within our power to avail ourselves of it in this world; but he admitted no assurance of any other world. "While you do not know life, what can you know of death?" he asked of those who desired his opinion on immortality.

The philosophy of his teaching undoubtedly helped to form the character and enhance the reputation of his nation as a people who practised plain dealing, and respected the sanctity of the oath. His thought was freely uttered and listened to by multitudes, for the authorities apparently at no time interfered with his activities, or set any curb upon his silver tongue. It was heard afar and created a gulf between the Chinese and Japanese in the days when, as yet, the

Muscovites knew little civilisation of any sort. Nippon's false gods had yet to lead them into perdition, for the words of Confucius were true enough: that nations only differ through their varying outlook upon what constitutes morality. He held the three cardinal preoccupations of life to be culture, learning and family, and the Orient indeed continues to respect family, attaching immense importance to all that is signified by relationship. But our latter-day Western philosophies dismiss this claim as a survival of no spiritual value.

Confucius explained that the first step to increased knowledge was the confession of ignorance, doubtless finding, as we do to-day, how few there are who have courage, willingly and frankly to confess it. Any such an avowal still appears to create a "loss of face" destructive of respect in private or public controversies.

The cult of isolation and complete estrangement from a hopeless world, persisting long under Christian inspirations, was an error in his opinion. He set his face against it, thought the hermit and ascetic to be mistaken, declared sack-cloth and ashes and solitary mortification a misuse and descration of life.

"It is impossible", he declared, "to withdraw from the world and associate with birds and beasts that have no affinity with us. With whom should I associate but suffering humanity? "

He must have resembled Epicurus in many aspects, for Mankind was his eternal prepossession; and similitude with a later saviour occurs to me, because, as did Jesus Christ in time to come, he was very apt to draw precepts and parables from the passing hour and the conditions surrounding him as he spoke to those at his side.

There is the story of how, travelling by a lonely way with his disciples, they met a woman suffering from manifold misfortunes and mourning her woes beside a newly-made grave. Confucius inquired as to the nature of her woe, and through her tears, she told him how that a tiger had slain no less than three of her beloved kinsmen. Her husband's father was the first to perish; next came her husband himself; while last and worst of all, her only son. Being asked why she could still remain within reach of such an enemy, and why she did not fly from this fatal region to another more secure, the widow made an astonishing reply. "I remain," she said, "because here the laws are gentle and we suffer no oppression from the government".

"Remember what you have heard, my children", commented Confucius. "Take note that oppressive government is a monster more terrible and worse to be feared than the tiger".

From *One Thing and Another,* Hutchinson Publishing Group, London, 1954

Leonard Woolf

A Civilised Man

I have always been fascinated by the life and character of Erasmus. He seems to me to have been a really civilised man, a very rare phenomenon in the world's history. Many people appear to believe that the history of spiritual and intellectual civilisation shows a steady curve of upward progress. This is a delusion. If you examine the past, at any rate of Europe, you will find that at rare intervals the world showed signs of becoming intellectually and socially civilised. There was such a moment at Athens four hundred years before Christ; another at the beginning of the sixteenth century; another, perhaps, at the beginning of the twentieth century. The essence of such intellectual and social civilisation is reason, tolerance, freedom, democracy, a kind of communal altruism and goodwill; the essence of barbarism is unreason, intolerance, tyranny, superstition, and a mystic belief that there is some virtue in making as many people as possible miserable. Now the curious fact is that whenever in Europe there has been any sign of a large number of people becoming civilised, immediately some appalling catastrophe has been let loose upon the world, the civilised people have been overwhelmed, and everyone has been plunged back again into the misery of barbarism. In Athens they contrived to blot out civilisation by one of the most futile wars that has ever been fought; the nascent civilisation of the Renaissance was overwhelmed by the savagery of Catholics and Reformers, an outbreak of religious barbarism which culminated in one of the most horrible events of history, the Thirty Years' War; in 1914 the Great War was only just in time to prevent Europe from becoming civilised.

The ordinary view of Erasmus, put forward by Froude and shared apparently by Professor Huizinga, who has written the latest biographical study of Erasmus, is that he ought to have thrown in his lot with Luther and the Reformers, and that the reason why he did not was, that he was weak and cowardly and prepared to compromise with lies. That, I think, is a superficial view both of Erasmus and of the Reformation. Erasmus agreed with Luther up to a point, and was himself a potent cause of the Reformation. He was a fighter all his life against superstition and the sordid corruption of the Church. But the end which he had in view was civilisation and a civilised life. He wanted Governments and Churches to be carried on according to reason and common sense, men and women to be able to know the truth and to be allowed to think and to say what they liked. He thought that it was a good thing that people should be happy and should, as much as possible, leave one another alone, each to be happy in his own way. He considered it important that ordinary people should live in good and comfortable houses, should have nice food to eat, should be clean, and should occasionally open their windows. He had a passion for learning and literature, and he did his best to make it possible for the rest of the world to share his own civilised pleasures. He liked conversation and argument and wit; to sit in a pleasant garden talking to men like More and Colet seemed to him a worthy occupation for a civilised man. He was a Christian who thought that Christians ought to live their lives in accordance with Christ's teachings, and that to persecute and massacre people because they did not hold your view about indulgences or consubstantiation or transsubstantiation was neither Christian nor civilised. He hated all violence as the crudest form of unreason and intolerance, and he was one of the first Europeans who refused to believe in the blessings of war.

Such were the general views of Erasmus. No man has ever been more consistent in carrying his beliefs and principles into the practise of his life. He refused absolutely at any time to join any party or faction, precisely because he was determined to keep his intellectual freedom, his freedom from dogma and prejudice. He was always on the right side, the side of reason and civilisation, and whenever he saw it changing through violence and superstition and fanaticism to the wrong side, he drew back. He saw with perfect clearness, whither Luther and the Reformers were going, to the persecutions and massacres of the Thirty Years' War, and he refused to follow them. He would have nothing to do with the argument by bonfire which was the ultimate argument of the Pope on one side and the Reformers on the other. As early as 1525 he wrote prophetically to Beda that when men begin by burning books they end by burning persons. Of course, Erasmus, with such views, seemed a weak man and a renegade to Luther, who, when the miserable peasants revolted and tried to put his own doctrines into practice, cried: "Therefore let all who are able, hew them down, slaughter and stab them, openly or in secret, and remember that there is nothing more poisonous, noxious, and utterly diabolical than a rebel. You must kill him as you would a mad dog; if you do not fall upon him, he will fall upon you and the whole land . . ." Who said of the Jews: "I would have their tongues torn out by the roots"; and who said that he heard the voice of the Devil, and that it resembled the grunting of a pig. Luther urged his disciples to hate Erasmus as "the worst enemy that Christ has had for a thousand years". Erasmus never hated Luther, but he hated the idea of killing peasants, tearing people's tongues out by the roots, and burning those who do not agree with you. It seemed to him uncivilised. Personally I incline to agree with him.

From *Essays on Literature, History, Politics, etc.,* Hogarth, London, 1927

G. M. Trevelyan

John Woolman, the Quaker

There are three religious autobiographies that I think of together—the *Confessions* of St. Augustine and of Rousseau and the *Journal* of John Woolman, the Quaker. Each of these men had soul-life abundantly, and the power of recording his experiences in that kind; and each gave the impulse to a great current in the world's affairs—the Mediaeval Church, the French Revolution, and the Anti-Slavery Movement. But Woolman is to me the most attractive, and I am proud to think that it was he who was the Anglo-Saxon—the "woolman" of old English trader stock.

There is an element of self in the finest ecstasies of St. Augustine, the spiritual parent of *Johannes Agricola in Meditation* as depicted by Robert Browning, and of all that hard soul-saving clan. He begins religion at the opposite end from Francis of Assisi, and they never meet. The African Saint started Western Europe on the downward course of religious persecution proper. Before him there had, indeed, been persecution of religions for racial or political reasons, but St. Augustine was perhaps the chief of those who supplied the religious motive for religious persecution, and turned God Himself into Moloch, a feat which no one but a really "good" man could have performed. Thenceforth, until the age of the much-abused Whigs and sceptics, all the best people in the world were engaged in torturing each other and making earth into hell. It was through St. Augustine rather than through Constantine that the Church drank poison. The torch was handed down from him through St. Dominic and St. Ignatius till it scorched the hand of St. John of Geneva by the pyre of Servetus. They were all, at least after their conversions, unusually "good" men, but not good all through like John Woolman.

Rousseau, at any rate, was not "good". We all ought to read his *Confessions*, but I fear the reason why many of us perform this duty is not always the highest. For this great spiritual reformer owns up to common weaknesses indulged to degrees that rise to an epic height. The story of the piece of ribbon thrills us with a moment's illusion that we are morally superior to the man who started the "religious reaction" and the love of mountains, as well as the French Revolution. And then he fulfilled the social contract by leaving his babies at the door of the foundling hospital. The imaginary story of the youth and manhood of one of those unfathered children of genius, say during the French Revolution, would be a fine theme for an historical fictionist of imagination and humor: Stevenson, for instance, would have loved to show by what strange routes through the Quartier Latin or elsewhere that deserted brood of the "old Serpent of Eternity" found their way to the Morgue—or perhaps to a bourgeois' easy-chair. O "Savoyard Vicar", first lover of the mountains, brother of the poor, shaker down of empires, how from such weakness as yours was born such strength? No wonder he puzzles his biographers, of whom himself was the first. No one can understand those who do not understand themselves.

Rousseau, having puzzled himself, inevitably puzzled Lord Morley, who had caught hold of simple Voltaire and packed him neatly into one small volume (with Frederick thrown in, to keep him company), while the insoluble problem of Rousseau trails on through two volumes—the more interesting but the less "final" of the twin biographies. Carlyle, though he posed Rousseau for "Hero as man of letters", did not even touch the problem. But the uncouth, rebellious child of nature struck in him sympathetic chords, and evoked outbursts of grim Carlylean humor, thus:

> He could be cooped into garrets, laughed at as a maniac, let to starve like a wild beast in his cage;—but he could not be hindered from setting the world on fire. His semi-delirious speculations on the miseries of civilised life, and suchlike, helped well to produce a whole delirium in France generally. True, you may well ask,—what could the world, the governors of the world, do with such a man? Difficult to say what the governors of the world could do with him! What he could do with them is unhappily clear enough,—*guillotine* a great many of them!

On another occasion, it is said, at a very English dinnertable, Carlyle was bored by a tribe of Philistines who were reiterating over their port our great insular doctrine that "political theories make no difference to practice". After listening long in silence he growled out: "There was once a man called Rousseau. He printed a book of political theories, and the nobles of that land laughed. But the next edition was bound in their skins". And so with a Scottish peasant's big chuckle, he fell silent again amid the apologetic coughs of the discomposed dinner-party.

John Woolman was a contemporary of Voltaire and Rousseau though he scarcely knew it. And the spirit of that age, "dreaming on things to come", spoke a new word through him also, bidding men prepare the ground for what we may call the Anglo-Saxon Revolution, the abolition of negro slavery. Woolman's *Journal* tells how this humblest and quietest of men used to travel round on foot, year after year, among these old-fashioned American Quakers, stirring their honest but sleepy consciences on this new point of his touching "the holding their fellow-men as property". A Quaker Socrates, with his searching, simple questions, he surpassed his Athenian prototype in love and patience and argumentative fairness, as much as he fell below him in intellect. And when the Friends found that they could not answer John's questions, instead of poisoning him or locking him up as an anarchist, they let their slaves go free! Truly, a most surprising outcome for the colloquy of wealthy and settled men with a humble and solitary pedestrian! Incredible as it may seem, they asked no one for "Compensation"! But then the Quakers always were an odd people.

Woolman's religious experience, from first to last, concerned his love and duty towards his fellow-creatures, and not the selfish salvation of his own soul. His conversion, we may say, dated from the following incident in his childhood:

> On going to a neighbour's house, I saw on the way a robin sitting on her nest, and as I came near she went off; but having young ones, she flew about and with many cries expressed her concern for them. I stood and threw stones at her, and one striking her she fell down dead. At first I was pleased with the exploit, but after a few minutes was seized with horror at having, in a sportive way, killed an innocent creature while she was careful for her young. I beheld her lying dead, and thought those young ones, for which she was so careful, must now perish for want of their dam to nourish them. After some painful

considerations on the subject, I climbed up the tree, took all the young birds and killed them, supposing that better than to leave them to pine away and die miserably. In this case I believed that Scripture proverb was fulfilled. *The tender mercies of the wicked are cruel.* I then went on my errand, and for some hours could think of little else but the cruelties I had committed, and was much troubled. Thus He whose tender mercies are over all His works hath placed a principle in the human mind, which incites to exercise goodness towards every living creature.

He was so filled with the spirit of love that he became, as it were, unconscious of danger and suffering when he was about the work dictated by this impelling force.

"Twelfth of sixth month", 1763, in time of war with the Red Indians, "being the first of the week and a rainy day, we continued in our tent, and I was led to think on the nature of the exercise which hath attended me. Love was the first motion, and thence a concern arose to spend some time with the Indians, that I might feel and understand their life and the spirit they live in, if haply I might receive some instruction from them, or they might be in any degree helped forward by my following the leadings of truth among them; and as it pleased the Lord to make way for my going at a time when the troubles of war were increasing, and when by reason of much wet weather travelling was more difficult than usual at that season, I looked upon it as a more favourable opportunity to season my mind and to bring me into a nearer sympathy with them". And so he went among the Indians to exchange with them what we should now call "varieties of religious experience", at a time when one section of them had proclaimed "war with the English", and were actually bringing back English scalps.

His objections to luxury, which he carried to the greatest lengths in his own case, were based not on any ascetic feeling, but on the belief that luxury among the well-to-do was a cause of their rapacity and therefore of their oppression of the poor. "Expensive living", he writes, "hath called for a large supply, and in answering this call the faces of the poor have been ground away and made thin through hard dealing". He was himself a man of but slender means, yet on this ground he denied himself things which he regarded as luxuries, and others would call common comforts. Humanity he thought of as a whole, not as a collection of individuals each busy saving his soul or amassing his own fortune. The rich, he held, were responsible for the miseries of the poor, and the "good" for the sins of the reprobate. "The law of Christ", he said, "consisted in tenderness towards our fellow-creatures, and a concern so to walk that our conduct may not be the means of strengthening them in error".

If the world would take John Woolman for an example in religion and politics instead of St. Augustine and Rousseau we should be doing better than we are in the solution of the problems of our own day. Our modern conscience-prickers often are either too "clever" or too violent. What they have said in one play or novel they must contradict in the next for fear of appearing simple. Or if they are frankly simple, they will set fire to your house to make you listen to their argument. "Get the writings of John Woolman by heart", said Charles Lamb—sound advice not only for lovers of good books but for would-be reformers.

They say John Brown in the ghost went marching along in front of the Northern armies. Then I guess John Woolman was bringing up the Ambulance behind. He may have lent a spiritual hand to Walt Whitman in the flesh, bandaging up those poor fellows. As to John Brown, to use a Balkan expression, he was a *comitadji*, "undaunted, true and brave". He could knock up families at night and lead out the fathers and husbands to instant execution, or be hung himself, with an equal sense of duty done, all in the name of the Lord, who he reckoned was antagonistic to negro slavery. And then came the war, those slaughter-ings by scores of thousands of the finest youthful manhood in the world, the grinding up of the seed-corn of Anglo-Saxon America, from which racially she can never wholly recover. And all because the majority of slave-owners, not being Quakers, had refused to listen to John Woolman. Close your ears to John Woolman one century and you will get John Brown the next, with Grant to follow.

The slave-owners in the British Empire were not Quakers, but fortunately for us they were a feeble folk, few enough to be bought out quietly. One of England's characteristic inventions is Revolution by purchase. It saves much trouble, but it is a luxury that only rich societies can afford. It was lucky for England that George III did not keep the Southern colonies when he lost us New England. It very nearly happened so, and if it had, then would Old England have been wedded to slavery. As it is she became John Woolman's best pupil.

The Anti-Slavery movement was quite as important as the French Revolution. For if the "Industrial Revolution" had been fully developed all the world over, while men still though it right to treat black men as machines, the exploitation of the tropics by the modern company-promoter on "Congo" lines would have become the rule instead of the exception. Central America, Africa, perhaps India and ultimately China, would be one hell, and Europe would be corrupted as surely as old Rome when she used the conquered world as a stud-farm to breed slaves for her *latifundia*. The Anti-Slavery movement came in the nick of time, just before machinery could universalize the slave system. Slavery on the scale of our modern industries, binding all the continents together in one wicked system of exploitation, would have been too big an "interest" for reformers to tackle. Even as it was, America was very nearly strangled by "cotton" in the Southern States, a more evil and far more formidable thing than the old eighteenth-century domestic slavery in the same region. But Wilberforce had by that time set the main current of the world's opinion the other way. So it was too late. But how would it have gone with the world if that poor Quaker clerk had kept to himself those first queer questionings of his about "holding fellow-men as property"? Woolman was not a bigwig in his own day, and he will never be a bigwig in history. But if there be a "perfect witness of all-judging Love", he may expect his meed of much fame in heaven. And if there be no such witness we need not concern ourselves. He was not working for "fame" either here or there.

From *Clio, a Muse, and Other Essays,* Longmans, London, 1930

Lytton Strachey

A Sidelight on Frederick the Great

The Memoirs of Henri de Catt have long been familiar to scholars; they were used by Carlyle in his *Life of Friedrich,* and an elaborate edition of the original manuscript forms one of the valuable series of publications issued from the Prussian State Archives. The book is an extremely interesting one. It is not as a piece of literature that this work is to be judged. Nor, except incidentally and indirectly, is it of any real importance from the historical and political point of view. The Frederick of history reaches us through other channels, and our estimate of that extraordinary career does not depend upon the kind of information which Catt provides. The interest of his book is entirely personal and psychological. It is like one of those photographs—old-fashioned and faded, perhaps, but still taken *sur le vif*—which one turns to with an eager curiosity, of some remarkable and celebrated man. The historian neglects Oliver Cromwell's warts; but it is just such queer details of physiognomy that the amateur of human nature most delights in. Catt shows us the queer details of Frederick's mental physiognomy, and some of them are very queer indeed.

His portrait has both the merits and the drawbacks of a photograph: it is true and it is stupid; and its very stupidity is the measure of its truth. There is not a trace of Boswellian artistry about it—of that power of selection and evocation which clothes its object with something of the palpable reality of life. There is hardly even a trace of criticism. "Let me have about me that are . . . not too clever", must have been Frederick's inward resolution after his disastrous experience with Voltaire; and obviously it was with some such feeling in his mind that, after a chance meeting on a boat in Holland, he engaged as his "reader" the pious, ingenuous, good-natured Swiss young man. The King's choice was amply justified: the young man was certainly not too clever; one gathers that Frederick actually almost liked him; and though the inevitable rupture came at last, it was delayed for more than twenty years. Catt was indeed the precise antithesis of Voltaire and his Memoirs are the precise antithesis of Voltaire's famous lampoon. The Frenchman's devastating sketch is painted with such brilliance that nobody can believe in it, and nobody can help believing in the bland acceptance of Catt's photographic plate.

The Memoirs only cover a period of two years, but it so happens, that these years contained the crisis of Frederick's life. Between 1758 and 1761 the hideous convulsion of the Seven Years' War reached its culmination. Frederick, attacked simultaneously by France, Austria and Russia, faced his enemies like a bear tied to the stake: disaster after disaster fell upon him; bloody defeats punctuated his ruinous marches and desperate manoeuverings; Berlin itself was taken; for many months it seemed certain that the doom of Prussia was sealed; more than once the hopeless King was on the brink of escaping the final humiliation by suicide. Catt, with a few brief intervals, was in daily intercourse with Frederick all through this period, and it is against this lurid background of frenzied struggle and accumulating horror that he shows us his portrait of his master. Every day, whether in camp under canvas, or in the cramped quarters of some wretched village, or amid the uncongenial splendours of some momentarily conquered palace, he was summoned at about five in the evening to the royal presence, where he remained, usually for at least two, and sometimes for four or five hours. His duties as "reader" were of a purely passive kind: it was his business not to read but to listen. And listen he did, while the King, putting aside at last the labours and agitations of the day, the coils of strategy and high politics, relaxed himself in literary chat, French declamations and philosophical arguments. Clearly enough, these evening *tête-a-têtes* with Catt were the one vestige left to him, in his terrible surroundings, of the pleasures of private life—of the life of intellectual cultivation and unofficial intercourse; and the spectacle of this grim old conqueror seeking out the company of a mediocre young man from Switzerland, with whom to solace himself in rhymes and rhapsodies, would be pathetic, if such a word were not so totally inapplicable to such a character. No, the spectacle is not pathetic, it is simply exceedingly curious. For what Catt shows us is a man for whom literature was not merely a pastime but a passion, a man of exaggerated sensibilities, a man who would devote ungrudging hours to the laborious imitation of French poetry, a man who would pass the evenings of days spent in scheming and slaughter reading aloud the plays of his favourite dramatist, until at last he would be overcome by emotion, and break down, in floods of tears. Frederick, in fact, appears in Catt's pages as a literary sentimentalist; he weeps at every opportunity, and is never tired of declaiming high sentiments in alexandrine verse. When he is cheerful, he quotes Chaulieu; when he is satirical he misquotes *Athalie*; when he is defeated in battle and within an ace of utter destruction, he greets his astonished Reader with a long tirade from *Mithridate*. After Frederick himself, Racine is the real hero of these Memoirs. His exquisite, sensuous and high-resounding oratory flows through them in a perpetual stream. It is a strange triumph for that most refined of poets: the sobs of Burrhus are heard in the ruined hamlets of Saxony, and the agonies of Zorndorf mingle with those of Phèdre.

And after Racine, Voltaire. Again and again Frederick recours, in accents of mingled anger and regret, to the Master whose art he worshipped, whose person he had once held in his clutches, and who had now escaped him forever. Voltaire was a rogue, no doubt, a heartless scoundrel, capable of any villainy—but his genius! — "Si son coeur égalait ses talents, quel homme, mon ami, quel homme! Et comme il nous humilierait tous! " And so Majesty bent once more over the screed of halting verses, struggling to polish them according to the precepts of the Patriarch, and so, when a letter came from Ferney, the royal countenance beamed with pleasure, and soldiers who had pilfered henroosts might hope for fewer lashes that day. Sometimes, when Frederick was particularly pleased with his compositions, he ventured to submit them to the critical eye of the great man. "Mon chér, croyez-vous que ma pièce soit assez bonne pour être envoyée au patriarche? " On one occasion he allowed his author's vanity to interfere even with his policy. He had concocted some highly scurrilous verses on Louis XV and Madame de Pompadour, and was so delighted with them that he proposed at once to send them to Ferney. He had never, he told Catt, done anything better; even the Patriarch would be unable to detect a single fault. Catt allowed the excellence of the verses, but sagaciously pointed out the danger of putting them in the hands of Voltaire—that heartless scoundrel, as his Majesty had so constantly remarked, capable of any villainy—at the very moment when the disasters of the campaign made it important to capture, if possible, the good graces of the French Court. Frederick reflected; agreed that Catt was right; and then in a day or two, unable to resist the temptation, secretly sent off the verses to Voltaire. The inevitable followed. On the receipt of the verses, Voltaire immediately despatched them to the French authorities, while he wrote to Frederick informing him that the royal letter had been apparently opened in the post, and that therefore, if copies had been taken of it and forwarded to certain quarters, he at any rate was not to blame. Frederick at once realised his folly. Voltaire, he declared to Catt, was a monster, a traitor and an old monkey. A few months later, a copy of *Candide* arrived from the author. Frederick read it; he read it again, and yet again. It was the best novel, he told Catt, that had ever been written, and Voltaire was the greatest man alive.

Never, surely, was the eighteenth-century theory of the "ruling-passion" more signally falsified than in the case of Frederick the Great. He was ambitious, no doubt; but ambitious for what? For political power? For military prestige? Or for the glory of satisfying an old monkey at Ferney that he could write a good alexandrine if he tried? The European bandit who sits up all night declaiming the noble sentiments of Racine's heroes, the hardened cynic who weeps for hours over his own elegies, is certainly a puzzling creature, hard to fit into a cut-and-dried system of psychology. So glaring, indeed, are these contradictions that Lord Roseberry suggests that Frederick posed to his Reader, that the tears and the literary emotions which Catt chronicles were "the result of dramatic art". When, in particular, Frederick expatiates on his desire for a life of retirement, devoted to the delights of friendship and aesthetic cultivation, Lord Roseberry is disposed to agree with the comment of the Swiss young man that "the whole was a little comedy". It may be so; but it is difficult to believe it. It is hard to see what object Frederick could have had in deluding Catt; and it is easier to suppose that a man should contradict himself, both in his thoughts and his feelings, than that he should spend years in keeping up an elaborate mystification with an insignificant secretary, for no apparent purpose. As a whole, the impression, produced by the Memoirs, of Frederick's sincerity is overwhelming. And perhaps the contradictions in his character, extreme as they are, are more apparent than real. Cynicism and sentimentality, so opposite in their effects, share at their root in a certain crudity; and Frederick, intellectually and spiritually, was crude. His ambitions, his scepticism, his admirations, his tastes—all were crude; on the one side this underlying quality came out in public Macchiavellisms and private cruelties, and on the other in highfalutin pathos and a schoolgirl's prostration before the literary man. On a smaller scale, such characters are not uncommon; what makes Frederick's case so extraordinary and at first sight so baffling is the extremity of difference to which the opposite tendencies were pushed. The explanation of this no doubt lies in the portentous, the terrific, energy of the man. His vehemence could be content with no ordinary moderation either in the callous or the lachrymose; and the same amazing force which made Prussia a Great Power created, in spite of incredible difficulties, in a foreign idiom, under the bondage of the harshest literary conventions ever known, that vast mass of fifth-rate poetising from which shuddering History averts her face.

From *Characters and Commentaries,* Chatto & Windus, London, 1933 (written in 1917)

Anonymous

Terror and Virtue

On May 6, 1758, there was born at Arras, in Picardy, Maximilien Francois Marie Isidore de Robespierre, who was for five years to play so considerable a part in the history of the French Revolution and finally to end on the scaffold, to which he had sent so many others. Looking back 200 years after his birth, his life seems less of an enigma than it did during the nineteenth century. The contrast between the prim middle-class existence, the powdered hair, and the neat clothes, and the terror which he advocated and directed, is less striking in 1958. Too many other precise dogmatists have signed death warrants since for the thing to be surprising. Even the real sincerity of a politician, who boasted of his incorruptibility and invoked a deist Supreme Being to approve his actions, recalls more recent and not less terrible apostles of virtue, Lenin and Hitler. In his report of February 5, 1794, Robespierre posed clearly enough the principles on which his political action was based: "virtue, without which terror is disastrous, and terror, without which virtue is powerless". He never seems to have perceived the revolutionary dilemma stated by his disciple Saint Just: "Virtue marries crime in times of anarchy". And it is strange how this mediocre little man, with his banal ideals gathered from Rousseau and his unprepossessing personality, should come to have such magnetic attraction that even to-day the name Robespierre furiously divides French historians. The answer seems to be that his clear, dogmatic, shallow mind, his thirst for absolutes, his lack of humour, his capacity for hard work typify certain qualities in the French petite bourgeoisie which have lasted till the present day, just as his economic ideas favoured the small business, the small holding, which still play so large a part in French life. For an Englishman his career can only confirm the belief that empiricism is the best approach to politics, and a cynical humanity the best qualification for politicians.

From *The Manchester Guardian,* leader of May 6, 1958

G. P. Gooch

Bismarck's Legacy

Makers of history from Julius Caesar to Adolf Hitler and Winston Churchill have felt an urge to write about themselves, to explain to posterity what they have done and tried to do, to justify the use they have made of their power, to cast the blame on others for what went wrong. Bismarck's apologia stands at the top of the list of political autobiographies, not merely because he is the greatest man who ever wrote a full-length narrative of his public career, and not merely owing to the earth-shaking events it describes, but because its utility as a manual of statesmanship is unsurpassed. It produces an almost overwhelming sense of power. So long as rulers desire guidance on the discharge of their perilous duties, and so long as students seek to unravel the tangled skein of European diplomacy, his volumes are likely to be read. Compared with their dynamic force and their majestic sweep, the lengthy narrations of Guizot and Bülow seem commonplace. Is it an exaggeration to describe the Iron Chancellor's political testament as the most authoritative treatise on the art of government since the "Prince" of Machiavelli? As a factual record and interpretation of events it is as open to criticism as any other work of its class. Its unique significance lies not only in the visualisation of the greatest figure of the nineteenth century except Napoleon, but in the maxims it enunciates and the warnings it suggests.

The lessons of Bismarck's political testament and unique career fall into two classes: those which concern statesmen of all times, and those specifically addressed to his own countrymen. The most important in the first category is enshrined in his celebrated aphorism: "Politics are the art of the possible", by which he meant the meticulous adjustment of ends to means. Qui trop embrasse mal étreint. Though nothing appears so obvious as the need for horse sense on the stony path or *haute politique,* no maxim has proved more difficult to apply by those who scale the giddy summits of power. The difference between practicable aims and *Cäsrenwahnsinn* was sharply illustrated by the careers of Frederick the Great and Napoleon. The former staked his fortunes on the seizure of Silesia, which events were to prove within his capacity to accomplish and retain. Though he cherished and fulfilled other territorial ambitions he never dreamt of fighting for them. Napoleon, on the other hand, intoxicated by his early victories in Italy, followed his delusive star and ended at St. Helena. The contrasted experiences of Bismarck and Hitler tell a similar tale. The former set out with a bold but limited resolve, and when he reached his goal he sheathed the sword. It was not a case of the Prussian eagle borrowing the silky plumes of a dove, but a cleareyed perception that there were limits to the strength of the Reich. Preventive wars he repudiated on the ground that no mortal could read the cards of Providence. The outstanding figure of the era of nationalism was neither an imperialist, for he never desired to impose German rule on alien races, nor a Pan-German, since he never aspired to bring all Germans into one fold. So long as he remained at the helm it could not be seriously argued that the new Reich had misused its strength. Hitler, on the other hand, neurotic, inexperienced and trusting to his intuitions, was spurred forward by ambition as insatiable as that of Napoleon, and even before his appointment as Chancellor he confided to Rauschning his fantastic dreams. Like Napoleon he never—in Byron's words—learned "that tempted fate will leave the loftiest star".

From this general principle of limiting risks stemmed a salutory exhortation to his countrymen, whose recurring temptation, located at the centre of the European chessboard without natural frontiers, has been to hit out in all directions. During the medieval *Kaiserzeit* it was an urge to the south, in the twentieth century the call of East and West. A weak and divided Germany has always been a tempting bait to greedy neighbours, a united and powerful Germany a potential threat. Though Bismarck solemnly adjured her rulers to avoid the simultaneous estrangement of East and West, the warning was in vain. In that well-organised state, it has been remarked, there was anarchy at the top. While Tirpitz, bent on challenging Britain's naval predominance, urged the covering of the German flank through an understanding with Russia, Bethmann advocated friendly relations with England as a condition of forward moves in the Middle East. Both policies had their advantages and their risks, and a choice should have been made between them, but there was no Bismarck to make it. Had he revisited the scenes of his triumphs in the opening decade of the twentieth century, he would have been appalled by the transformation of a friendly England and a neutral Russia into potential foes. Had he returned for a second time at the close of the second decade, he would have pointed in grief and anger to the result of a policy of uninsurable risks. Like the Emperor Augustus after the defeat of Varus in the battle of the Teutoburger Wald, he might have murmured: "Give me back my legions".

Statesmen can learn much of their trade in Bismarck's school but not the whole. *Raison d'état* is a polite name for an ugly thing—the divorce of politics from morals. This gospel of anarchy, formulated though not invented by Machiavelli, has been practised, if not always professed, by men of all races and creeds, by good and bad alike. "If I see my opportunity", exclaimed Frederick the Great when the sudden death of the Emperor Charles VI opened the road to Breslau, "shall I not take it?" Napoleon dismissed as *ideologues* men who, as he believed, refused to look facts in the face. In the latter half of the nineteenth century Cavour and Bismarck played the familiar game with complete lack of moral scruple and with consummate skill. "If we did for ourselves what we do for our country", remarked the maker of United Italy, "what rascals we should be". Among the most ingenious of his strategems was the dispatch of a beautiful countess to win the support of Napoleon III in expelling the Austrians from Lombardy. Though Bismarck stressed the importance of *imponderabilia,* when the right hour struck he acted without hesitation and let the world say what it liked. It is an error to regard Prussia as more of an aggressor than Piedmont and Bismarck as morally inferior to Cavour. It was not till the shattering experience of the first World War revealed the insufficiency of the sovereign state in an increasingly interdependent world that Woodrow Wilson, General Smuts, Lord Cecil and other practical idealists launched a crusade for a system which seemed to promise less tragic results.

A second weakness in Bismarckian statesmanship was his neglect to train his countrymen for self-government. His grant of adult suffrage suggested confidence in their wisdom and patriotism; but the Reichstag proved—and was intended to prove—little more than a fig-leaf, to use Liebknecht's drastic expression, to cover the nakedness of autocracy. That the power of the purse might have been put to better use is true enough, but the core of the Bismarckian constitution was the retention of final decisions in non-elective hands. A further bar to the democratisation of Germany was the maintenance of the Three Class voting system invented by Frederick Wilhelm IV for Prussia, which contained two-thirds of the population of the Reich and in which the rapidly growing army of urban workers did not count. So obsessed was Bismarck by the principle of undivided responsibility that, though he was prepared to admit to office Bennigsen, the trusty leader of the National Liberal, he declined the request to bring two of his Parliamentary colleagues with him, and the project of broadening the basis of government was dropped. When the Hohenzollern Empire fell with a crash in 1918 the problems of Weimar Germany had to be faced by amateurs.

It was not solely the fault of the Chancellor, for there was little demand for parliamentary government except among the Socialists and the Radicals. Collaboration worked well enough in South Germany, but the Emperor and the army chiefs, the Junkers and the great industrialists of the Rhineland, objected to entrusting the proletariat with a substantial share of power. Conservative historians such as Hans Delbrück and Adalbert Wahl regarded the Bismarckian constitution as a model blending of popular representation with an irremovable executive, thus ensuring continuity in foreign policy and national defence. Liberal scholars, on the other hand, such as Ziekursch and Erich Eyck, censure him for ignoring the world-wide demand for parliamentary government. He could not live for ever, and no other superman was in sight. Officials nominated or dominated by the ruler are as liable to make mistakes as Ministers responsible to Parliament.

Bismarck bequeathed to his grateful countrymen a superb inheritance: a nation-state, a Triple Alliance to ensure its safety, a federal constitution which satisfied the *amour propre* of the rulers of the component states, the beginnings of social security, colonial territory, and a prestige unknown since the Emperor Barbarossa. Almost all these assets were thrown away by the shortsighted successors who forgot that politics are the art of the possible. It is one of the ironies of history that his most enduring monument should be a book which would never have been written but for the accident of his dismissal. The action of a young ruler, so hotly resented by his victim, unwittingly set the seal on his immeasurable renown.

Bismarck spoke disdainfully of "Professor Gladstone", but are the practitioners of Realpolitik as much wiser as they believe? Their weakness is to think too much of immediate returns and too little of the long-range results of their hammer-strokes. Vast and splendid as was his intellect, he could see nothing and imagine nothing beyond the sovereign state pursuing exclusively its own supposed interests. For him Europe was only a geographical expression. The vision of an organised world, an international order, resting on a willing partnership of self-governing national units, was beyond his ken. The presupposition of all profitable political and economic planning is a firm grasp of the unity of civilisation, but to the shaping of the human spirit for that supreme adventure he contributed nothing. He laboured exclusively for his countrymen—first for Prussia and later for a Prussianised Reich—and was satisfied with their applause. In a word, he dates, for we have learned by bitter experience that nationalism is not enough. Yet the twentieth century will have little right to throw stones at the nineteenth until all the Great Powers begin to operate a system more conducive to human welfare than that which the Iron Chancellor practised and preached.

From *Catherine the Great and Other Studies,* Longmans, London, 1954

Richard Church

Winston S. Churchill

To introduce Winston Churchill to-day is rather like getting up at dawn to announce the rising of the sun. It is the action of a crank or an imbecile. This man, whose force of character and subtly-simple personality were for five years concentrated upon leading the British Commonwealth of Nations to victory, has stood for so long before the glare of publicity that he is a part of world history, and will be discussed accordingly for centuries to come. I can only remark here, therefore, upon the double aspect of his genius, and show how oddly, almost anachronistically, it is placed in time.

We had begun to think that the possibility of a man excelling both in the world of action and the world of letters had vanished. The world of action had become too vast, too specialized and departmentalized. The world of letters, in reflecting that other growth, had become too widely spread, and language had accordingly worn thin and threadbare. Could it be possible for one man to exercise again the classical gift of universal synthesis; to grasp with one hand the control of human affairs, and with the other a pen to record that control? It had been possible in the miniature Greek States during the Golden Age. It had been possible even in Imperial Rome, where the conditions of life were approximating more to those of our modern bureaucratic life. It had been possible, under certain retarded conditions, even as late as the beginning of the nineteenth century, as we see from the life and work of Goethe. But modern life and politics were too complicated, loaded with precedent and increasingly technical formality, to permit of divided service. We see how Henry Adams in America had to relinquish his political ambition in order to remain a historian. We see how Lord Macaulay in England, by remaining a historian and critic, carried the methods of his art into Parliament, and was little more than an ornament there.

Obvious conclusions were to be drawn from these examples; conclusions based on a study of facts and tendencies. Winston Churchill overthrew those conclusions, and in doing so returned us to a looser freer estimate of the age of civilization, and of its latent capacity for surprising us. He has made it young again, more elastic and adventurous. Its sophistications, its subservience to the spider-like control of the money-market, are challenged by his leadership. For, in effect, as in character, he is an artist, and in estimating the nature of his administrative method, its directness and dependence upon humane contacts and considerations, we have always to bear this in mind. And in the end, this recollection may help us to explain why Winston Churchill has always stood outside the political party machinery, its dullness, its routine, its clumsiness, while at the same time manipulating it with a skill that has made him suspect among the dunderheads and the office-mongers.

Along with that public life, he has been a writer. He entered the army at the age of twenty-one. He published his first commentary three years later (The Story of the Malakand Field Force). For nearly half a century since that first double overture, he has maintained that method of life. He acts first. Then he retires a little and digests his experience, before recording it as a well-considered body of facts, still warm in his grasp, but now ordered and knit together into an artistic significance. And the medium for that presentation is a prose as ample as his own personal gesture. It is part of his field of action. It is his courage and his genius for oratory brought to the study and demonstrated in privacy; that privacy of pen and ink which in the end is the greatest publicity of all; because more enduring than action, and more confiding than deeds. As will be seen from his three outstanding books, *My Early Life, The World Crisis,* and *Marlborough,* he is always the man of action, the shrewd and instant assessor of character and situation. It is this tremendous dynamic which fills his prose style, and makes it an ample vehicle for the man.

From *British Authors,* Longmans, London, 1943

Literature and Art

Graham Greene

The Lost Childhood

Perhaps it is only in childhood that books have any deep influence on our lives. In later life we admire, we are entertained, we may modify some views we already hold, but we are more likely to find in books merely a confirmation of what is in our minds already: as in a love affair it is our own features that we see reflected flatteringly back.

But in childhood all books are books of divination, telling us about the future, and like the fortune teller who sees a long journey in the cards or death by water they influence the future. I suppose that is why books excited us so much. What do we ever get nowadays from reading to equal the excitement and the revelation in those first fourteen years? Of course I should be interested to hear that a new novel by Mr. E. M. Forster was going to appear this spring, but I could never compare that mild expectation of civilized pleasure with the missed heartbeat, the appalled glee I felt when I found on a library shelf a novel by Rider Haggard, Percy Westerman, Captain Brereton or Stanley Weyman which I had not read before. No, it is in those early years that I would look for the crisis, the moment when life took a new slant in its journey towards death.

I remember distinctly the suddenness with which a key turned in a lock and I found I could read—not just the sentences in a reading book with the syllables coupled like railway carriages, but a real book. It was paper-covered with the picture of a boy, bound and gagged, dangling at the end of a rope inside a well with the water rising above the waist—an adventure of Dixon Brett, detective. All a long summer holiday I kept my secret, as I believed: I did not want anybody to know that I could read. I suppose I half consciously realised even then that this was the dangerous moment. I was safe so long as I could not read—the wheels had not begun to turn, but now the future stood around on bookshelves everywhere waiting for the child to choose—the life of a chartered accountant perhaps, a colonial civil servant, a planter in China, a steady job in a bank, happiness and misery, eventually one particular form of death, for surely we choose our death much as we choose our job. It grows out of our acts and our evasions, out of our fears and out of our moments of courage. I suppose my mother must have discovered my secret, for on the journey home I was presented for the train with another real book, a copy of Ballantyne's Coral Island with only a single picture to look at, a coloured frontispiece. But I would admit nothing. All the long journey I stared at the one picture and never opened the book.

But there on the shelves at home (so many shelves for we were a large family) the books waited—one book in particular, but before I reach that one down let me take a few others at random from the shelf. Each was a crystal in which the child dreamed that he saw life moving. Here in a cover stamped dramatically in several colours was Captain Gilson's *The Pirate Aeroplane.* I must have read that book six times at least—the story of a lost civilization in the Sahara and of a villainous Yankee pirate with an aeroplane like a box kite and bombs the size of tennis balls who held the golden city to ransom. It was saved by the hero, a young subaltern who crept up to the pirate camp to put the aeroplane out of action. He was captured and watched his enemies dig his grave. He was to be shot at dawn, and to pass the time and keep his mind from uncomfortable thoughts the amiable Yankee pirate played cards with him—the mild nursery game of Kuhn Kan. The memory of that nocturnal game on the edge of life haunted me for years, until I set it to rest at last in one of my own novels with a game of poker played in remotely similar circumstances.

And here is *Sophy of Kravonia* by Anthony Hope—the story of a kitchen-maid who became a queen. One of the first films I ever saw, about 1911, was made from that book, and I can hear still the rumble of the Queen's guns crossing the high Kravonian pass beaten hollowly out of a single piano. Then there was Stanley Weyman's *The Story of Francis Cludde,* and above all other books at that time of my life *King Solomon's Mines.*

This book did not perhaps provide the crisis, but it certainly influenced the future. If it had not been for that romantic tale of Allan Quartermain, Sir Henry Curtis, Captain Good, and, above all, the ancient witch Gagool, would I at 19 have studied the appointments list of the Colonial Office, and very nearly picked on the Nigerian Navy for a career? And later, when surely I ought to have known better, the odd African fixation remained. In 1935 I found myself sick with fever on a camp bed in a Liberian native's hut with a candle going out in an empty whisky bottle and a rat moving in the shadows. Wasn't it the incurable fascination of Gagool with her bare yellow skull, the wrinkled scalp that moved and contracted like the hood of a cobra, that led me to work all through 1942 in a little stuffy office in Freetown, Sierra Leone? There is not much in common between the land of the Kukuanas, behind the desert and the mountain range of Sheba's Breast, and a tin-roofed house on a bit of swamp where the vultures moved like domestic turkeys and the pi-dogs kept me awake on moonlight nights with their wailing, and the white women yellowed by atebrin drove by to the club; but the two belonged at any rate to the same continent, and, however distantly, to the same region of the imagination—the region of uncertainty, of not knowing the way about. Once I came a little nearer to Gagool and her witch hunters, one night in Zigita on the Liberian side of the French Guinea border, when my servants sat in their shuttered hut with their hands over their eyes and someone beat a drum and a whole town stayed behind closed doors while the big bush devil—whom it would mean blindness to see—moved between the huts.

But *King Solomon's Mines* could not finally satisfy. It was not the right answer. The key did not quite fit. Gagool I could recognize—didn't she wait for me in dreams every night in the passage by the linen cupboard, near the nursery door? and she continues to wait, when the mind is sick or tired, though now she is dressed in the theological garments of Despair and speaks in Spenser's accents:

> *The longer life, I wote the greater sin.*
> *The greater sin, the greater punishment.*

Yes, Gagool has remained a permanent part of the imagination, but Quartermain and Curtis—weren't they, even when I was only ten years old, a little too good to be true? They were men of such unyielding integrity (they would only admit to a fault in order to show how it might be overcome) that the wavering personality of a child could not rest for long against those monumental shoulders. A child, after all, knows most of the game—it is only an attitude to it that he lacks. He is quite well aware of cowardice, shame, deception, disappointment. Sir Henry Curtis perched upon a rock bleeding from a dozen wounds but fighting on with the remnant of the Greys against the hordes of Twala was too heroic. These men were like Platonic ideas: they were not life as one had already begun to know it.

But when—perhaps I was fourteen by that time—I took Miss Marjorie Bowen's *The Viper of Milan* from the library shelf, the future for better or worse really struck. From that moment I began to write. All the other possible futures slid away: the potential civil servant, the don, the clerk had to look for other incarnations. Imitation after imitation of Miss Bowen's magnificent novel went into exercise books—stories of sixteenth-century Italy or twelfth-century England marked with enormous brutality and a despairing romanticism. It was as if I had been supplied once and for all with a subject.

Why? On the surface *The Viper of Milan* is only the story of a war between Gian Galeazzo Visconti, Duke of Milan, and Mastino della Scala, Duke of Verona, told with zest and cunning and an amazing pictorial sense. Why did it creep in and colour and explain the terrible living world of the stone stairs and the never quiet dormitory? It was no good in that real world to dream that one would ever be a Sir Henry Curtis, but della Scala who at last turned from an honesty that never paid and betrayed his friends and died dishonoured and a failure even at treachery—it was easier for a child to escape behind his mask. As for Visconti, with his beauty, his patience and his genius for evil, I had watched him pass by many a time in his black Sunday suit smelling of mothballs. His name was Carter. He exercised terror from a distance like a snowcloud over the young fields. Goodness has only once found a perfect incarnation in a human body and never will again, but evil can always find a home there. Human nature is not black and white but black and grey. I read all that in *The Viper of Milan* and I looked round and I saw that it was so.

There was another theme I found there. At the end of *The Viper of Milan*—you will remember if you have once read it—comes the great scene of complete success—della Scala is dead, Ferrara, Verona, Novara, Mantua have all fallen, the messengers pour in with news of fresh victories, the whole world outside is cracking up, and Visconti sits and jokes in the wine light. I was not on the classical side or I would have discovered, I suppose, in Greek literature instead of in Miss Bowen's novel the sense of doom that lies over success—the feeling that the pendulum is about to swing. That too made sense; one looked around and saw the doomed everywhere—the champion runner who one day would sag over the tape; the head of the school who would atone, poor devil, during forty dreary undistinguished years; the scholar . . . and when success began to touch oneself too, however mildly, one could only pray that failure would not be held off for too long.

One had lived for fourteen years in a wild jungle country without a map, but now the paths had been traced and naturally one had to follow them. But I think it was Miss Bowen's apparent zest that made me want to write. One could not read her without believing that to write was to live and to enjoy, and before one had discovered one's mistake it was too late—the first book one does enjoy. Anyway she has given me my pattern—religion might later explain it to me in other terms, but the pattern was already there—perfect evil walking the world where perfect good can never walk again, and only the pendulum ensures that after all in the end justice is done. Man is never satisfied, and often I have wished that my hand had not moved further than *King Solomon's Mines,* and that the future I had taken down from the nursery shelf had been a district office in Sierra Leone and twelve tours of malarial duty and a finishing dose of blackwater fever when the danger of retirement approached. What is the good of wishing? The books are always there, the moment of crisis waits, and now our children in their turn are taking down the future and opening the pages. In his poem "Germinal" A.E. wrote:

> *In ancient shadows and twilights*
> *Where childhood had strayed*
> *The world's great sorrows were born*
> *And its heroes were made.*
> *In the lost boyhood of Judas*
> *Christ was betrayed.*

From *The Lost Childhood and Other Essays,* Viking, New York, 1951

Hamlet

Few critics have ever admitted that Hamlet the play is the primary problem, and Hamlet the character only secondary. And Hamlet the character has had an especial temptation for that most dangerous of critics: the critic with a mind which is naturally of the creative order, but which through some weakness in creative power exercises itself in criticism instead. These minds often find in Hamlet a vicarious existence for their own artistic realisation. Such a mind had Goethe, who made of Hamlet a Werther; and such had Coleridge, who made of Hamlet a Coleridge; and probably neither of these men in writing about Hamlet remembered that his first business was to study a work of art. The kind of criticism that Goethe and Coleridge produced, in writing of Hamlet, is the most misleading kind possible. For they both possessed unquestionable critical insight, and both make their critical aberrations the more plausible by the substitution—of their own Hamlet for Shakespeare's—which their creative gift effects. We should be thankful that Walter Pater did not fix his attention on this play.

Two writers of our time, Mr. J. M. Robertson and Professor Stoll of the University of Minnesota, have issued small books which can be praised for moving in the other direction. Mr. Stoll performs a service in recalling to our attention the labours of the critics of the seventeenth and eighteenth centuries, observing that "they knew less about psychology than more recent Hamlet critics, but they were nearer in spirit to Shakespeare's art; and as they insisted on the importance of the effect of the whole rather than on the importance of the leading character, they were nearer, in their old-fashioned way, to the secret of dramatic art in general".

Qua work of art, the work of art cannot be interpreted; there is nothing to interpret; we can only criticise it according to standards, in comparison to other works of art; and for "interpretation" the chief task is the presentation of relevant historical facts which the reader is not assumed to know. Mr. Robertson points out, very pertinently, how critics have failed in their "interpretation" of Hamlet by ignoring what ought to be very obvious: that Hamlet is a stratification, that it represents the efforts of a series of men, each making what he could out of the work of his predecessors. The Hamlet of Shakespeare will appear to us very differently if, instead of treating the whole action of the play as due to Shakespeare's design, we perceive his Hamlet to be superposed upon much cruder material which persists even in the final form.

We know that there was an older play by Thomas Kyd, that extraordinary dramatic (if not poetic) genius who was in all probability the author of two plays so dissimilar as the *Spanish Tragedy* and *Arden of Feversham;* and what this play was like we can guess from three clues: from the *Spanish Tragedy* itself, from the tale of Belleforest upon which Kyd's Hamlet must have been based, and from a version acted in Germany in Shakespeare's lifetime which bears strong evidence of having been adapted from the earlier, not from the later, play. From these three sources it is clear that in the earlier play the motive was a revenge motive simply; that the action or delay is caused, as in the *Spanish Tragedy,* solely by the difficulty of assassinating a monarch surrounded by guards; and that the "madness" of Hamlet was feigned in order to escape suspicion, and successfully. In the final play of Shakespeare, on the other hand, there is a motive which is more important than that of revenge, and which explicitly "blunts" the latter; the delay in revenge is unexplained on grounds of necessity or expediency; and the effect of the "madness" is not to lull but to arouse the king's suspicion. The alteration is not complete enough, however, to be convincing. Furthermore there are verbal parallels so close to the *Spanish Tragedy* as to leave no doubt that in places Shakespeare was merely *revising* the text of Kyd. And finally there are unexplained scenes—the Polonius-Laertes and the Polonius-Reynaldo scenes—for which there is little excuse; these scenes are not in the verse style of Kyd, and not beyond doubt in the style of Shakespeare. These Mr. Robertson believes to be scenes in the original play of Kyd reworked by a third hand, perhaps, Chapman, before Shakespeare touched the play. And he concludes, with very strong show of reason, that the original play of Kyd was, like certain other revenge plays, in two parts of five acts each. The upshot of Mr. Robertson's examination is, we believe, irrefragable; that Shakespeare's Hamlet, so far as it is Shakespeare's, is a play dealing with the effect of a mother's guilt upon her son, and that Shakespeare was unable to impose this motive successfully upon the "intractable" material of the old play.

Of the intractability there can be no doubt. So far from being Shakespeare's masterpiece, the play is most certainly an artistic failure. In several ways the play is puzzling, and disquieting as is none of the others. Of all the plays it is the longest and is possibly the one on which Shakespeare spent most pains; and yet he has left in it superfluous and inconsistent scenes which even hasty revision should have noticed. The versification is variable. Lines like

> *Look, the morn, in russet mantle clad,*
> *Walks o'er the dew of yon high eastern hill,*

are of the Shakespeare of *Romeo and Juliet.* The lines in Act V, Sc. 2,

> *Sir, in my heart there was a kind of fighting*
> *That would not let me sleep . . .*
> *Up from my cabin,*
> *My sea-gown scarf'd about me, in the dark*
> *Grop'd I to find out them: had my desire;*
> *Finger'd their packet . . .*

are of his quite mature. But workmanship and thought are in unstable position. We are surely justified in attributing the play, with that other profoundly interesting play of "intractable" material and astonishing versification, *Measure for Measure,* to a period of crisis, after which follow the tragic successes which culminate in *Coriolanus. Coriolanus* may not be as "interesting" as *Hamlet,* but it is, with *Antony and Cleopatra,* Shakespeare's most assured artistic success. And probably more people have thought *Hamlet* a work of art because they found it interesting, than have found it interesting because it is a work of art. It is the "Mona Lisa" of literature.

The grounds of Hamlet's failure are not immediately obvious. Mr. Robertson is undoubtedly correct in concluding that the essential emotion of the play is the feeling of a son towards his guilty mother: "[Hamlet's] tone is that of one who has suffered tortures on the score of his mother's degradation. . . . The guilt of a mother is an almost intolerable motive for drama, but it had to be maintained and emphasized to supply a psychological solution, or rather a hint of one".

This, however, is by no means the whole story. It is not merely the "guilt of a mother" that cannot be handled as Shakespeare handled the suspicion of Othello, the infatuation of Antony, or the pride of Coriolanus. The subject might conceivably have expanded into a tragedy like these, intelligible, self-complete, in the sunlight. *Hamlet,* like the Sonnets, is full of some stuff that the writer could not drag to light, contemplate, or manipulate into art. And when we search for this feeling, we find it, as in the sonnets, very difficult to localize. You cannot point to it in the speeches; indeed, if you examine the two famous soliloquies you see the versification of Shakespeare, but a content which might be claimed by another, perhaps by the author of the *Revenge of Bussy d'Ambois,* Act V, Sc. 1. We find Shakespeare's Hamlet not in the action, not in any quotations that we might select, so much as in an unmistakable tone which is unmistakably not in the earlier play.

The only way of expressing emotion in the form of art is by finding an "objective correlative"; in other words, a set of objects, a situation, a chain of events which shall be the formula of that *particular* emotion; such that when the external facts, which must terminate in sensory experience, are given, the emotion is immediately evoked. If you examine any of Shakespeare's more successful tragedies, you will find this exact equivalence; you will find that the state of mind of Lady Macbeth walking in her sleep has been communicated to you by a skilful accumulation of imagined sensory impressions; the words of Macbeth on hearing of his wife's death strike us as if, given the sequence of events, these words were automatically released by the last event in the series. The artistic "inevitability" lies in this complete adequacy of the external to the emotion; and this is precisely what is deficient in Hamlet. Hamlet (the man) is dominated by an emotion which is inexpressible, because it is in *excess* of the facts as they appear. And the supposed identity of Hamlet with his author is genuine to this point: that Hamlet's bafflement at the absence of objective equivalent to his feelings is a prolongation of the bafflement of his creator in the face of his artistic problem. Hamlet is up against the difficulty that his disgust is occasioned by his mother, but that his mother is not an adequate equivalent for it; his disgust envelops and exceeds her. It is thus a feeling which he cannot understand; he can not objectify it, and it therefore remains to poison life and obstruct action. None of the possible actions can satisfy it; and nothing that Shakespeare can do with the plot can express Hamlet for him. And it must be noticed that the very nature of the *données* of the problem precludes objective equivalence. To have heightened the criminality of Gertrude would have been to provide the formula for a totally different emotion in Hamlet; it is just *because* her character is so negative and insignificant that she arouses in Hamlet the feeling which she is incapable of representing.

The "madness" of Hamlet lay to Shakespeare's hand; in the earlier play a simple ruse, and to the end, we may presume, understood as a ruse by the audience. For Shakespeare it is less than madness and more than feigned. The levity of Hamlet, his repetition of phrase, his puns, are not part of a deliberate plan of dissimulation, but a form of emotional relief. In the character of Hamlet is the buffoonery of an emotion which can find no outlet in action; in the dramatist it is the buffoonery of an emotion which he can not express in art. The intense feeling, ecstatic or terrible, without an object or exceeding its object, is something which every person of sensibility has known; it is doubtless a subject of study for pathologists. It often occurs in adolescence: the ordinary person puts these feelings to sleep, or trims down his feelings to fit the business world; the artist keeps them alive by his ability to intensify the world to his emotions. The Hamlet of Laforgue is an adolescent; the Hamlet of Shakespeare is not, he has not that explanation and excuse. We must simply admit that here Shakespeare tackled a problem which proved too much for him. Why he attempted it at all is an insoluble puzzle; under compulsion of what experience he attempted to express the inexpressibly horrible, we cannot ever know. We need a great many facts in his biography; and we should like to know whether, and when, and after or at the same time as what personal experience, he read *Montaigne*, II, xii, *Apologie de Raimond Sebond*. We should have, finally, to know something which is by hypothesis unknowable, for we assume it to be an experience which, in the manner indicated, exceeded the facts. We should have to understand things which Shakespeare did not understand himself.

From *Selected Essays,* Faber & Faber, London, 1919

Hilaire Belloc

King Lear

The great unity which was built up two thousand years ago and was called Christendom in its final development split and broke in pieces. The various civilisations of its various provinces drifted apart, and it will be for the future historian to say at what moment the isolation of each from all was farthest pushed. It is certain that the point is passed.

In the task of reuniting what was broken—it is the noblest work a modern man can do—the very first mechanical act must be to explain one national soul to another. That act is not final. The nations of Europe, now so divided, still have more in common than those things by which they differ, and it is certain that when they have at last revealed to them their common origin they will return to it. They will return to it, perhaps, under the pressure of war waged by some not Christian civilisation, but they will return. In the meanwhile, of those acts not final, yet of immediate necessity in the task of establishing unity, is the act of introducing one national soul to another.

Now this is best accomplished in a certain way which I will describe. You will take that part in the letters of a nation which you maturely judge most or best to reflect the full national soul, with its qualities, careless of whether these be great or little; you will take such a work as reproduces for you as you read it, not only in its sentiment, but in its very rhythm, the stuff and colour of the nation; this you will present to the foreigner, who cannot understand. His efforts must be laborious, very often unfruitful, but where it is fruitful it will be of a decisive effect.

Thus let anyone take some one of the immortal things that Racine wrote and show them to an Englishman. He will hardly ever be able to make anything of it at first. Here and there some violently emotional passage may faintly touch him, but the mass of the verse will seem to him dead. Now, if by constant reading, by association with those who know what Racine is, he at last sees him—and these changes in the mind come very suddenly—he will see into the soul of Gaul. For the converse task, today not equally difficult but once almost impossible, of presenting England to the French intelligence—or indeed to any other alien intelligence—you may choose the play *King Lear*.

That play has every quality which does reflect the soul of the community in which and for which it was written. Note a few in their order. First, it is not designed to its end; at least it is not designed accurately to its end; it is written as a play and it is meant to be acted as a play, and it is the uniform opinion of those versed in plays and in acting that in its full form it could hardly be presented, while in any form it is the hardest even of Shakespeare's plays to perform. Here you have a parallel with a thousand mighty English things to which you can turn. Is there not institution after institution to decide on, so lacking a complete fitness for its end, larger in a way than the end it is to serve, and having, as it were, a life of its own which proceeds apart from its effect? This quality which makes so many English things growths rather than instruments is most evident in the great play.

Again, it has that quality which Voltaire noted, which he thought abnormal in Shakespeare, but which is the most national characteristic in him, that a sort of formlessness, if it mars the framework of the thing and spoils it, yet also permits the exercise of an immeasurable vitality. When a man has read *King Lear* and lays down the book, he is like one who has been out in one of those empty English uplands in a storm by night. It is written as though the pen bred thoughts. It is possible to conjecture as one reads, and especially in the diatribes, that the pen itself was rapid and the brain too rapid for the pen. One feels the rush of the air. Now, this quality is to be discovered in the literature of many nations, but never with the fullness which it has in the literature of England. And note that in those phases of the national life when foreign models have constrained this instinct of expansion in English verse, they never have restrained it for long, and that even through the bonds established by those models the instinct of expansion breaks. You see it in the exuberance of Dryden and in the occasional running rhetoric of Pope, until it utterly loosens itself with the end of the eighteenth century.

The play is national again, in that permanent curiosity upon knowledgable things—nay, that mysterious half-knowledge of unknow-able things—which, in its last forms, produced the mystic, and which is throughout history so plainly characteristic of these Northern Atlantic islands. Every play of Shakespeare builds with that material, and no writer, even of the English turn, has sent out points farther into the region of what is not known than Shakespeare has in sudden flashes of phrase. But *King Lear,* though it contains a lesser number of lines of this mystical and half-religious effect than, say, *Hamlet,* yet as a general impression is the more mystical of the two plays. The element of madness, which in *Hamlet* hangs in the background like a storm-cloud ready to break, in *King Lear* rages; and it is the use of this which lends its amazing psychical power to the play. It has been said (with no great profundity of criticism) that English fiction is chiefly remarkable for its power of particularization of character, and that where French work, for instance, will present ideas, English will present persons. The judgement is grossly insufficient, and therefore false, but it is based upon a proof which is very salient in English letters, which is that, say, in quite short and modern work the sense of complete unity deadens the English mind. The same nerve which revolts at a straight road and at code of law, revolts against one tone of thought; and the sharp contrast of emotional character, not the dual contrast which is common to all literatures, but the multiple contrast, runs through *King Lear* and gives the work such a tone that one seems as one reads it to be moving in a cloud.

The conclusion is perhaps Shakespearean rather than English, and in a fashion escapes any national labelling. But the note of silence which Shakespeare suddenly brings in upon the turmoil, and with which he is so fond of completing what he has done, would not be possible were not that spirit of expansion and of a kind of literary adventurousness present in all that went before.

It is indeed this that makes the play so memorable. And it may not be fantastic to repeat and expand what has been said above in other words, namely, that King Lear has something about him which seems a product of English landscape and English weather, and if its general movement is a storm its element is one of those sudden silences that come sometimes with such magical rapidity after the booming of the wind.

From *Selected Essays,* Methuen, London, 1948

Robert Lynd

Robinson Crusoe

Robinson Crusoe is as familiar a figure in the general imagination as Jack the Giant-Killer. He is, I think, the only hero of a long novel who has frequently been the centre of a Christmas pantomime. I do not suppose one person in a hundred reads *Robinson Crusoe* after the school age. Even so, most people feel that they know Robinson Crusoe, with his dog, his cats, his parrot, and his man Friday, as one of the immortal legends.

And there could be no better adventure story to read at any age. Compare it with the travel books that are so popular nowadays—and *Robinson Crusoe* is largely a travel book in the form of fiction—and how many of them approach it in variety of excitement, observation and interest? It would be the perfect travel book if it were true, and while we read it we believe that it is in fact true. We enjoy in it at once the excitements of fiction and of the old voyagers' tales.

Never elsewhere in popular fiction, I think, have we had a hero who, during at least half the story, never even speaks to another human being. (I am referring, I should say, only to the first volume of *Robinson Crusoe,* which is all that is published in many editions, and which is all that most boys read.) Yet seldom for a page do we cease to follow the alterations in the life of the solitary castaway with fascinated curiosity. There are some people who maintain that Robinson Crusoe is not a very real character, and that it is in his adventures rather than in himself that we are interested. I do not agree with them.

Robinson Kreuznaer—Bob Crusoe, as his schoolfellows called him—seems to me to use the very speech of reality from the time when first, without his father's consent, he leaves Hull on a ship bound for London. In his follies, his hopes, and his fears, he reflects moods that all human beings know, and, all through his life, from the time of his capture and enslavement by the Moors, he moves in the light of the sun, an ordinary human being flung into extraordinary circumstances. A hundred attempts have been made to explain the spell of *Robinson Crusoe,* but none of them can be successful which ignores the reality of Crusoe himself, and the fact that even from a psychological point of view he is more truly observed and created than the heroes of most of the so-called psychological novels of modern times.

The truth is that Robinson is an exceedingly deft mixture of several of the elements of good fiction. It is at once about a real person and a figure in a fairy-tale; it is both realistic and sensational; it fulfills the dream of every child about a little island of its own and at the same time excites all the inherited fears of solitude and danger.

Without some such variety of imaginative appeal, the story would have been bound to be monotonous. Some critics, indeed, have underestimated the imaginative quality of Defoe's writing: they even complain that he has not brought the scenery of Crusoe's island clearly before our eyes.

I wonder, however, if any other scenery in fiction is much more vivid in the memory than the long level of the sandy beach of the island on which the ship was wrecked. It is brought home to us in sentence after sentence, as Crusoe swims and staggers through the shallow water with the great breaker pursuing him. A retreating wave leaves him almost dry, and he scrambles to his feet.

Struggling towards the land, he looks back apprehensively and "I saw", he says, "the sea come after me like a great hill, and as furious as an enemy, which I had no means or strength to contend with. . . . The wave that came upon me again buried me at over twenty or thirty feet in its own body, and I could feel myself carried with a mighty force and swiftness towards the shore a very great way; but I held my breath, and assisted myself to swim still forward with all my might". Clearly, Defoe himself saw that shallow shore as vividly as though it had been outside his study window, and he makes us see it with the same vividness.

He is a master, indeed, of the kind of detail that brings a whole scene to life. How well he brings home the loneliness of Crusoe, and the sense of the loss of his comrades when he makes him write of them: "As for them, I never saw them afterwards, or any sign of them, except three of their hats, one cap and two shoes that were not fellows". Those "two shoes that were not fellows" might be used as a text for a sermon on the secrets of good writing.

Robinson Crusoe is the oldest novel in the English language that has survived for the general reader, and it has survived largely through Defoe's genius for particularity. The realist of to-day gives us plenty of insignificant detail. Defoe gives us only significant detail. He loves making catalogues of things, like a child writing a letter about the Christmas presents it has received; and everything that Crusoe recovers on his journeys to the wreck before it finally disappears—the three bags full of nails and spikes, the great screw-jack, the seven muskets, the three large runlets of rum, and the pair of large scissors—becomes as interesting to us as a Christmas present in the nursery. Descriptions of the utensils in a large English house might well become wearisome, but even a bagful of stale chicken food is treasure trove on a desert island when, on being thrown out as worthless, it may sprout into crops of corn and rice. For *Robinson Crusoe* is a story of magic as well as of character.

Magic alone would not have made a great story, as readers of the *Swiss Family Robinson* will agree; and character might have resulted merely in a tragic story of a miserable wretch, if there had not been good fairies to provide Crusoe with the wherewithal to shoot, to cook, to till the ground, to build boats, to surround himself with a small menagerie of pets, and even, till the ink ran down, to write. All the offices of the good fairies, however, do not detract from the moral triumph of Crusoe (during the twenty-four years before he rescued Friday from the cannibals and so added a second human being to the population of the island) in housing, feeding, and clothing himself, and maintaining not only sanity, but a kind of cheerfulness. "I had never handled a tool in my life", says Crusoe, and yet, as builder, farmer, slaughterman, tailor, and carpenter, he had in the course of time achieved an all-round success surpassing anything recorded in Smile's *Self-Help*. Even if we did not sympathise with him, we should respect him as (in the modern phrase) "the man who made good".

But we do sympathise with him at every turn of his fortunes—when his boat is carried out to sea on the current, and, thinking he is lost, he longs for the island as "home"—when, seeing the print of the naked foot in the sand, he flies to his castle and passes a sleepless night in terror—when, having observed the cannibal visitors at their orgies, he meditates wrathfully on putting five or six pounds of gunpowder under the place where they made their fire to blow them up, and then begins to wonder whether it is right to murder even cannibals—when he has rescued Friday and taught him English and the Protestant religion, and finds it difficult to answer his objection: "If God much strong, much might as the devil, why God no kill the devil, so make him no more do wicked? " Defoe is not much praised for humour, but there is a quiet smile in the story at times that lights up Crusoe and makes him a more than ever attractive figure. We like him the better even for laughing at his grotesque appearance in his goat-skin cap, goat-skin jacket and breeches, with the "great clumsy, ugly, goat-skin umbrella" over his head, and wondering what would be thought of him if he travelled in such a dress through Yorkshire. We like him immensely in the comical description of himself and his "little family" sitting down to dinner—the dog sitting at his right hand, the two cats at opposite sides of the table, and the parrot, "the only person permitted to talk to me". Here he becomes an oddity as well as an ordinary man. There are few more irresistible combinations in fiction.

Mrs. Thrale in her *Anecdotes* quotes Dr. Johnson as saying: "Alas, Madam, how few books are there of which one can even possibly arrive at the last page! Was there ever yet anything written by mere man that was wished longer by its readers, except *Don Quixote, Robinson Crusoe* and the *Pilgrim's Progress*? " That is a tribute with which everybody would agree if Defoe had not written the second part, and with which most of us would agree, even though the second part falls short of the interest of the first.

From *Books and Writers,* Dent, London, 1952 (written in 1934)

Virginia Woolf

The Novels of Turgenev

Rather more than fifty years ago Turgenev died in France and was buried in Russia, appropriately it may seem, if we remember how much he owed to France and yet how profoundly he belonged to his own land. The influence of both countries is to be felt if we look at his photograph for a moment before reading his books. The magnificent figure in the frock coat of Parisian civilisation seems to be gazing over the houses far away at some wider view. He has the air of a wild beast who is captive but remembers whence he came. "C'est un colosse charmant, un doux géant aux cheveux blancs, qui a l'air du bienveillant génie d'une montagne ou d'une fôrêt", the brothers Goncourt wrote when they met him at dinner in 1863. "Il est beau, grandement beau, énormément beau, avec du bleu du ciel dans les yeux, avec le charme du chantonnement de l'àccent russe, de cette cantilène où il y a un rien de l'enfant et du nègre". And Henry James noted later the great physical splendour, the Slav languor and "the air of neglected strength, as if it had been part of his modesty never to remind himself that he was strong. He used sometimes to blush like a boy of sixteen". Perhaps something of the same combination of qualities is to be found if we turn to his books.

At first, after years of absence it may be, they seem to us a little thin, slight and sketchlike in texture. Take *Rudin,* for instance—the reader will place it among the French school, among the copies rather than the originals, with the feeling that the writer has sat himself an admirable model, but in following it has sacrificed something of his own character and force. But the superficial impression deepens and sharpens itself as the pages are turned. The scene has a size out of all proportion to its length. It expands in the mind and lies there giving off fresh ideas, emotions and pictures much as a moment in real life will sometimes only yield its meaning long after it has passed. We notice that though the people talk in the most natural speaking voices, what they say is always unexpected; the meaning goes on after the sound has stopped. Moreover, they do not have to speak in order to make us feel their presence; "Volintsev started and raised his head, as though he had just waked up"—we had felt him there though he had not spoken. And when in some pause we look out of the window, the emotion is returned to us, deepened, because it is given through another medium, by the trees or the clouds, by the barking of a dog, or the song of a nightingale. Thus we are surrounded on all sides—by the talk, by the silence, by the look of things. The scene is extraordinarily complete.

It is easy to say that in order to gain a simplicity so complex Turgenev has gone through a long struggle of elimination beforehand. He knows all about his people, so that when he writes he chooses only what is most salient without apparent effort. But when we have finished *Rudin, Fathers and Children, Smoke, On the Eve* and the others, many questions suggest themselves to which it is not so easy to find an answer. They are so short and yet they hold so much. The emotion is so intense and yet so calm. The form is in one sense so perfect, in another so broken. They are about Russia in the fifties and sixties of the last century, and yet they are about ourselves at the present moment. Can we then find out from Turgenev himself what principles guided him—had he, for all his seeming ease and lightness, some drastic theory of art? A novelist, of course, lives so much deeper down than a critic that his statements are apt to be contradictory and confusing; they seem to break in the process of coming to the surface, and do not hold together in the light of reason. Still, Turgenev was much interested in the art of fiction, and one or two of his sayings may help us to clarify our impressions of the famous novels. Once, for example, a young writer brought him the manuscript of a novel to criticize. Turgenev objected that he had made his heroine say the wrong thing. "What then ought she to have said? " the author asked. Turgenev exploded: "Trouver l'expression propre, c'est votre affaire! " But, the youth objected, he could not find it. "Eh bien! vous devez la trouver. . . . Ne pensez pas, que je sais l'espression et que je ne veux pas vous la dire. Trouver, en la cherchant, une expression *propre* est impossible: elle doit couler de source. Quelquefois même, il faut créer l'expression ou le mot". And he advised him to put away his manuscript for a month or so, when the expression might come to him. If not—"Si vous n'y arrivez pas, cela voudra dire que vous ne ferez jamais rien qui vaille". From this it would seem that Turgenev is among those who hold that the right expression, which is of the utmost importance, is not to be had by observation, but comes from the depths unconsciously. You cannot find by looking. But then again he speaks of the novelist's art, and now he lays the greatest emphasis upon the need of observation. The novelist must observe everything exactly, in himself and in others. "La douleur passera et la page excellente reste". He must observe perpetually, impersonally, impartially. And still he is only at the beginning. "Il faut encore lire, toujours étudier, approfondir tout ce qui entoure, non seulement tâcher de saisir la vie dans toutes les manifestations, mais encore la comprendre, comprendre les lois, d'après lesquelles elle se meut et qui ne se montrent pas toujours". That was, how he himself worked before he grew old and lazy he said. But one has need of strong muscles to do it, he added; nor, if we consider what he is asking can we accuse him of exaggeration.

For he is asking the novelist not only to do many things but some that seem incompatible. He has to observe facts impartially, yet he must also interpret them. Many novelists do the one; many do the other—we have the photograph and the poem. But few combine the fact and the vision; and the rare quality that we find in Turgenev is the result of this double process. For in these short chapters he is doing two very different things at the same time. With his infallible eye he observes everything accurately. Solomin picks up a pair of gloves; they were "white chamois-leather gloves, recently washed, every finger of which had stretched at the tip and looked like a finger-biscuit". But he stops when he has shown us the glove exactly; the interpreter is at his elbow to insist that even a glove must be revelant to the character, or to the idea. But the idea alone is not enough; the interpreter is never allowed to mount unchecked into the realms of imagination; again the observer pulls him back and reminds him of the other truth, the truth of fact. Even Bazarov, the heroic, packed his best trousers at the top of his bag when he wanted to impress a lady. The two partners work in closest alliance. We look at the same thing from different angles, and that is one reason why the short chapters hold so much; they contain so many contrasts. On one and the same page we have irony and passion;

the poetic and the commonplace; a tap drips and a nightingale sings. And yet, though the scene is made up of contrasts, it remains the same scene; our impressions are all relevant to each other.

Such a balance, of course, between two very different faculties is extremely rare, especially in English fiction, and demands some sacrifices. The great characters, with whom we are so familiar in our literature, the Micawbers, the Pecksniffs, the Becky Sharps, will not flourish under such supervision; they need, it seems, more license; they must be allowed to dominate and perhaps to destroy other competitors. With the possible exception of Bazarov and of Harlov in *A Lear of the Steppes* no one character in Turgenev's novels stands out above and beyond the rest so that we remember him apart from the book. The Rudins, the Larretskys, the Litvinovs, the Elenas, the Lisas, the Mariannas shade off into each other, making with all their variations, one subtle and profound type rather than several distinct and highly individualized men and women. Then, again, the poet-novelists like Emily Brontë, Hardy or Melville, to whom facts are symbols, certainly give us a more overwhelming and passionate experience in *Wuthering Heights* or *The Return of the Native* or *Moby Dick* than any that Turgenev offers us. And yet, what Turgenev offers us not only affects us as poetry, but his books are perhaps more completely satisfying than the others. They are curiously of our own time, undecayed, and complete in themselves.

For the other quality that Turgenev possesses in so great a degree is the rare gift of symmetry, of balance. He gives us, in comparison with other novelists, a generalized and harmonized picture of life. And this is not only because his scope is wide—he shows us different societies, the peasant's, the intellectual's, the aristocrat's, the merchant's—but we are conscious of some further control and order. Yet such symmetry. as we are reminded, perhaps, by reading *A House of Gentlefolk,* is not the result of a supreme gift for storytelling. Turgenev, on the contrary, often tells a story very badly. There are loops and circumlocutions in his narrative—". . . we must ask the reader's permission to break off the thread of our story for a time", he will say. And then for fifty pages or so we are involved in great-grandfathers and great-grandmothers, much to our confusion, until we are back with Lavretsky at O—"where we parted from him, and whither we will now ask the indulgent reader to return with us". The good storyteller, who sees his book as a succession of events, would never have suffered that interruption. But Turgenev did not see his books as a succession of events; he saw them as a succession of emotions radiating from some character at the centre. A Bazarov, a Harlov seen in the flesh, perhaps once in the corner of a railway carriage, becomes a paramount importance and acts as a magnet which has the power to draw things mysteriously belonging, though apparently incongruous, together. The connexion is not of events but of emotions, and if at the end of the book we feel a sense of completeness, it must be that in spite of his defects as a storyteller Turgenev's ear for emotion is so fine that even if he uses an abrupt contrast, or passes away from his people to a description of the sky or of the forest, all is held together by the truth of his insight. He never distracts us with incongruity—the introduction of an emotion that is false, or a transition that is arbitrary.

It is for this reason that his novels are not merely symmetrical but make us feel so intensely. His heroes and heroines are among the few fictitious characters of whose love we are convinced. It is a passion of extraordinary purity and intensity. The love of Elena for Isarov, her anguish when he fails to come, her despair when she seeks refuge in the chapel in the rain; the death of Bazarov and the sorrow of his old father and mother remain in the mind like actual experiences. And yet, strangely enough, the individual never dominates; many other things seem to be going on at the same time. We hear the hum of life in the fields; a horse champs his bit; a butterfly circles and settles. And as we notice, without seeming to notice, life going on, we feel more intensely for the men and women themselves because they are not the whole of life, but only part of the whole. Something of this, of course, is due to the fact that Turgenev's people are profoundly conscious of their relation to things outside themselves. "What is my youth for, what am I living for, why have I a soul, what is it all for? " Elena asks in her diary. The question is always on their lips.

It lends a profundity to talk that is otherwise light, amusing, full of exact observation. Turgenev is never, as in England he might have been, merely the brilliant historian of manners. But not only do they question the aim of their own lives but they brood over the question of Russia. The intellectuals are always working for Russia; they sit up arguing about the future of Russia till the dawn rises over the eternal samovar. "They worry and worry away at that unlucky subject, as children chew away at a bit of india-rubber", Potugin remarks in *Smoke.* Turgenev, exiled in body, cannot absent himself from Russia—he has the almost morbid sensibility that comes from a feeling of

inferiority and suppression. And yet he never allows himself to become
a partisan, a mouthpiece. Irony never deserts him; there is always the
other side, the contrast. In the midst of political ardour we are shown
Fomushka and Fimushka, "chubby, spruce little things, a perfect pair
of little pollparrots", who manage to exist very happily singing glees in
spite of their country. Also it is a difficult business, he reminds us, to
know the peasants, not merely to study them. "I could not *simplify*
myself", wrote Nezhdanow, the intellectual, before he killed himself.
Moreover, though Turgenev could have said with Marianna " . . . I
suffer for all the oppressed, the poor, the wretched in Russia", it was
for the good of the cause, just as it was for the good of his art, not to
expatiate, not to explain. "Non, quand tu as énoncé le fait, n'insiste
pas. Que le lecteur le discute et le comprenne lui-même. Croyez-moi,
c'est mieux dans l'intérêt même des idées qui vous sont chères". He
compelled himself to stand outside; he laughed at the intellectuals; he
showed up the windiness of their arguments, the sublime folly of their
attempts. But his emotions and their failure, affect us all the more
powerfully now because of that aloofness. Yet, if this method was
partly the result of discipline and theory, no theory, as Turgenev's
novels abundantly prove, is able to go to the root of the matter and
eliminate the artist himself; his temperament remains ineradicable.
Nobody, we say over and over again as we read him, even in a
translation, could have written this except Turgenev. His birth, his race,
the impressions of his childhood, pervade everything that he wrote.

But though temperament is fated and inevitable, the writer has a
choice, and a very important one, in the use he makes of it. "I" he must
be; but there are many different "I's" in the same person. Shall he be
the "I" who has suffered this slight, that injury, who desires to impose
his own personality, to win popularity and power for himself and his
views; or shall he suppress that "I" in favour of the one who sees as far
as he can impartially and honestly, without wishing to plead a cause or
to justify himself? Turgenev had no doubt about his choice; he refused
to write "élégamment et chaudement ce que vous ressentez à l'aspect de
cette chose ou de cette homme". He used the other self, the self which
has been so rid of superfluities that it is almost impersonal in its intense
individuality; the self which he defines in speaking of the actress
Violetta:

She has thrown aside everything subsidiary, everything superfluous, and *found herself;* a rare, a lofty delight for an artist! She

had suddenly crossed the limit, which it is impossible to define, beyond which is the abiding place of beauty.

That is why his novels are still so much of our own time; no hot and personal emotion has made them local and transitory; the man who speaks is not a prophet clothed with thunder but a seer who tries to understand. Of course there are weaknesses; one grows old and lazy as he said; sometimes his books are slight, confused, and perhaps sentimental. But they dwell in "the abiding place of beauty" because he chose to write with the most fundamental part of his being as a writer; nor, for all his irony and aloofness, do we ever doubt the depth of his feelings.

From *The Captain's Death Bed and Other Essays,* Hogarth, London, 1950 (written in 1933)

D. H. Lawrence

The Grand Inquisitor

It is a strange experience, to examine one's reaction to a book over a period of years. I remember when I first read *The Brothers Karamazov,* in 1913, how fascinated yet unconvinced it left me. And I remember Middleton Murry* saying to me: "Of course the whole clue to Dostoievsky is in that Grand Inquisitor story". And I remember saying: "Why? It seems to me just rubbish".

And it was true. The story seemed to me just a piece of showing off: a display of cynical-satanical pose which was simply irritating. The cynical-satanical pose always irritated me, and I could see nothing else in that black-a-vised Grand Inquisitor talking at Jesus at such length. I just felt it was all pose; he didn't really mean what he said; he was just showing off in blasphemy.

Since then I have read *The Brothers Karamazov* twice, and each time found it more depressing because, alas, more drearily true to life. At first it had been lurid romance. Now I read *The Grand Inquisitor* once more, and my heart sinks right through my shoes. I still see a trifle of cynical-satanical showing off. But under that I hear the final and unanswerable criticism of Christ. And it is a deadly, devastating summing up, unanswerable because borne out by the long experience of humanity. It is reality versus illusion, and the illusion was Jesus', while time itself retorts with the reality.

*Editor's Note: Before this preface was published the name of Katherine Mansfield was substituted for that of Middleton Murry (Preface to the Grand Inquisitor story, translated by S. S. Koteliansky, London, 1930).

If there is any question: Who is the grand Inquisitor? —then surely we must say it is Ivan himself. And Ivan is the thinking mind of the human being in rebellion, thinking the whole thing out to the bitter end. As such he is, of course, identical with the Russian revolutionary of the thinking type. He is also, of course, Dostoievsky himself, in his thoughtful, as apart from his passionate and inspirational self. Dostoievsky half hated Ivan. Yet, after all, Ivan is the greatest of the three brothers, pivotal. The passionate Dmitri and the inspired Alyosha are, at last, only offsets to Ivan.

And we cannot doubt that the Inquisitor speaks Dostoievsky's own final opinion about Jesus. The opinion is, baldly, this: Jesus, you are inadequate. Men must correct you. And Jesus in the end gives the kiss of acquiescence to the Inquisitor, as Alyosha does to Ivan. The two inspired ones recognise the inadequacy of their inspiration: the thoughtful one has to accept the responsibility of a complete adjustment.

We may agree with Dostoievsky or not, but we have to admit that his criticism of Jesus is the final criticism, based on the experience of two thousand years (he says fifteen hundred) and on a profound insight into the nature of mankind. Man can but be true to his own nature. No inspiration whatsoever will ever get him permanently beyond his limits.

And what are the limits? It is Dostoievsky's first profound question. What are the limits to the nature, not of Man in the abstract, but of men, mere men, everyday men?

The limits are, says the Grand Inquisitor, three. Mankind in the bulk can never be "free", because man on the whole makes three grand demands on life, and cannot endure unless these demands are satisfied.

1. He demands bread, and not merely as foodstuff, but as a miracle, given from the hand of God.

2. He demands mystery, the sense of the miraculous in life.

3. He demands somebody to bow down to, and somebody before whom all men shall bow down.

These three demands, for miracle, mystery and authority, prevent men from being "free". They are man's "weakness". Only a few men, the elect, are capable of abstaining from the absolute demand for bread, for miracle, mystery, and authority. These are the strong, and they must be as gods, to be able to be Christians fulfilling all the Christ-demand. The rest, the millions and millions of men throughout time, they are as babes or children or geese, they are too weak, "impotent, vicious, worthless and rebellious" even to be able to share out the earthly bread, if it is left to them.

This, then, is the Grand Inquisitor's summing up of the nature of mankind. The inadequacy of Jesus lies in the fact that Christianity is too difficult for men, the vast mass of men. It could only be realised by the few "saints" or heroes. For the rest, man is like a horse harnessed to a load he cannot possibly pull. "Hadst Thou respected him less, Thou wouldst have demanded less of him, and that would be nearer to love, for his burden would be lighter".

Christianity, then, is the ideal, but it is impossible. It is impossible because it makes demands greater than the nature of man can bear. And therefore, to get a livable, working scheme, some of the elect, such as the Grand Inquisitor himself, have turned round to "him", that other great Spirit, Satan, and have established Church and State on "him". For the Grand Inquisitor finds that to be able to live at all, mankind must be loved more tolerantly and more contemptuously than Jesus loved it, loved, for all that, more truly, since it is loved for itself, for what it is, and not for what it ought to be. Jesus loved mankind for what it ought to be, free and limitless. The Grand Inquisitor loves it for what it is, with all its limitations. And he contends his is the kinder love. And yet he says it is Satan. And Satan, he says at the beginning, means annihilation, and not-being.

As always in Dostoievsky, the amazing perspicacity is mixed with ugly perversity. Nothing is pure. His wild love for Jesus is mixed with perverse and poisonous hate of Jesus: his moral hostility to the devil is mixed with secret worship of the devil. Dostoievsky is always perverse, always impure, always an evil thinker and a marvellous seer.

It is true that mankind demands, and will always demand, miracle, mystery, and authority? Surely it is true. To-day, man gets his sense of the miraculous from science and machinery, radio, aeroplanes, vast ships, zeppelins, poison gas, artificial silk: these things nourish man's sense of the miraculous as magic did in the past. But now, man is master of the mystery, there are no occult powers. The same with mystery: medicine, biological experiment, strange feats of the psychic people, spiritualists, Christian scientists—it is all mystery. And as for authority, Russia destroyed the Tsar to have Lenin and the present mechanical despotism, Italy has the rationalised despotism of Mussolini, and England is longing for a despot.

Dostoievsky's diagnosis of human nature is simple and unanswerable.

We have to submit, and agree that men are like that. Even over the question of sharing the bread, we have to agree that man is too weak, or vicious, or something, to be able to do it. He has to hand the common bread over to some absolute authority, Tsar or Lenin, to be shared out. And yet the mass of men are *incapable* of looking on bread as a mere means of sustenance, by which man sustains himself for the purpose of true living, true life being the "heavenly bread". It seems a strange thing that men, the mass of men, cannot understand that *life* is the great reality, that true living fills us with vivid life, "the heavenly bread", and earthly bread merely supports this. No, men cannot understand, never have understood that simple fact. They cannot see the distinction between bread, or property, money, and vivid life. They think that property and money are the same thing as vivid life. Only the few, the potential heroes or the "elect", can see the simple distinction. The mass *cannot* see it, and will never see it.

Dostoievsky was perhaps the first to realise this devastating truth, which Christ had not seen. A truth it is, none the less, and once recognised it will change the course of history. All that remains is for the elect to take charge of the bread—the property, the money—and then give it back to the masses as if it were really the gift of life. In this way, mankind might live happily, as the Inquisitor suggests. Otherwise, with the masses making the terrible mad mistake that money is life, and that therefore no one shall control the money, men shall be "free" to get what they can, we are brought to a condition of competitive insanity and ultimate suicide.

So far, well and good, Dostoievsky's diagnosis stands. But is it then to betray Christ and turn over to Satan if the elect should at last realise that instead of refusing Satan's three offers, the heroic Christian must now accept them? Jesus refused the three offers out of pride and fear: he wanted to be greater than these, and "above" them. But we now realise, no man, not even Jesus, is really "above" miracle, mystery, and authority. The one thing that Jesus is truly above, is the confusion between money and life. Money is not life, says Jesus, therefore you can ignore it and leave it to the devil.

Money is not life, it is true. But ignoring money and leaving it to the devil means handing over the great mass of men to the devil, for the mass of men *cannot* distinguish between money and life. It is hard to believe: certainly Jesus didn't believe it: and yet, as Dostoievsky and the Inquisitor point out, it is so.

Well, and what then? Must we therefore go over to the devil? After all, the whole of Christianity is not contained in the rejection of the three temptations. The essence of Christianity is a love of mankind. If a love of mankind entails accepting the bitter limitation of the mass of men, their inability to distinguish betwen money and life, then accept the limitation, and have done with it. Then take over from the devil the money (or bread), the miracle, and the sword of Caesar, and, for the love of mankind, give back to men the bread, with its wonder, and give them the miracle, the marvellous, and give them, in a hierarchy, someone, some men, in higher and higher degrees, to bow down to. Let them bow down, let them bow down *en masse,* for the mass, who do not understand the difference between money and life, should always bow down to the elect, who do.

And is that serving the devil? It is certainly not serving the spirit of annihilation and not-being. It is serving the great wholeness of mankind, and in that respect, it is Christianity. Anyhow, it is the service of Almighty God, who made men what they are, limited and unlimited.

Where Dostoievsky is perverse is in his making the old, old, wise governor of men a Grand Inquisitor. The recognition of the weakness of man has been a common trait in all great, wise rulers of people, from the Pharaohs and Darius through the great patient Popes of the early Church right down to the present day. They have known the weakness of men, and felt a certain tenderness. This is the spirit of all great government. But it was not the spirit of the Spanish Inquisition. The Spanish Inquisition in 1500 was a new-fangled thing, peculiar to Spain, with her curious death-lust and her bullying, and, strictly, a Spanish-political instrument, not Catholic at all, but rabidly national. The Spanish Inquisition actually was diabolic. It could not have produced a Grand Inquisitor who put Dostoievsky's sad questions to Jesus. And the man who put those sad questions to Jesus could not possibly have been a Spanish Inquisitor. He could not possibly have burnt a hundred people in an *auto-da-fé.* He would have been too wise and far-seeing.

So that, in this respect, Dostoievsky showed his epileptic and slightly criminal perversity. The man who feels a certain tenderness for mankind in its weakness or limitation is not therefore diabolic. The man who realises that Jesus asked too much of the mass of men, in asking them to choose between earthly and heavenly bread, and to judge between good and evil, is not therefore satanic. Think how difficult it is to know the difference between good and evil! Why, sometimes it is evil to be good. And how is the ordinary man to understand that? He can't. The extraordinary men have to understand it for him. And is that going over to the devil? Or think of the difficulty in choosing between the earthly and heavenly bread. Lenin, surely a pure soul, rose to great power simply to give men—what? The earthly bread. And what was the result? Not only did they lose the heavenly bread, but even the earthly bread disappeared out of wheat-producing Russia. It is most strange. And all the socialists and the generous thinkers of to-day, what are they striving for? The same: to share out more evenly the earthly bread. Even *they* who are practising Christianity *par excellence,* cannot properly choose between the heavenly and earthly bread. For the poor, they choose the earthly bread, and once more, as soon as it is really chosen, the earthly bread begins to disappear. It is a great mystery. But to-day, the most passionate believers in Christ believe that all you have to do is to struggle to give earthly bread (good houses, good sanitation, etc.) to the poor, and that is in itself the heavenly bread. But it isn't. Especially for the poor, it isn't. It is for them the loss of heavenly bread. And the poor are the vast majority. Poor things, how everybody hates them to-day! For benevolence is a form of hate.

What then is the heavenly bread? Every generation must answer for itself. But the heavenly bread is life, is living. Whatever makes life vivid and delightful is the heavenly bread. And the earthly bread must come as a by-product of the heavenly bread. The vast mass will never understand this. Yet it is the essential truth of Christianity, and of life itself. The few will understand. Let them take the responsibility.

Again, the Inquisitor says that it is a weakness in men, that they must have miracle, mystery and authority. But is it? Are they not bound up in our emotions, always and for ever, these three demands of miracle, mystery, and authority? If Jesus cast aside miracle in the Temptation, still there is miracle again in the Gospels. And if Jesus refused the earthly bread, still he said: "In my Father's house are many mansions". And for authority: "Why call ye me Lord, Lord, and do not the things which I say? "

The thing Jesus was trying to do was to supplant physical emotion by moral emotion. So that earthly bread becomes, in a sense, immoral, as it is to many refined people to-day. The Inquisitor sees that this is the mistake. The earthly bread must in itself be the miracle, and be bound up with the miracle.

And here, surely, he is right. Since man began to think and to feel vividly, seed-time and harvest have been the two great sacred periods of miracle, rebirth, and rejoicing. Easter and harvest-home are festivals of the earthly bread, and they are festivals which go to the roots of the soul. For it is the earthly bread as a miracle, a yearly miracle. All the old religions saw it: the Catholic still sees it, by the Mediterranean. And this is not weakness. This is *truth*. The rapture of the Easter kiss, in old Russia, is intimately bound up with the springing of the seed and the first footstep of the new earthly bread. It is the rapture of the Easter kiss which makes the bread worth eating. It is the absence of the Easter kiss which makes the Bolshevist bread barren, dead. They eat dead bread, now.

The earthly bread is leavened with the heavenly bread. The heavenly bread is life, is contact, and is consciousness. In sowing the seed man has his contact with earth, with sun and rain: and he *must not* break the contact. In the awareness of the springing of the corn he has his ever-renewed consciousness of miracle, wonder, and mystery: the wonder of creation, procreation, and re-creation, following the mystery of death and the cold grave. It is the grief of Holy Week and the delight of Easter Sunday. And man must not, must not lose this supreme state of consciousness out of himself, or he has lost the best part of him. Again, the reaping and the harvest are another contact, with earth and sun, a rich touch of the cosmos, a living stream of activity, and then the contact with harvesters, and the joy of harvest-home. All this is life, life, it is the heavenly bread which we eat in the course of getting the earthly bread. Work is, or should be, our heavenly bread of activity, contact and consciousness. All work that is not this, is anathema. True, the work is hard; there is the sweat of the brow. But what of it? In decent proportion, this is life. The sweat of the brow is the heavenly butter.

I think the older Egyptians understood this, in the course of their long and marvellous history. I think that probably, for thousands of years, the masses of the Egyptians were happy, in the hierarchy of the State.

Miracle and mystery run together, they merge. Then there is the third thing, authority. The word is bad: a policeman has authority, and no one bows down to him. The Inquisitor means: "that which men bow down to". Well, they bowed down to Caesar, and they bowed down to Jesus. They will bow down, first, as the Inquisitor saw, to the one who has the power to control the bread.

The bread, the earthly bread, while it is being reaped and grown, it is life. But once it is harvested and stored, it becomes a commodity, it becomes riches. And then it becomes a danger. For men think, if they only possessed the hoard, they need not work; which means, really, they need not live. And that is the real blasphemy. For while we live we must live, we must not wither or rot inert.

So that ultimately men bow down to the man, or group of men, who can and dare take over the hoard, the store of bread, the riches, to distribute it among the people again. The lords, the givers of bread. How profound Dostoievsky is when he says that the people will forget that it is their own bread which is being given back to them. While they keep their own bread, it is not much better than stone to them—inert possessions. But given back to them from the great Giver, it is divine once more, it has the quality of miracle to make it taste well in the mouth and in the belly.

Men bow down to the lord of bread, first and foremost. For, by knowing the the difference between earthly and heavenly bread, he is able calmly to distribute the earthly bread, and to give it, for the commonalty, the heavenly taste which they can never give it. That is why, in a democracy, the earthly bread loses its taste, the salt loses its savour, and there is no one to bow down to.

It is not man's weakness that he needs someone to bow down to. It is his nature, and his strength, for it puts him into touch with far, far greater life than if he stood alone. All life bows to the sun. But the sun is very far away to the common man. It needs someone to bring it to him. It needs a lord: what the Christians call one of the elect, to bring the sun to the common man, and put the sun in his heart. The sight of a true lord, a noble, a nature-hero puts the sun into the heart of the ordinary man, who is no hero, and therefore cannot know the sun direct.

This is one of the real mysteries. As the Inquisitor says, the mystery of the elect is one of the inexplicable mysteries of Christianity, just as the lord, the natural lord among men, is one of the inexplicable mysteries of humanity throughout time. We must accept the mystery, that's all.

But to do so is not diabolic.

And Ivan need not have been so tragic and satanic. He had made a discovery about men, which was due to be made. It was the rediscovery of a fact which was known universally almost till the end of the eighteenth century, when the illusion of the perfectibility of men, of all men, took hold of the imagination of the civilised nations. It was an illusion. And Ivan has to make a restatement of the old truth, that most men *cannot* choose between good and evil, because it is so extremely difficult to know which is which, especially in crucial cases: and that most men *cannot* see the difference between life-values and money-values: they can only see money-values; even nice simple people who *live* by the life-values, kind and natural, yet can only estimate value in terms of money. So let the specially gifted few make the decision between good and evil, and establish the life-values against the money-values. And let the many accept the decision, with gratitude, and bow down to the few, in the hierarchy. What is there diabolical or satanic in that? Jesus kisses the Inquisitor: Thank you, you are right, wise old man! Alyosha kisses Ivan: Thank you, brother, you are right, you take a burden off me! So why should Dostoievsky drag in Inquisitors and *autos-da-fé,* and Ivan wind up so morbidly suicidal? Let them be glad they've found the truth again.

From *Selected Literary Criticism,* Heinemann, London, 1955 (written in 1930)

John Lehmann

The Life of the Prodigal Son

At one time in my life I wanted to write poetry above all things, and I went to Vienna to devote myself to it. I don't quite know why I chose Vienna—I am sure the reasons I gave myself and others at the time only partly expressed the truth—but it seems to me now that I was drawn on by obscure impressions of childhood, things told me or overheard by me or seen in picture books, and sustained by the thought that I should be absolutely alone. And one of the few books I took with me, perhaps the one I was most careful to pack, was an English translation of Rilke's *Notebook of Malte Laurids Brigge.*

It was not my first acquaintance with this extraordinary book, which I now think one of the most original and beautiful books of the twentieth century; I had already, at various times, dipped into it, and I had already fallen under the spell of Rilke's poetry that has worked so powerfully on my generation; but I was now going to immerse myself in it under the conditions in which it demands to be read; in solitude, in a strange city, and with poetry in my head. It stayed with me, my favourite reading, all that late summer and autumn. Much of it I found hermetic, even incomprehensible, and impossible to relate to any central pattern; for it demands not only some knowledge of Rilke's own life to explain its riddles, but also a marriage of experiences and conceptions of which I was still too young to be aware. Again and again, however, I came upon passages that enthralled and haunted me, and one passage in particular that I read and re-read and tried to absorb into myself with all my assimilative power of mind, the passage in which Malte describes how to be a poet:

Verses amount to so little when one begins to write them young. One ought to wait and gather sense and sweetness a whole life long, and a long life if possible, and then, quite at the end, one might perhaps be able to write ten good lines. For verses are not, as people imagine, simply feelings (we have these soon enough); they are experiences. In order to write a single verse, one must see many cities, and men and things; one must get to know animals and the flight of birds, and the gesture that the little flowers make when they open out in the morning. One must be able to return in thought to roads in unknown regions, to unexpected encounters, and to partings that had been long foreseen; to days of childhood that are still indistinct, and to parents whom one had to hurt when they sought to give one some pleasure which one did not understand (it would have been a pleasure to someone else); to childhood's illnesses that so strangely begin with such a number of profound and grave transformations, to days spent in rooms withdrawn and quiet, and to mornings by the sea, to the sea itself, to oceans, to nights of travel that rushed along loftily and flew with all the stars—and still it is not enough to be able to think of all this. There must be memories of many nights of love, each one unlike the others, of the screams of women in labour, and of women in childbed, light and blanched and sleeping, shutting themselves in. But one must also have been beside the dying, must have sat beside the dead in a room with open windows and with fitful noises. And still it is not enough yet to have memories. One must be able to forget them when they are many, and one must have the immense patience to wait until they come again. For it is the memories themselves that matter. Only when they have turned to blood within us, to glance and gesture, nameless and no longer to be distinguished from ourselves—only then can it happen that in a most rare hour the first word of a poem arises in their midst and goes forth from them.

This seemed to me then one of the most wonderful releasing statements about poetry that I had ever read. It is, I can now see, an ideal which might lead to the writing of a great deal of very bad poetry, unless corrected by what one might call the *grammarian's* attitude which had been in fashion in the circles I moved in at Cambridge and directly after: the view that the first essential for the poet is to be able to think clearly and to use words precisely, and to express a certain intellectual energy in his views by his *wit,* in the sense of the term defined by T. S. Eliot. If the ultra-romantic view was responsible for a great deal of showy nonsense, this grammarian's view, admirable in its due place and proportion, was in danger, if slavishly followed, of producing mere arid exercises, the purely masculine without that feminine and intuitive element which is essential to poetry; all the more arid and marginal if the poet had also come under the influence of the equally fashionable 'clinical' view, which insisted that poetry was the resolution in words of obscure psychological tensions in the mind of its author. Rilke's words, so eloquent, so simple and so evocative, avoiding so carefully the exalted peaks of the claims made by the great romantics such as Shelley, seemed to me to present exactly what was missing in these views; a vision of how poetry was created or should be created in our post-romantic age, not by taking great themes and giving them the noblest treatment one was capable of, but by allowing the whole of experience, of years of thought and feeling and observation to be distilled in the depth of one's imagination, unforced and unhurried, to form their precious fluid. And, above all, it presented a design for the dedicated life a poet should lead, not merely for his working hours but for the whole preparation of himself before and between those (perhaps very brief) periods.

This ideal, of a life devoted to poetry, planned to provide the opportunity for every kind of experience that might nurture the poetic being and avoid every experience and entanglement that might be destructive to it, was grand enough when Rilke wrote the *Notebook* before the first world war. It is grander, in fact it is heroic now, when the wars and revolutions of our age have destroyed the old Europe, in which leisure was possible even if only for the more fortunate classes and those to whom they acted as patrons, and when the cancerous development of state control and interference has created an environment where everything conspires to ruin the inner life.

The fulfillment of the inner life was Rilke's own supreme object, and the passion with which he endowed Malte. Almost the last words in the *Notebook* are:

> Long ago he had detached himself from the accidents of fate to which men cling, but now even whatever of pleasure and pain were necessary lost their spicy after taste and became pure and nourishing to him. From the roots of his being there sprang the sturdy, evergreen plant of a fertile joy. He was wholly engrossed

in learning to handle what constituted his inner life; he wanted to omit nothing, for he doubted not that his love dwelt and grew in all this. Indeed, his inward serenity went so far that he resolved to overtake the most important of those things which he had hitherto been unable to accomplish, the things he had simply allowed to slip past while he waited.

The *Notebook* itself can be described as the record of how Rilke learnt, in the first period of his life as a poet, to 'handle his inner life'; it is a distillation of experience, through the invented character of the young Danish poet, that follows remarkably faithfully the prescription for a poet's life Rilke gives within it. All the wanderings, both over Europe and inside his own world of thought, all the emotions and spiritual struggles, all the provocative outward events and inward imaginative discoveries of six years of Rilke's life are mirrored in Malte's notebook; and the history of its development is a fascinating study of his creative processes at work.

We know from Maurice Betz, with whom Rilke collaborated in the French translation of the *Notebook* during his stay in Paris in 1925, that the original germ was Rilke's discovery of a book called *The Diary of a Priest,* by Sigbjorn Obstfelder, a young Norwegian writer who had come to live in Paris and died there at the early age of thirty-two. Rilke read this story of the struggles of a tormented soul to find God, a pursuit that ends in madness, at a time when his enthusiasm for anything Scandinavian was at its height; and the fact that Obstfelder had, like Rilke, been a stranger alone in Paris as a young man, made a special bond of sympathy. Rilke seems to have been haunted by the Norwegian from the beginning: and in the end his imaginative occupation of his life became so intense that he speaks of Malte as if he were a living person, always beside him; who was, as it were, dictating the book. 'I must not advance beyond him and his suffering too far,' he says in a letter to his wife in 1908, 'otherwise I will no longer understand him.' It is always in this strain that he speaks of the book; and his description of the sudden sprouting of the seed that Obstfelder's work had planted in his mind is like the account of a spiritual possession. Maurice Betz reports Rilke as telling him the story as follows:

At that time I was in Rome. I had been living for several

months in a little studio which had been lent me in the park of
the Villa Strohl-Fern. The Italian spring diasppointed me by its
undue haste, and my reading of Jacobsen awakened my longing
for that Northern country where I knew no one except the good
Ellen Key, to whom I had dedicated *The Stories of God.* I wrote
a series of dialogues between a young man and a young girl who
confide their little secrets to each other. The young man told the
girl a great deal about a Danish poet, a certain Malte, whom he
had known and who died young in Paris. The girl wanted to know
more about Malte, and the young man was indiscreet enough to
tell her that his friend had left a diary, while he admitted that he
himself had never looked into it yet. The girl begged him to let
her see it. I succeeded in keeping her waiting for several days by
various subterfuges, but her curiosity increased and in the end she
began to build up her own picture of Malte. I realized that it was
not permissible for me to offer resistance any longer, and so I
interrupted the dialogue and began to write Malte's own diary
without troubling any more with the subsidiary personages who
had led me to him almost against my will.

From that moment in 1904 the *Notebook* was always in Rilke's
mind; and from 1906 to 1910 with occasional intervals of a few weeks
or months when Malte's problems became too difficult for him to solve
and he had to turn away from the 'heavy, heavy book', it was his major
preoccupation as a writer. During that time he was restless and
dissatisfied, with frequent breakdowns in health, always moving from
one place to another, but experiencing new scenes and making new
friends—among them, one of the most important in his whole life,
Rodin—the stimulus of which can be traced again and again in the
Notebook. There was, first of all, the excitement of getting to know
Denmark, the country he was to make Malte's own. It is probably true,
as Countess Wydenbruck suggests in her book,* that the friends he
made during these years among the north German Lutheran nobility,
were probably as important, or even more important than his brief
experiences of Denmark itself, in providing him with material for
building up the background of Malte's family. Nevertheless, the Danish
visit was responsible for at least one of the most striking and

---

*Rilke: Man and Poet, a book to which I am immensely indebted in the
preparation of this study.

characteristic passages in the *Notebook,* where the young Malte and his mother visit the family of the Schulins, the great central wing of whose manor-house has recently been burnt down. Rilke describes the arrival by sleigh, in darkness and snowstorm:

> One might have imagined one saw the church tower on the left, but suddenly the outline of the park wall appeared, high up, almost on top of us, and we found ourselves in the long avenue. The tinkling of the bells no longer ceased abruptly; it seemed to hang in clusters right and left on the trees. Then we swung in and drove around something, passed something else on the right, and came to a halt in the centre.
>
> Georg had quite forgotten that the house was no longer there, and for all of us at that moment it was there. We ascended the front steps that led up to the old terrace, and only wondered at finding all in darkness. Suddenly a door opened below and behind us on the left, and someone cried, 'This way! ' at the same time lifting and swinging a dim lantern. My Father laughed: 'We are wandering about here like ghosts,' and he helped us down the steps again.
>
> 'But still there was a house there just now,' said Mother. . . .

The actual experience from which this episode was created, is related in a letter to Lou Andreas Salome in December 1904. He describes how he went to visit his Danish friend Ellen Key in a lonely country house that belonged to her brother:

> We found ourselves in the courtyard, enclosed by the small lateral wings of the chateau. But there, where four flights of steps ascended with a great effort from the deep snow of the courtyard to the terrace, on which a balustrade with ornamental vases appeared to herald the chateau itself, there was nothing except a few snow-covered shrubs and a grey, glimmering sky, against which I could distinguish snowflakes falling through the twilight. I had to remind myself that the building no longer existed, that I had been told how it had burnt down to the ground years ago, but still I could not help feeling that there must be something there, that the air behind the balustrade was not the same as the air around, but was still divided into passages and rooms and a great central hall, a high, empty, forsaken, twilit hall. . . .

Thus the actual description in the *Notebook* is taken almost exactly from Rilke's own experiences at Oby, but he transforms and enlarges it by making it pass through the wondering mind of a small boy who, quickly taking up the hint dropped by his mother, is overcome by the idea of this phantom house, tries to slip away to see it again, and *believes* in it in spite of the laughter of the others: ' "Of course they only go when it is not there", I thought contemptuously; "if Mother and I lived here, it would always be there". Mother looked distraught, while the others were all talking at once. She was certainly thinking of the house'.

Another striking example of Rilke's way of refashioning the experience of these years to make them part of the *Notebook* is the passage towards the end, where Malte is once more reminded of Abelone, vividly and with a new insight, by a girl he meets at a salon one afternoon in Venice. The famous description of Venice, not 'the soft, narcotic Venice' that is the illusion of the 'somnolent foreigners', but the real Venice of winter that reveals itself when they have gone, 'awake, brittle to breaking-point, and not in the least dream-like: this Venice willed into being in the midst of nothing and set on sunken forests, created by force, and in the end so thoroughly manifest', 'this inventive state that bartered the salt and glass of its poverty for the treasures of the nations', was directly inspired by the winter he spent in the city of 1907. The same images occur in a letter he wrote to his wife at the time, and in the poem *Spaetherbst in Venedig* which he published in *New Poems:*

> *Aber vom Grund aus alten Waldskeletten*
> *Steigt willen auf: als sollte über Nacht*
> *der General des Meeres die Galeeren*
> *verdoppeln in dem wachen Arsenal. . . .*

Even more fundamental to the purpose of the book was the vision of Paris he conjured up, in the opening passages of the *Notebook,* out of his early experiences when he went there for the first time in 1902, and his later impressions in 1907, when he shut himself up in his room in the Rue Cassette and worked at the *New Poems,* the book on Rodin and the *Notebook* itself throughout the summer and autumn. Again, nothing could be less sentimental than the vision this poet, who has so often been accused of sentimentality, created of Paris: for him it seemed always to be a city of macabre happenings, of suffering and poverty (except when he thought of it as the home of Rodin):

People come here, then, to live? I should rather have thought that they came here to die. I have been out, and I saw hospitals. I saw a poor fellow stagger and fall. People gathered round him; so I was spared the rest. I saw a pregnant woman. She dragged herself heavily along a high, warm wall, now and again groping for it as if to assure herself it was still there. . . .

These are the opening words of the *Notebook,* and they set the tone for all that comes after. His very first letter to his wife from Paris, in 1902, records the same impression, and shows that Malte's, that Obstfelder's nightmares had been his own: 'I am appalled at the great number of hospitals here. Legions of sick people, armies of dying men, populations of corpses—I have never felt this as strongly in any other city'. Even the man with St. Vitus's Dance appears first of all as a person actually observed and described in one of his letters a year later. And the macabre episode of the medical student in the room next door, whose eyelid refused to stay open and who in his misery and nervous exhaustion stamped up and down while a noise repeated itself—'the noise made by any round, tin object, such as the lid of a canister, when it slips from one's grasp'—this, too, came directly out of his own experience, while he was working at the *Notebook* in the Rue Cassette.

All these scenes, these moments of intense imaginative apprehension, Rilke was able to work into the fabric of the *Notebook,* while preserving the thematic wholeness of the book, with an art that reveals itself as more consummate with every reading. The method he had chosen, the apparently random record of an intimate journal, allowed him considerable latitude; and as he later admitted to Maurice Betz, his idea of giving it the air of incompleteness that the journal of the dead Obstfelder might well have had, so took possession of him that he did not even collect all the fragments he had written at one time or another for use in it. But the book is one; as a poem of loneliness and suffering, of death in all its mysterious and terrible aspects, the spiritual voyage through a haunted darkness of a young man who strives to recapture the beauty and meaning of his childhood; and to fulfil what he had left there incomplete and unsatisfied, by reliving the memories and using all his maturer powers to understand where and why he had failed to answer all the demands of heart and imagination made on him. The *Notebook* was to Rilke a 'heavy, heavy book', causing him such disturbance and exhaustion of spirit, because it was a delving into his own failures in the inner life; and yet, unlike Malte, he finally surmounted these failures to a miraculous degree by the very fact of writing out Malte's suffering. 'The creative artist is not permitted to select or to turn away from any form of existence', he wrote in an illuminating letter on Baudelaire's poem *La Charogne* in October 1907, 'surely among his earlier works there must be some where he overcame himself with a mighty effort, right to the utmost limits of love. Beyond this surrender lies saintliness, beginning with small things, the simple existence of a love that has passed the test, and, without boasting, approaches everything'. He was about to make that surrender himself, and the anticipation of it lies in what follows: 'Suddenly (for the first time) I understood Malte Laurids's fate. Is it not that the ordeal was too great for him, that he could not pass the actual test, though he was theoretically convinced of its necessity, so much so that he sought it out instinctively until it haunted him? The book of Malte Laurids once it is written, will be nothing but the story of this insight, exemplified in one for whom it was too mighty. . . .'

It was this insight which drew Malte to the story of the Prodigal Son, which forms part of the great coda to the *Notebook,* and out of which Rilke made one of the most beautiful of his shorter poems. Rilke and Malte then become one in what was perhaps the crucial spiritual problem of the poet's earlier years. 'It will be difficult to persuade me', writes Malte, 'that the story of the Prodigal Son is not the legend of one who did not want to be loved. When he was a child everybody in the house loved him. He grew up knowing nothing else, and as a child he became accustomed to their tenderness. But as a growing boy he sought to lay aside these habits . . . what he then desired was that inner indifference of spirit, which, sometimes, of an early morning in the fields, seized him so unalloyed that he began to run, that he might have neither time nor breath to be more than a transient moment in which the morning became conscious of itself'.

The impulse which, obscurely but so intensely, racks the Prodigal Son, is surely the deep instinct of the artist in one of its many disguises—the artist who must, as he becomes conscious of being an artist, learn to apprehend everything for himself and create his own universe before he can go back to the allegiances and habits of his childhood, so as to be strong enough to treat with them on equal terms. The desire not to be 'more than a transient moment in which the morning becomes conscious of itself' is not unlike Keats's idea that a poet must be capable of being everything and nothing and has no identity, and his confession that 'if a sparrow comes before my window I take part in its existence and pick about the gravel'. The similarity becomes even more striking when Malte goes on to describe, in a passage evidently inspired by Rilke's own holiday in Provence in the spring of 1909, the shepherd's life of the Prodigal Son: 'That was the time which began with his feeling himself a part of the universe and anonymous, like a lingering convalescent. He did not love unless it were that he loved to live. The lowly affection of his sheep did not weigh upon him; like light falling through clouds it dispersed itself about him and gleamed softly on the meadows. In the innocent track of their hunger he strode silently across the pastures of the world. Strangers saw him on the Acropolis; and perhaps he was for a long time one of the shepherds in Les Baux, and saw the petrified age outlast that lofty race which, despite all its acquisition of sevens and threes, could not master the sixteen rays of its star. . . .'

With Rilke, however, the mood of the Prodigal Son was not simply the impulse of the artist to become anonymous; it was at the same time the struggle against loving and being loved, a struggle that had in the end to be abandoned because the complete person, the complete artist (like Baudelaire) learns to love and be loved without shrinking, and the Prodigal Son (not Malte, but Rilke himself) comes home at last. These two themes are introduced in the *Notebook;* but the book is even more than the exploration of the artist's need to lose himself and the Prodigal Son's attempt to escape love, because Rilke's unique poetic faculty makes out of all the groupings within the spirit and journeyings in the outer world, a demonstration of his extraordinary sensibility so vivid and convincing that one feels one has acquired a new kind of perception. One actually sees with him a woman, too suddenly disturbed in her private thoughts, leaving her face in her hands and exposing something flayed and terrible to the onlooker, or one comes to think of death as a being that possesses (has always, in a slow process of growth, possessed) the dying creature and finally enacts its own individual drama—'one *had* it, and that gave one a singular dignity, a quiet pride'. And more than that, with its movement from Malte's own childhood reminiscences, the way of life in the old country houses, to his wanderings in the great cities, and from them to re-creations of legends and famous moments of history, it achieves an evocation of the ancient Europe, a four-dimensional evocation of a haunting resonance and depth. How deliberately this was in Rilke's design, one cannot be sure, but once one has observed how as an artist he loves to present symbols and drop hints within his work of what the work as a whole is fulfilling, one remembers in this connection the picture at the end of the *Notebook* of the sage, the older man who has travelled much in his youth and has long been considered eccentric, as the light burns late in his study:

> He does not always remain bent over his pages; he often leans back and closes his eyes on a line he has read again and again, and its meaning passes into his blood. Never before has he been so certain of the ancient past. He could almost smile at the generations that have mourned it as a lost drama, in which they would have liked to play a part. Now he instantly understands the dynamic significance of that early world-unity, which was something like a new and simultaneous gathering up of all human labour. . . .

In writing the *Notebook* Rilke felt, in a strange way, that he was exploring deeper even than in the poetry he had written hitherto. In his letters we find him talking of going back to the 'discipline of writing verses' and seeking renewal in nature, so that the inner world from the depths of which the *Notebook* was emerging should be 'strengthened and tautened by the influences of the external world'—as if his poetry, compared with his prose, was part of that external world; and in a letter to Rodin, in December 1908, he says, 'In writing poetry one is always helped, and even carried along, by the rhythm of external things—the waters, the winds, the night. But to acquire the rhythms of prose one must go deep down into oneself and find the anonymous and manifold rhythms of the blood'.

It was indeed out of these depths that the *Notebook of Malte Laurids Brigge* was created, and because Rilke was courageous and persistent enough, in spite of illness and misery and the resistance of the wounded memory, to explore them fully, it stands out, ever more clearly as the years go by, as a masterpiece. No book of our time is more passionately dedicated to the inner life, more completely infused with the belief in the primacy of the imagination, of the poetic way of apprehending life; and as the threat to all that it means increases like the deafening roar of a flight of super bombers in the sky, so we instinctively reach out to hold such precious things closer to us.

From *The Open Night,* Longmans, London, 1952

Ford Madox Ford

The Apotheosis of John Galsworthy

He made towards supreme Honours a tranquil course that suggested that of a white-sailed ship progressing inevitably across a halcyon sea. You would have said that he had every blessing that kings and people and providence had to bestow. Having refused a knighthood he was awarded the highest honour the King had at his disposal—that of the Order of Merit. He presided in Paris at the dinner of the international P.E.N. Club, which is the highest honour that the members of his craft could find for him; and, in the end, the Nobel Prize Committee honoured itself by selecting him for one of its laureates. It seemed, all this, appropriate and inevitable, for, in honouring him, the world honoured one of its noblest philanthropists.

The last time I saw him was in Paris when he gave his presidential address to his beloved P.E.N. And singularly, as he emerged above the shadow of all those hard French writers, there re-emerged, at any rate for me, the sense of his frailty . . . of his being something that must be shielded from the harder earnestnesses of the world. I don't know that he was conscious on that last public triumph of the really bad nature of the hard men who surrounded him. The world had moved onward since the days when he had read Maupassant and Turgenev for what he could learn from them. Both those writers were what he called dissolvents and the Paris littérateurs now wanted above all constructive writing and would have agreed with him if he had said—as he did in one of the last letters he wrote—that Tolstoi was a greater writer than Turgenev.

But, there, he said nothing of the sort. He seemed to float, above all those potential assassins, like a white swan above a gloomy mere, radiating bright sunlight . . . and with his gentle, modest French words he made statements that ran hissing through Paris as if he had drawn a whip across all those listening faces.

For the French writers of to-day, Maupassant is the Nihilist Enemy—an enemy almost as hated as the late Anatole France.

And Turgenev is an alien ugly duckling who once disgusted the paving-stones of Paris with his foreign footsteps. Nothing indeed so infuriates the French of to-day as to say that Turgenev was really a French writer. . . . And there enthroned and smiling, poor Galsworthy told that audience that shivered like tigers in a circus cage that, if he had trained himself to have any art, and if that training had landed him where he was, that art had been that of French writers.

A sort of buzzing of pleasurable anticipation went all round that ferocious assembly. The author of "Fort comme la Paix" looked at the author of "Nuits Ensoleillées" and thought: "Aha, my friend, this is going to be a bitter moment for you. When I consider the dédicace of the ignoble volume that this barbarian chieftain presented yesterday to me . . . when I consider the fulsome, but nevertheless deserved, praise that he wrote on that fly-leaf, I don't have a doubt who he is going to claim as his Master". And the author of the "Nuits Ensoleillées" looked back at the author of the other classic and thought exactly the same thing—with the necessary change in the identity of the author. And every French author present looked at every other French author and thought Thoughts similar. And when the applause subsided poor Jack went on:

Yes, he repeated, all the art he had had he had had of the French. If he stood where he was; if he was honoured as he was; it was because all his long life he had studied the works, he had been guided by the examples of . . . Guy de Maupassant and of him who though a foreigner by birth was yet more French in heart than any Frenchman—Ivan Turgenev!

I have never seen an audience so confounded. If an invisible force had snatched large, juicy joints of meat from the very jaws of a hundred Bengal tigers the effect would have been the same. They simply could not believe their ears . . . As for me, I was so overwhelmed with confusion that I ran out of the place and plunged, my cheeks still crimson, into the salon of the author of "Vasco", who was preparing to give a tea-party at the end of the Île St. Louis. And the news had got there before me. It was in the salon of every author of the Île, of the

Rue Guynemer, of the Rues Madame, Jacob, Tombe Issoire and Notre Dame des Champs before the triumphant Galsworthy had finished his next sentence. . . . For that was the real triumph of his radiant personality, that not one of the fierce beasts quivering under his lash so much as raised a protest. No other man in the world could have brought that off!

From *Ford Madox Ford*, Vol. I, Bodley Head, London, 1933

Thomas Mann

It is extraordinary, as one gets into these stories, how soon one forgets that Thomas Mann is a German. For the Germany he represents is like the lost continent of Atlantis of which he seems one of the few survivors, a Germany full of people like ourselves. Not a breath of politics disturbs these five hundred and fifty pages; the war occurs casually between Death in Venice and a dog story; the inflation gives rise to a study of a grandfather's feelings for his grandchild—even Mario the Magician will easily stand without its allegorical significance. Yes, here is a great artist writing for thirty years about a vanished and submerged race, a people who are as if they had never been, writing in exile of an enormous cultivated bourgeoisie, dignified, liberal, art-loving; bringing forth a certain amount of juvenile and morbid delinquents, but apparently for thirty years secure in the saddle, and now quite extinct, extinct as those early films, Destiny, Dr. Caligary, Warning Shadows, Dr. Mabuse, which once thrilled us with their hints of macabre patrician vices.

What makes the world of Thomas Mann so particularly remote is his own cultural background, the formative influences of his early years. These influences are clearly of the 'nineties, that is to say, they derive from the Flaubertian conception of art and the artist. Writing is a high calling exacting great labour and patience and a certain self-sacrifice from those who profess it. One can't expect to make much money, and one must be content to remain an observer of life and of one's own life, often deprived of the experiences which render more rounded and full those of other human beings. The artist is a being naturally isolated who cannot or should not seek admission to the organized body of society, he is an aristocratic ivory-towering hermit vowed from his birth to sensibility, austerity, loneliness and fame. To this ideal of the 'seventies and 'eighties the next decade added a delicious "art nouveau" touch. The artist should travel. And so there grew up a literature of these travelling artists; the romance of the liner and the wagon-lit appears, and a nostalgia for villages seen from trains, or for certain hotels, which increases among the writers of the nineteen-hundreds—till after Firbank, Larbaud, Morand, the new restrictions and the new currencies put an end to the travelling epoch. We now "read most of the night and go march on Sundays". It is interesting to compare the Venice of the "Aspern Papers" with that of "Tod in Venedig", the latter so full of hotels and "l'affreux lido", of carefully-built-up local colour exaggerated in a fin de siècle manner. Henry James' long short story of the 'eighties, on the other hand, is scrupulously reticent about the obvious charms of Venice, and is confined to the existence of two old ladies in a shabby palazzo in an unfashionable quarter—without the poster quality of Thomas Mann's story of 1914.

> He did not like to be aware of the hour or the day of the week, and, moreover he had no truck with the calendars. Some time ago he had lost the habit of knowing the day of the month or even the month of the year. Everything must be in the air—so he put it in his mind, and the phrase was comprehensive though rather vague. After all, was it not enough for him to know more or less what season it was? "It is more or less autumn", he thought, gazing out into the damp and gloomy train-shed. "More I do not know. Do I even know where I am? "

In this delicious aestheticism of 1899 we are at once reminded of the early Gide and the early Valéry. As the stories grow (although there are trains in nearly all of them), two themes emerge as those most congenial to his talent: studies of the nature of the artist—that being who, for Thomas Mann, combines the integrity and self-discipline of a puritan banker with the emotional depravity of a criminal—and studies of adolescence, often on a note of idealised homosexuality. In the best stories these two themes are combined, as in Tonio Kröger, Death in Venice or Felix Krull which is their satirical counterpart. They thus illustrate the extraordinary affinity which exists between his work and Gide's and, in a lesser degree, between him and the Henry James of the short stories, and E. M. Forster and the earlier Lawrence.

Landscape, Denmark 1903:

Sometimes it was still and summery there. The sea lay idle and smooth, in stripes of blue and russet and bottle green, played all across with glittering silvery lights. The seaweed shrivelled in the sun and the jellyfish lay steaming. Then grey stormy days would come. The waves lowered their heads like bulls and charged against the beach; they ran and ramped high up the sands and left them strewn with shining wet seagrass, driftwood and mussels. He went landward by lonely meadowpaths, and was swallowed up in the beachgroves that clothed the rolling landscape near and far. Here he sat down on the moss, against a tree, and gazed at the strip of water he could see between the trunks. Sometimes the sound of surf came on the wind—a noise like boards collapsing at a distance.

Death in Venice 1914:

His head burned, his body was wet with clammy sweat, he was plagued by intolerable thirst. He looked about for refreshment, of whatever sort, and found a little fruit-shop where he bought some strawberries. They were overripe and soft; he ate as he went. The street he was on opened out into a little square, one of those charmed, forsaken spots he liked. Grass grew between the stones and rubbish lay about. A waft of carbolic acid was borne on a warm gust of wind.

There he sat, the master: this was he who had found a way to reconcile art with honours, who had written The Abject, and in a style of classic purity renounced bohemianism and all its works, all sympathy with the abyss and the troubled depths of the outcast human soul. His eyelids were closed, there was only a swift sidelong glint of the eyeballs now and again, something between a question and a leer; while the rouged and flabby mouth uttered single words of the disordered sentences shaped in his brain by the fantastic logic that governs our dreams.

Dog-days 1918:

Certainly the meeting in the open of two dogs, strangers to each other is one of the most painful, thrilling, and pregnant of all conceivable encounters; it is surrounded by an atmosphere of the last uncanniness, presided over by a constraint for which I have no precise name; they simply cannot pass each other, their

mutual embarrassment is frightful to behold. . . . 'Go away', I
repeat in a lower voice. But Bashan does not go away, he sticks in
his distress the closer to me, making as brief a pause as he can at a
tree trunk to perform the accustomed rite. I can see the other dog
doing the same. We are now within twenty paces, the suspense is
frightful. The strange dog is crawling on his belly, like a cat, his
head thrust out. He is under a spell; he is bound to the other dog;
they are bound to each other with some obscure and equivocal
bond which may not be denied. We are now within two paces.
They cannot pass each other, they probably want to, they turn
away their heads, rolling their eyes sideways; evidently the same
sense of guilt weighs on them both.

These two quotations may show something of the many-sidedness
of this great, vigorous, and sensitive writer. It is obvious that the
later stories are the best; Mario the Magician, Disorder and Early
Sorrow, are little masterpieces; A Man and His Dog is remarkable.
Death in Venice is a borderline case. For one thing, alone among these
stories, it is not well translated. I am inclined to think that though
perfect in many details, and in form especially, there is something a
little artificial, almost arty, about the homosexual element—which is
not deep and honest enough—and something a little vulgar about the
thick palette which is used to describe the plague in Venice—but how, if
one can't read German, can one lay down the law?
    Death in Venice is based on a fundamental but neglected principle of
tragedy: the sequence of cause and effect. When von Aschenbach, the
austere great writer, is suddenly prompted to go to Venice by the
appearance of a wayfarer in a Munich cemetery, we feel that he is
doomed as any bull that enters the arena, creature of equal dignity or
fire. All von Aschenbach's elaborate spartanism crumbles under the
strain of his passion for a Polish boy whom he sees when he arrives on
the Lido. During the whole book they never speak, but Aschenbach
goes through all the stages of a desperate and irremediable passion,
blundering through Venice in pursuit of his idol as the bull blunders
after the sword that will kill it, and as the one sinks down to die, its
back planted with absurd streamers, so Aschenbach, now painted,
powdered, and rejuvenated by dyed hair, is carried off by the plague.
The plague in Venice forms the background, as if the author had
understood that the city's essential spirit, torrid, sinister, pagan and
decayed could reveal itself only in such a décor. Death appears in many

shapes through the book which, in spite of the Wagnerian union of love and death and the heavy quality of German Hellenism, has the frozen completeness of a work of art, a classic example of the tragic breaking-up of a fine character through the fatal abandon of age to its "sola et sera voluptas"—love for what Proust called "la jeuness féroce et légère".

Stories of Three Decades is not really a book to recommend to writers, for to those who wish to write well it is disheartening to find so much of themselves already expressed thirty years ago and in another language, and to those who don't care, Thomas Mann will prove only too easy to imitate. But for the disinterested this book presents, in the most readable way possible, the picture of a fine writer and his time, a writer who may lack the emotions which sweep over us to-day, but who stands master of a complete world and of his attitude to it, an attitude of great fertility, that of the artist, in all his sensuality, in all his distinction.

From *The Condemned Playground, Essays 1927-1944,* Routledge & Kegan Paul, London, 1945 (written in 1936)

Edward Charles Sackville-West

The Legacy of Germany in
Music and Literature

How indicate such riches in so small a space, otherwise than by a string of names? Should I sacrifice Mozart to Bach and Haydn, because of the Italian nature Mozart's music; Schumann and Weber to Beethoven and Schubert; rush past Liszt to dwell on Mendelssohn and Brahms; find no space for Wolf because Wagner takes up too much; and glancing at Mahler, Strauss and Schönberg, end the list with Hindemith? Should I, turning to literature ignore Winckelmann and Herder in favour of Lessing; confound Schiller and Goethe in a single pert phrase; dwell on Hölderlin and pass over Novalis, Jean-Paul, Hoffmann, Lenau, in silence; allow the bitterness of Heine to etch away the tender qualities of Chamisso, von Arnim, Brentano; consider the dramas of Kleist but not those of Grillparzer and Hebbel; ignore the Tennysonian beauties of Mörike, Eichendorff and Stifter; and wind up again with Thomas Mann, because I lack space for Rilke, George, Kafka? Better perhaps to attempt the largest possible view and try to discern, from above that vast Ruysdaelian landscape, the features which unify it—here the spire, there the spreading tree or windmill, the bird on the wing or the peasant with the plough. It is a beautiful, diverse, yet homely landscape; but the sky above it is neither clear nor unbroken: a thunderstorm approaches from the right background, sinister shafts of light pick out a group of houses; and the colours are those of autumn.

Like England, Germany is a land of poets; and poetry includes music, for there is no musical version of prose. Its nearest equivalent would perhaps be the fugue, and it is significant that Bach's music was the perfect expression of the Reformation spirit, by which Luther deprived Germany of the mythology she has ever since been striving to recapture. Here, I think, is the crux of the matter. The history of German art, no less in music than in literature, is that of a search for a mythology adequate to the needs of the teutonic soul. The tragedy of that search lies in its inevitable baulking by a soul so much at odds with itself that no mythology could satisfy it. Symbols must not be self-contradictory. Moreover, a mythology remains inert unless it is believed true, and to believe it true, is to live under the spell of its mysteries—to be content not to perceive its underpinning; for to understand a thing fully is to surpass it, and a mythology completely understood becomes a fable.

Christianity, Greece, the Nordic Sagas: from Winckelmann to Wagner, German poets and composers have wrestled with those incompatible gods, in the effort to achieve that final synthesis of opposites which Hegel asserted to be the key to human life, but which may be only the expression of a peculiarly German dilemma.

On the coast of Colombia stands one of the strangest and most fascinating towns in the world. Cartagena was founded by Charles V, who left it unfinished. The Indians, instead of undoing his work and rebuilding the town on their own lines, contented themselves with finishing the Renaissance buildings in a style of their own; so that the modern visitor is astounded by the sight of an elegant classical portal surmounted by a crazily ornate superstructure. The effect of an entire town built on these lines is bizarre and extravagant in the extreme, but not more so than the spectacle afforded by the great German romantics in an effort to fit the art and thought of the ancient world into the procrustean bed of their own strange sensibility. This attempt, which was initiated by Winckelmann in the middle of the eighteenth century, reached its height in the poetry of Hölderlin, and achieved a lurid sunset in the pseudo-philosophy of Nietzsche and the esoteric theories of Stephan George.

The whole movement, which produced all the best of German literature and some of the greatest poetry in the world, was in essence the outcome of the teutonic yearning for a mythology that should be their very own—a search the deplorable results of which we observe in the "new" Germany of to-day. "He bears his own pains more easily who sees his god suffer too", remarked Heine piercingly; and the hypostatisation of reality, whether in the interest of art or of life, is a game at which the Germans have always shown themselves to be proficient. To see life steadily and whole is a programme which fails to commend itself to this strange people, for, as Professor Butler observes, in her capital book, The Tyranny of Greece over Germany: "Accurate knowledge has little inspirational value".

Now German knowledge of Greek art was never accurate: it has little chance to be, since it was inaugurated by a man whose neurotic, if genuine, sensibility led him to see, not what was there, but what he wanted to see. Poor Winckelmann's disabilities (the expression imposes itself) landed him in the fatal error of finding all he wanted of Greece in Rome, and of refusing to look further. It was left to Lessing, a far greater man, and to Goethe, to discover the error; but neither was more successful in rectifying it. *Iphigenia,* though a poetic masterpiece, proved in the outcome to be quite as unsuited as the Laocoon group to exemplify the serenity and noble grandeur which Winckelmann laid down as the essential qualities of Greek art. The tragedy of Goethe's attempt to scale this Everest lay in the essential un-Greekness of his mind, though in this respect he was undoubtedly nearer to his ideal than the writers who followed in his wake.

If Goethe was in some ways able to surmount the inconsistencies and unrealities of his Hellenism, Hölderlin remained the martyr of the whole disastrous movement, for his mind was soon destroyed by the Frankenstein monsters of his own (and Goethe's and Schiller's) creation. Hölderlin's poem, *Bread and Wine,* is the bridge that, in their heart of hearts, both Goethe and Schiller longed to build—and which Goethe did, to some extent, build, in *Hermann and Dorothea.* There it stands; but, as Miss Butler points out, no orthodox Christian would dare attempt to cross it. Only a weightless spirit could pass safely across: Hölderlin did so, and in *Der Einzige* yielded to Christ. But the gods of his imaginary Greece—the Greece of his so often exquisite novel, *Hyperion*—had their revenge in the end.

To Heine, in some ways an even more tragic figure, the problem presented itself from a rather different angle—the sceptical, iconoclastic angle of the exile and the Jew. Apart from this fact, the parallel with Baudelaire is instructive, and one is not surprised that the lover of Crescentia Mirat, a stupid, selfish sensualist who corresponds so strikingly to Baudelaire's Jeanne Duval, should have ended, after many gyrations in substituting Dionysos for the Apollo of Goethe and Winckelmann. Nietzsche saw the possibility of making the best of both worlds, and stated the problem with a new and startling eloquence, in *The Birth of Tragedy*. But the eventual result in *Zarathustra*, was something more wildly un-Greek than anything Nietzsche's predecessors could have dreamed of, and "the deepest book in the German language" becomes, with the years, ever less convincing. Thenceforward, the battle may be considered lost, in spite of the attempts of distinguished poets, such as Carl Spitteler and Stefan George, to rejoin it.

To see life steadily and whole seems all but impossible to the supercharged mind of the Teuton; only Goethe perhaps, achieved that wisdom, and then only at the cost of his creative power—his demon. For us English it has been otherwise: the world of Shakespeare is our world, and his philosophy—an empirical one, which Mr. T. S. Eliot has called a rag-bag philosophy—is the one we still steer by. The pathos of the German passion for Shakespeare is an effect of their inability to accept the view of life which his dramas imply. Likewise, in their pursuit of Greek beauty, they ended by embracing a shadow: Faust's Helen is really Brünnhilde in disguise, while the method of the Ring is finally the result of a misconception of Greek drama which, under the aegis of Lessing, arose with Goethe's *Iphigenia* and Schiller's *Bride of Messina*. and continued with Kleist's *Penthesilea* and the stiff but noble plays of Grillparzer.

To put the matter differently: the tragedy of the German creative writers of the nineteenth century was that they strove to do what their brothers, the composers, were doing better; for it is only in music that spiritual opposites can truly be dissolved into an organic whole. It was Beethoven, not Goethe, who achieved this miracle of synthesis: the *Ninth Symphony* fuses the pagan and Christian sacraments into a whole not achieved even by that masterpiece of German poetry, Hölderlin's *Brot und Wein*. Yet this poem is one of the keystones of German literature; it has the supercharged quality I have mentioned—the brimming, elegiac passion peculiar to the music of German hexameters —the music of Goethe's *Euphrosyne,* or Rilke's *Duineser Elegien* (another keystone)—that unique quality which, translated into another kind of harmony, fills the Clarinet Quintets of Mozart and Brahms, saturates Beethoven's Mass in D (the Mount Everest of music, an unscalable peak), and can still be heard in what is perhaps the greatest symphony since the classical Viennes period—Mahler's *Ninth.*

After the composition of the *Eroica,* the complexities of human emotion tended, in the teutonic mind, to resolve themselves in the free language of music. For the metaphysical struggle which I have represented as the basis of German art finds its most natural outlet in the allegory. Now allegory is the soul of opera, but it is the enemy of the novel. In the hundred years which stretch from *Wilhelm Meister* to *der Zauberberg,* what of real importance has the German novel to offer? Freytag's *Soll und Haben,* no doubt, the novels and stories of Adalbert Stifter (an Austrian) and *Der Grüne Heinrich* of Gottfried Keller (a Swiss). But no *Lys dans la Vallée* no *Madame Bovary,* no *Middlemarch.* Poetic psychology, the development of which produced a spate of masterpieces in England, France and Russia during the nineteenth century, in Germany took form in the song-cycles of Schubert and Schumann, to issue eventually in the Wagnerian leitmotiv. In place of *Anna Karenina, Tristan and Isolde;* instead of *David Copperfield, Die Meistersinger;* instead of the *Mayor of Casterbridge,* Wolf's *Prometheus;* and Schumann's *Kreisleriana* have outlived the stories (admirable as these are) which inspired them.

Yet the demonic element in the teutonic soul has not always been dominant, and quite other qualities, no less strong, have produced three interrelated kinds of masterpiece: the lyric, the short story and the song. The turn of the eighteenth century was Germany's Elizabethan age. The songs of Shakespeare and Ford and Beaumont remained unequalled until Goethe put words into the mouth of Mignon, and the simplicity of the German *Lied* is the subtlest thing their art has achieved. Schubert, Schumann and Wolf; Brentano, Heine, Mörike and Eichendorff; Tieck, Jean-Paul, Hoffmann, Keller, Stifter: the names evoke a long series of lyrical comments on the extraordinary things which happen to ordinary folk and what they feel about them. They are discreet and perfect, the single cries of a passionate and naive people in love with the magic and mystery of Nature; they ring like a tuning-fork. It is the world of *Hermann und Dorothea* we are in now—the landscape of the Rhineland in September. We are back in the country of *Brot und Wein;* but it is the cosy homeliness, the towheaded child biting into an apple, the young lovers in the sunset, that meet our eyes now.

German art is commonly accused of excessive romanticism. Certainly Wagner, and before him Beethoven, have much to answer for.

The new styles they evolved gave vast scope to the nimiety of thought and feeling, the weathercock emotionalism, that has ever been the bane of Germany. Luckily for her, however, Providence has injected her with a ceaseless yearning after the classical south; Austria has been (and will be again) her corrective, and behind Austria, Italy. Few events in modern history have been so ironically symbolic as the forced marriage which Germany's ambivalent feeling towards Italy foisted upon her. Goethe and Christine Vulpius together brought forth the *Roman Elegies;* it was too much to expect that Ribbentrop and Ciano would be able to repeat a miracle of that order.

From *Inclinations,* Secker & Warburg, London, 1949 (written in 1938)

J. B. Priestley

Orchestras Tuning Up

We are told that some Oriental visitor, attending one of our symphony concerts for the first time, was particularly delighted by what he thought was the opening piece on the programme, the sound of the orchestra tuning up. But I am not sure that he was wrong. *Is* there in fact anything more delightful in all the symphonies, concertos and tone-poems that follow than this anonymous opening piece, so enormous in its promise, so cunningly anticipatory of the best of what is to come. What else that we hear during the evening takes such a hold on the imagination? It is, if you like, a chaos, this tuning-up-and-trying-the-instrument-and-having-a-go-at-the-difficult-bit noise; but it is a chaos caught at the supreme moment, immediately before Creation. Everything of order and beauty shortly to be revealed is already there in it. Moreover, it never fails us, unlike some of the compositions that will follow it. We never find ourselves groaning over its interminable slow movements, its tedious crescendos. It is never pretentious, never bogus. It is as delightful, crammed with as much promise, the hundredth time we hear it as it was the first: and indeed I think it grows on us. Moreover, it belongs to all schools, smiling at old Haydn and yet nodding to Schönberg, and so is always in fashion. All the instruments, from the piccolo to the contra-bassoon, play their part in it. And it conducts itself and asks for no applause. Is there a good gramophone record of it? If so, my birthday is the 13th of September.

From *Delights,* No. 89, Heinemann, London, 1949

Neville Cardus

Mozart, the Unparalleled

Over two hundred years ago Mozart was born at Salzburg on 27th January. His star was temporarily obscured by the post-Beethoven Wagnerian aesthetic, dramatical-symphonical, quasi-symphonical, hero-ical-ethical and pastoral, the aesthetic of the fertilisation of music by drama. But to-day it shines more luminously, certainly more constantly than any other in the sky. Hans Richter was once asked to name the composer who, in his opinion was the greatest of them all. Without hesitation he said, "Beethoven, undoubtedly". The questioner expressed surprise at a reply so positive. "Undoubtedly, Herr Doktor? But I thought you might have considered Mozart". "Oh", replied Richter, "I didn't understand that you were bringing Mozart into the argument; I thought you were referring to the rest".

Less than half a century ago, in fact in the lifetime of many of us not yet tottering, Mozart's position in musical history had once and for all been established by the authorities as "classical"; he was almost docketed a "period" composer, plus genius, a genius no doubt having gifts towards drama as well as for the strictly musical forms, but born as an opera composer perhaps too soon; for not yet had the expressive and plastic technique of music-drama been brought under control. Mozart was obliged to compose operas in forms derived very much from instrumental music. "Mozart's most dramatic finales and concerted numbers", wrote Bernard Shaw, "are more or less in sonata-form, like symphonic movements ... and sonata-form dictates repetitions and recapitulations from which the perfectly unconventional form adopted by Wagner is free". Shaw admits, with an insight uncanny half a century ago, that Mozart was a dramatist comparable to Molière. I shall try to show presently that as a dramatist he, in his own art, went beyond Molière.

The great miracle of his achievements, most of them a separate miracle, is that though bound to his period's "absolute" patterns of music, undramatically shaped, he composed opera which in 1957 we can see, now that the Wagnerian mists are clearing and we can dwell on other peaks in the range, as unparalleled for breadth of characterisation in all phases of human activity, from the ridiculous to the sublime, from Papageno to Sarastro, from the comedic to the pathetic, from Figaro to the Countess, from the rogue-picaresque to the traditional romantic seducer, from Leporello to Don Giovanni. He can embody in a melody which an infant can sing the vivacity of a Zerlina, or the awakening ardours of the boy Cherubino. By a few chords in the trombones Mozart can evoke the shape and presence of the majestically spectral; in simple notes for a bass singer, almost displaying the lowest spectacularly, he wrote for Sarastro the only music which, as Shaw said, we might decently conceive coming out of the mouth of God. The "Non mi dir" air in *Don Giovanni* is none the less expressive and in character even if it does end in virtuoso vocal embellishments. Mozart had no need to invent leading-motives to identify his characters; all the music each of them sings is nearly always in character. I cannot explain—and nobody has enlightened me on this point—why "Lá ci darem" comes naturally from the mouth of Don Giovanni though really it is the most childlike of tunes, ideal for performances on the chimes which on sunny afternoons at Salzburg have delighted the ear as we have sat outside the Glockenspiel café. The strains of the March of the Priests in *Zauberflöte* evoke feelings of awe and majesty, of solemn temples and the insubstantial pageant; yet they are strains of a harmony scarcely going beyond the stage of study reached by the first-year pupil coping with elementary inversions. Other composers, Bach and Gluck for example, had composed dramatic music before Mozart came to the scene, using forms not fashioned or evolved from a dramatic intent or impulse. But they had been obliged by the limitations of the dominant musical patterns to confine themselves to a general and not particular dramatic suggestiveness. Mozart, with much the same material and moulds, created a whole "Comédie Humaine". This was the wonder, the miracle, of him. His instrumental works, his "absolute" compositions, are for all their perfections of style and diversity to be explained in terms of a flowering to genius of an eighteenth-century musical culture. By means of forms and tones not yet associated with precise expression, not yet rendered dramatically significant and plastic, he breathed life into figures which in their different libretti are more or less the lay stock puppets of the hack theatre scribbler.

He was the least consciously expressive as he was the most comprehensively ranged composer. He contributed to every kind and shape of music, secular and sacred, opera and symphony, all manner of chamber combinations, all manner of concerted pieces, all manner of "occasional" pieces, including a composition for a musical clock. He seldom went to work directed by an aesthetic theory. No sweat of notebooks for him. "I made it a little long on purpose", he writes to his father of the aria he had written for Raaff the singer, "for it is always easy to cut down, but not easy to lengthen". If the tenor engaged to sing in *Don Giovanni* is unequal to "Il mio tesoro", well then let him try "Dalla sua pace". If Elvira wants another "number" perhaps she will be placated by "Mi tradi". And if "Mi tradi" does not quite seem to fit into the context, heard only with the ear of logic and dramatic sequence, the Mozartian style will in time reconcile the irreconcilable. All is changed in the twinkling of an eye from earth to heaven. Shaw, as we have seen, compared Mozart as a dramatist to Molière, and he was right to think of him as a being essentially informed by the Comic Spirit. Whether the characters in Mozart's operas are living vitally in laughter, or suddenly softened by pathos or possessed by the daemonic, or harried, like Elvira, by jealously outraged pride and contumely which are ironically a proof of the love that is a constant wound to the self, no matter how often these people may strike home to our ordinary hearts, yet we can never come truly to know them, any more than we can come to know Mozart. They are aloof, masked like their creator, who surveys his work as though "sub specie aeternitatis". Mozart transcended the comedy of Molière; and he brought to it a Platonic ideality and finality.

He would be moved to astonishment and perplexity if he could revisit us and learn that he is safe with the greatest of those who have illumined and transfigured existence here below. His attitude to his art was almost professional; he composed much as craftsmen making Chippendale. He described himself as "soaked" in music; he composed habitually. In the last year of his life he composed *La Clemenza di Tito* and *Zauberflöte*, the *Requiem*, the E flat Quintet, an adagio for harmonica, a work (K.617) for harmonica, flute, oboe, viola and 'cello, three pieces for a mechanical organ, his last piano concerto, the clarinet concerto, the beatific "Ave verum corpus". In six weeks he composed the E flat, G minor and C major symphonies.

> I gave to-day to the mail coach the symphony which I composed in Linz for Old Count Thun, and also four concertos. I am not particular about the symphony, but I ask you to have the four concertos copied at home, for the Salzburg copyists are as little to be trusted as the Viennese . . .

This is another passage in a letter to his father; and the symphony he thought of little value, tossed off for the "Old Count", is as near to perfection as human genius can reasonably hope to approach. Sometimes Mozart's inexhaustible gift to compose had inevitably to nourish itself on notes and ingenuity. The flawless execution happened as instinctively as the weaving of a bird's nest, which of course is one of the wonders of creation. He remains the most enigmatic and inexplicable of composers; we shall not know his like again. That a Mozart was born once, and once and for all, is a happening and consummation which beggars understanding and all known science, all psychology, biology, physics and metaphysics, and all cosmogony whatsoever.

From *Talking of Music,* Collins, London, 1957

George Bernard Shaw

Beethoven's Centenary

A hundred years ago a crusty old bachelor of fifty-seven, so deaf that he could not hear his own music played by a full orchestra, yet still able to hear thunder, shook his fist at the roaring heavens for the last time, and died as he had lived, challenging God and defying the universe. He was Defiance Incarnate: he could not even meet a Grand Duke and his Court in the street without jamming his hat tight down on his head and striding through the very middle of them. He had the manners of a disobliging steamroller (most steamrollers are abjectly obliging and conciliatory); and he was rather less particular about his dress than a scarecrow; in fact he was once arrested as a tramp because the police refused to believe that such a tatterdemalion could be a famous composer, much less a temple of the most turbulent spirit that ever found expression in pure sound. It was indeed a mighty spirit; but if I had written the mightiest, which would mean mightier than the spirit of Handel, Beethoven himself would have rebuked me; and what mortal man could pretend to a spirit mightier than Bach's? But that Beethoven's spirit was the most turbulent is beyond all question. The impetuous fury of his strength, which he could quite easily contain and control, but often would not and the uproariousness of his fun, go beyond anything of the kind found in the work of other composers. Greenhorns write of Syncopation now as if it were a new way of giving the utmost impetus to a musical measure; but the rowdiest jazz sounds like The Maiden's Prayer after Beethoven's Leonore III Overture; and certainly no negro corroboree that I ever heard could inspire the blackest dancer with such diable en corps as the last movement of the

Seventh Symphony. And no other composer has ever melted his hearers into complete sentimentality by the tender beauty of his music and then suddenly turned on them with derisive trumpet blasts for being such fools. Nobody but Beethoven could govern Beethoven; and when, as happened when the fit was on him, he deliberately refused to govern himself, he was ungovernable.

It was this turbulence, this deliberate disorder, this mockery, this reckless and triumphant disregard of conventional manners, that set Beethoven apart from the musical geniuses of the ceremonious seventeenth and eighteenth centuries. He was a giant wave in that storm which produced the French Revolution. He called no man master. Mozart, his greatest predecessor in his own department, had from his childhood been washed, combed and beautifully behaved in the presence of royal personages and peers. His childish outburst at the Pompadour, "Who is this woman who does not kiss me? The Queen kisses me", would be incredible of Beethoven, who was still an unlicked cub even when he had grown into a very grizzly bear. Mozart had the refinement of convention and society as well as the refinement of nature and of the solitudes of the soul. Mozart and Gluck are refined as the Court of Louis XIV was refined: Haydn is refined as the most cultivated country gentlemen of his day were refined: compared to them Beethoven was an obstreperous Bohemian: a man of the people. Haydn, so superior to envy that he declared his junior, Mozart, to be the greatest composer that ever lived, could not stand Beethoven: Mozart, more far seeing, listened to his playing and said "You will hear of him some day"; but the two would never have hit it off together had Mozart lived long enough to try. Beethoven had a moral horror of Mozart, who in Don Giovanni had thrown a halo of enchantment round an aristocratic blackguard, and then, with the unscrupulous moral versatility of a born dramatist, turned round and cast a halo of divinity round Sarastro, setting his words to the only music yet written that would not sound out of place in the mouth of God.

Beethoven was no dramatist: moral versatility was to him revolting cynism. Mozart was still to him the master of masters (this is not an empty eulogistic superlative: it means literally that Mozart is a composer's composer much more than he has ever been a really popular composer); but he was a Court flunkey in breeches whilst Beethoven was a Sansculotte, and Haydn also was a flunkey in the old livery: the Revolution stood between them as it stood between the eighteenth and the nineteenth centuries. But to Beethoven Mozart was worse than Haydn because he trifled with morality by setting vice to music as magically as virtue. The Puritan who is in every true Sansculotte rose up against him in Beethoven, though Mozart had shown him all the possibilities of nineteenth century music. So Beethoven cast back for a hero to Handel, another crusty old bachelor of his own kidney, who despised Mozart's hero Gluck, though the Pastorale Symphony in the Messiah is the nearest thing in music to the scenes in which Gluck, in his Orfeo, opened to us the plains of Heavens.

Thanks to broadcasting millions of musical novices will hear the music of Beethoven this anniversary year for the first time with their expectations raised to an extraordinary pitch by hundreds of newspaper articles piling up all the conventional eulogies that are applied indiscriminately to all the great composers. And like his contemporaries they will be puzzled by getting from him not merely a music they did not expect, but often an orchestral hurlyburly that they may not recognize as what they call music at all, though they can appreciate Gluck and Haydn and Mozart quite well. The explanation is simple enough. The music of the eighteenth century is all dance music. A dance is a symmetrical pattern of steps that are pleasant to move to; and its music is a symmetrical pattern of sound that is pleasant to listen to even when you are not dancing to it. Consequently the sound patterns, though they begin by being as simple as chessboards get lengthened and elaborated and enriched with harmonies until they are more like Persian carpets; and the composers who design these patterns no longer expect people to dance to them. Only a whirling Dervish could dance a Mozart symphony: indeed I have reduced two young and practised dancers to exhaustion by making them dance a Mozart overture. The very names of the dances are dropped: instead of suites consisting of sarabands, pavanes, gavottes and jigs, the designs are presented as sonatas and symphonies consisting of sections called single movements and labelled according to their speed (in Italian) as allegros, adagios, sherzos and prestos. But all the time, from Bach's preludes to Mozart's Jupiter Symphony, the music makes a symmetrical sound pattern and gives us the dancer's pleasure always as the form and foundation of the piece.

Music, however, can do more than make beautiful sound patterns. It can express emotion. You can look at a Persian carpet and listen to a Bach prelude with a delicious admiration that goes no further than itself; but you cannot listen to the overture to Don Giovanni without being thrown into a complicated mood which prepares you for a tragedy of some terrible doom overshadowing an exquisite but Satanic gaiety. If you listen to the last movement of Mozart's Jupiter Symphony, you hear that it is as much a riotous corroboree as the last movement of Beethoven's Seventh Symphony: it is an orgy of ranting drumming tow-row-row, made poignant by an opening strain of strange and painful beauty which is woven through the pattern all through. And yet the movement is a masterpiece of pattern designing all the time.

Now what Beethoven did, and what made some of his greatest contemporaries give him up as a madman with lucid intervals of clowning and bad taste, was that he used music altogether as a means of expressing moods, and completely threw over pattern designing as an end in itself. It is true that he used the old patterns all his life with dogged conservatism (another Sansculotte characteristic, by the way); but he imposed on them such an overwhelming charge of human energy and passion, including the highest passion which accompanies thought, and reduced the passion of the physical appetites to mere animalism that he not only played Old Harry with their symmetry but often made it impossible to notice that there was any pattern at all beneath the storm of emotion. The Eroica Symphony begins by a pattern (borrowed from an overture which Mozart wrote when he was a boy), followed by a couple more very pretty patterns; but they are tremendously energised, and in the middle of the movement the patterns are torn up savagely; and Beethoven from the point of view of the mere pattern musician, goes raving mad, hurling out terrible chords in which all the notes of the scale are sounded simultaneously, just because he feels like that and wants you to feel like it.

And there you have the whole secret of Beethoven. He could design patterns with the best of them; he could write music whose beauty will last you all your life; he could take the driest stick of themes and work them up so interestingly that you find something new in them at the hundredth hearing; in short, you can say of him all that you can say of the greatest pattern composers; but his diagnostic, the thing that marks him out from all the others, is his disturbing quality, his power of unsettling us and imposing his giant moods on us. Berlioz was very angry with an old French composer who expressed the discomfort Beethoven gave him by saying "J'aime la musique qui me berce", "I like music that lulls me". Beethoven's music is music that wakes you up; and the one mood when you shrink from it is the mood when you want to be let alone.

When you understand this you will advance beyond the eighteenth century and the oldfashioned dance band (jazz, by the way, is the old dance band Beethovenized), and understand not only Beethoven's music, but what is deepest in post-Beethoven music as well.

From *Selected Prose,* Constable, London, 1933 (written in 1927)

Aldous Huxley

Popular Music

There is a certain jovial, bouncing, hoppety little tune with which any one who has spent even a few weeks in Germany, or has been tended in childhood by a German nurse, must be very familiar. Its name is "Ach, Du lieber Augustin". It is a merry little affair in three-four time; in rhythm and melody so simple, that the village idiot could sing it after a first hearing; in sentiment so innocent that the heart of the most susceptible maiden would not quicken by a beat a minute at the sound of it. Rum ti-tiddle, Um tum tum, Um tum tum, Um tum tum; Rum ti-tiddle, Um tum tum, Um tum tum, TUM. By the very frankness of its cheerful imbecility the thing disarms all criticism.

Now for a piece of history. "Ach, Du lieber Augustin" was composed in 1770, and it was the first waltz. The first waltz! I must ask the reader to hum the tune to himself, then to think of any modern waltz with which he may be familiar. He will find in the difference between the tunes a subject richly suggestive of interesting meditations.

The difference between "Ach, Du lieber Augustin" and any waltztune composed at any date from the middle of the nineteenth century onwards, is the difference between one piece of music almost completely empty of emotional content and another, densely saturated with amorous sentiment, languor and voluptuousness. The susceptible maiden who, when she hears "Ach, Du lieber Augustin", feels no emotions beyond a general sense of high spirits and cheerfulness, is fairly made to palpitate by the luscious strains of the modern waltz. Her soul is carried swooning along, over waves of syrup; she seems to breathe an atmosphere heavy with ambergris and musk. From the jolly little thing it was at its birth, the waltz has grown into the voluptuous, heart stirring affair with which we are now familiar.

And what has happened to the waltz has happened to all popular music. It was once innocent but is now provocative; once pellucid, now richly clotted; once elegant, now deliberately barbarous. Compare the music of *The Beggar's Opera* with the music of a contemporary revue. They differ as life in the Garden of Eden differed from life in the artistic quarters of Gomorrah. The one is prelapsarian in its airy sweetness, the other is rich, luscious and loud with conscious savagery.

The evolution of popular music has run parallel on a lower plane with the evolution of serious music. The writers of popular tunes are not musicians enough to be able to invent new forms of expression. All they do is to adapt the discoveries of original geniuses to the vulgar taste. Ultimately and indirectly, Beethoven is responsible for all the languishing waltz tunes, all the savage jazzings, for all that is maudlin and violent in our popular music. He is responsible because it was he who first devised really effective musical methods for the direct expression of emotion. Beethoven's emotions happened to be noble; moreover he was too intellectual a musician to neglect the formal, architectural side of music. But unhappily he made it possible for composers of inferior mind and character to express in music their less exalted passions and vulgar emotions. He made possible the weakest sentimentalities of Schumann, the baroque grandiosities of Wagner, the hysterics of Scriabine; he made possible the waltzes of the Strausses, from the *Blue Danube* to the waltz from *Salome*. And he made possible at a still further remove, such masterpieces of popular art as "You made me love you" and "That coal black mammy of mine".

For the introduction of a certain vibrant sexual quality into music, Beethoven is perhaps less directly responsible than the nineteenth century Italians. I used often to wonder why it was that Mozart's operas were less popular than those of Verdi, Leoncavallo and Puccini. You couldn't ask for more, or more infectiously "catchy" tunes than are to be found in *Figaro* or *Don Giovanni*. The music though "classical" is not obscure, nor forbiddingly complex. On the contrary it is clear, simple with that seemingly easy simplicity which only consummate genius can achieve and thoroughly engaging. And yet for every time *Don Giovanni* is played, *La Bohème* is played a hundred. *Tosca* is at least fifty times as popular as *Figaro*. And if you look through a catalogue of gramophone records you will find that, while you can buy *Rigoletto* complete in thirty discs, there are not more than three records of *The Magic Flute*. This seems at first sight extremely puzzling. But the reason is not really far to seek. Since Mozart's day composers have learned the art of making music throatily and palpitatingly sexual. The Arias of Mozart have a beautiful clear purity which renders them utterly insipid compared with the sobbing, catch-in-the-throaty melodies of the nineteenth century Italians. The public, having accustomed itself to this stronger and more turbid brewage, finds no flavour in the crystal songs of Mozart.

No essay on modern popular music would be complete without some grateful reference to Rossini, who was, so far as I know, the first composer to show what charms there are in vulgar melody. Melodies before Rossini's days were often exceedingly commonplace and cheap; but almost never do they possess that almost indefinable quality of low vulgarity which adorns some of the most successful of Rossini's airs, and which we recognize as being somehow a modern, contemporary quality. The methods which Rossini employed for the achievement of his melodic vulgarity are not easy to analyse. His great secret, I fancy, was the very short and easily memorable phrase frequently repeated in different parts of the scale. But it is easiest to define by example. Think of Moses' first Aria in *Moses of Egypt*. That is an essentially vulgar melody; and it is quite unlike the popular melodies of an earlier date. Its affinities are with the modern popular tune. It is to his invention of vulgar tunes that Rossini owed his enormous contemporary success. Vulgar people before his day had to be content with Mozart's delicate airs. Rossini came and revealed to them a more congenial music. That the world fell down and gratefully worshipped him is not surprising. If he has long ceased to be popular, that is because his successors, profiting by his lessons, have achieved in his own vulgar line triumphs of which he could not have dreamed.

Barbarism has entered popular music from two sources—from the music of barbarous people, like the negroes, and from serious music which has drawn upon barbarism for its inspiration. The technique of being barbarous effectively has come, of course, from serious music. In the elaboration of this technique no musicians have done more than the Russians. If Rimsky-Korsakoff had never lived, modern dance music would not be the thing it is.

Whether, having grown inured to such violent and purely physiolo-gical stimuli as the clashing and drumming, the rhythmic throbbing and wailing glissandos of modern jazz music can supply, the world will ever revert to something less crudely direct, is a matter about which one cannot prophesy. Even serious musicians seem to find it hard to dispense with barbarism. In spite of the monotony and the appalling lack of subtlety which characterise the process, they persist in banging away in the old Russian manner, as though there were nothing more interesting or exciting to be thought of. When as a boy I first heard Russian music, I was carried off my feet by its wild melodies, its persistent, its relentlessly throbbing rhythms. But my excitement grew less and less with every hearing. To-day no music seems to me more tedious. The only music a civilised man can take unfailing pleasure in is civilised music. If you were compelled to listen every day of your life to a single piece of music, would you choose Stravinsky's "Oiseau de Feu" or Beethoven's "Grosse Fugue"? Obviously you would choose the fugue, if only for its intricacy and because there is more in it to occupy the mind than in the Russians' too simple rhythms. Composers seem to forget that we are, in spite of everything and though appearances may be against us, tolerably civilised. They overwhelm us not only with Russian and negroid noises, but with Celtic caterwaulings on the black notes, with dismal Spanish wailings, punctuated by the rattle of the castanets and the clashing harmonies of the guitar. When serious composers have gone back to civilised music—and already some of them are turning from barbarism—we shall probably hear a corresponding change for the more refined in popular music. But until serious musicians lead the way, it will be absurd to expect the vulgarisers to change their style.

From *Along the Road,* Harper, New York, 1925, 1953

Neville Cardus

The Closed Mind

It is inevitable and very natural that the day comes to all of us sooner or later, especially if we are professional critics, when we are charged with having closed our minds. And, frankly, there is often something in the accusation. After 30 or 40 years of harvesting, the mind might easily be so fully stored that there is little room left. It takes years thoroughly to get a sight of the bottom of even one great composer, to know his language inside out in some relation to what he is saying, or some general assumption of what he is saying. There is no fool so foolish as the old man who goes about slapping his thighs saying he's as young as ever, ready for everything. The dilettante is even worse, the dabbler quick for the latest fashion. Oscar Wilde reminded us that it is the duty of the auctioneer to appreciate all schools of art. Wisdom in criticism is content to realise that a man's tastes and antennae, his standards and aesthetic responses, have been produced, cultivated, and developed in a certain soil and period. He can't extend the base of his pyramid. If he is sensible he will consolidate the gains of his impressionable years. Vintage implies, even with critical judgements, some lengthy cellarage.

The irony about the position of those of us called "Diehards" and "Crusted Reachmaries" is that once on a time we also fought the fight of modernity. None of the present-day young lions is raging more fiercely about his favourite contemporaries than the young lions of yesteryear raged about Strauss, Debussy, Sibelius, Stravinsky—the same Stravinsky who is still, in the year 1958, a leader of the avant-garde. It is no doubt beyond belief to young people of to-day that audiences put fingers to their ears when they heard the "battle" music in Strauss's "Ein Heldenleben"; and old men at Hallé Concerts and elsewhere were seen crossing themselves at the first chord or harmony of "L'aprèsmidi d'un faune". "Punch" was regarded as fantastically sarcastic when in some verses it hinted that the day would dawn on which we should cry out:

O for the good old tunes
Of Strauss and Debussy.

It has come to pass. Audiences of the early nineteen-hundreds, including musicians supposedly as up to date and alert then as the next exponent of the dodecaphonic mysteries, could not for long get used to the transitions of Ochs's "Keine Nacht" waltz in "Der Rosenkavalier". We can see now that Strauss was always a traditionalist, diatonic at bottom. Why could a fact as obvious as this not have been seen half a century ago? In every period the critical vision is best focused in a certain way; it can achieve definition only when the object is situated or presented at a certain point. At a rehearsal of one of Schoenberg's most esoteric works one of the woodwind players lost his way entirely, and afterwards went to the composer to apologise. But Schoenberg had apparently listened with satisfaction: "But do you mean to say, Master", said the woodwind player, "that even you don't know when your own music is being performed all wrong? " "No", answered Schoenberg, "I don't—not always. But my grandchildren will".

The critic born and nurtured in the social, religious, and aesthetic scene of pre-1914 years might to-day as well have been born in the moon as far as his genuine qualifications to deal justly with much contemporary art are concerned. Before 1914 there had been in music a chain of logical development, reaching across a century at least, in the main technical procedure and vocabulary. There was a general consistency, with natural modifications according to the dominant aesthetic. Since the eruption of two wars the entire habitation of every artist has been transformed. The nineteenth century saw the flowering of the individual in most activities, aesthetic and other. It was the age in music of free will and of self-assertion. There was also the influences of religion and ethics. An oratorio was supposed, the form itself and its associations, to set a composer well away towards the sources of plenary inspiration. Beauty was regarded by artists as essential to expression. "Beauty once sat enthroned over all the arts", wrote Langford 30 years ago, "but we have come to a time, almost, when it is never even mentioned". We have come, in fact, to the scientific age; and music must respond to the urges of the Time Spirit. Men are engaged in music now, composers and critics, who are not artists really but mathematicians in the wrong profession. In the nineteenth century the movement no doubt was overdone to "fertilise" music with literature, poetry, and whatnot. Music as an abstract ideal harmony, sounding air and numbers (Why doesn't Mr. Keller write for us a Pythagorean symphony?), is no new thing. Each age receives the music it deserves and lives with most comfortably. Time levels matters. But the critic of years and experience cannot be expected to turn here and there, sharing the principles of a weathercock. When all has been said of closed minds and the fossilisation of the tastes of the Mandarins, the fact remains that hardly any of them have yet been proved blind to Britten, Bartok, Stravinsky. It is absolutely certain that the mind is unmistakably bolted and barred that won't accommodate What's-his-Name and Never Mind.

At any stage a man's mind can only hold so much. Whether the years bring wisdom is frequently arguable. The young eye and ear can act swiftly and certainly as the arrow. But even in these days it is not infallible. It is easily led astray by the desire to prove a case; youth in general is occupied not so much with forming aesthetic judgements as with propaganda. Once, I confess, I could myself lose a night's sleep because I had failed to convince somebody that Mahler was a great composer, and Elgar more original than Bartok, Sibelius more "progressive" than Scriabin. To-day I am indifferent to nearly all opinions except those I have come by from my own study and devotion. A young man went to Strauss saying that, though he admired most of his works ardently, he could not really enjoy "Der Rosenkavalier". "How sad for you", said Strauss. A critic contemplating the harvest glory of his years, the full store he has gathered to himself, must be more modest than Strauss, and be content to hope that his younger colleagues one day may bring in as many sheaves. He might also set an example to them in manners and proportion if he refers them to Goethe's saying: "People always fancy that we must become old to be wise; but in truth, as the years advance, it is hard to keep ourselves as wise as we were. . . ."

From the *Manchester Guardian*, March 1, 1958

Peter Quennell

Epilogue, from The Sign of the Fish

A small hollow object in rugged dark bronze stands opposite me on the corner of my desk. Not much bigger than a large Victorian thimble, it is certainly over two thousand years old and may possibly have been created during an even more remote period; nothing about it reveals its exact age; it is the casual everyday product of an extraordinarily long and vigorous tradition. Besides worshipping at Bubastis the cat- or lion-faced goddess Bast, the ancient Egyptians kept a multitude of cats which ran freely around their palaces and houses, and placed cat-heads as decorative finials on many pieces of domestic furniture. Such a head I happen to have acquired; and innumerable similar relics are now distributed through the world's museums. No expert Egyptologist would allow my head a second glance: in its context it is almost as unimportant as a late-Victorian doorknob. Yet, for its owner at least, it possesses a mysterious gift of stirring the senses and quickening the imagination. That the household cat remains a wild animal, the Egyptian craftsman makes completely clear. Deep, dusky triangular eye-sockets—once filled with coloured faience eyeballs or perhaps with fragments of semi-precious stone—give the narrow, thin-cheeked mask a look of fierce, unblinking expectancy. The muzzle is lengthy but blunted, as in the modern Abyssinian breed; and the tall flattened, thick-furred ears—each pierced towards the base to receive a miniature jewelled ring—project sentinel-wise from the rounded cranium, as the cat raises its lean neck to confront some unfamiliar challenge. The Egyptians, unlike the Japanese, very seldom portrayed a cat asleep. What they admired in the half-tamed animal was its attitude of vigilant, aggressive pride—the pride of life peculiar to a race cherished and protected by the mighty mother-goddess Bast, who numbered "The Lady of Life" among her various solemn titles. On that aspect of the splendid creature before him, the craftsman dwelt with especially loving care. Between himself and its alien existence he seems to have established a strong imaginative bond; and from the contact sprang a sudden minute explosion of the life-enriching quality we call "art".

Microscopic the spark is; yet there it still gleams after twenty centuries—imperishable and unmistakable as a scrap of pure gold in a barren, dried-up stream-bed; and to have caught and fixed even that single spark few efforts would not be worth enduring. The theme of the present book is the background of art, studied chiefly through the art of literature; and although, while I pursued my subject, I have often wandered very far afield, the time has now come to cut short my journey and prelude its close with an unashamed confession. For nearly as long as I can remember, I have wished to be some kind of artist, and have believed that no other activity brought the same rewards or had quite the same value. In my early youth, I suppose, I should have agreed with Cyril Connolly's stern dictum that the "true function of a writer" is simply "to produce a masterpiece" and that no less ambitious aim is of the slightest consequence. To be memorable, I thought, a work must also be "great", an achievement of heroic magnitude, large and grandiose and breath-taking as *Paradise Lost,* Michelangelo's *Night* and *Day* or Piero della Francesca's painted visions at Arezzo. Today, however, the scale of a work seems relatively unimportant, partly no doubt because I no longer expect to succeed in creating a masterpiece myself, partly because my ideas of the artist's function have since undergone a gradual change. Thus I have begun to think of art as a quality that may illumine the most trivial objects, and to value an artist both for his ability to raise us high above the world and for his gift, simultaneously exercised, of intensifying and enlarging our sense of life. This he may help to do, if he is an imaginative writer, by encouraging us, in our own experience, to distinguish the essential from the inessential. Art is the essential residue of life: literature, a record of experience from which the inessentials have been carefully removed, the essential elements being further purified during their translation into imaginative imagery. An artist cannot unriddle the universe; but he alone formulates an insoluble problem in terms that the human mind can grasp. Shakespeare's tragedies provide no answers; but they put forward a series of age-old questions with such commanding grace and skill that they reconcile us to the unaltered human condition and deprive uncertainty of half its terrors.

"As the influence of religion declines", once suggested Aldous Huxley, "the social importance of art increases". And, were the artist to drop out of the social system, who nowadays could take his place? Not only does he illuminate the landscape of the present; but he throws an airy bridge between the present and the future. In a thousand years, if our descendants can reach us, it will be through the works of art that we have left behind, just as we ourselves, handling a scrap of bronze cast a thousand or two thousand years ago, enjoy a sensation of electric sympathy with the artificer who kneaded the wax model. Nothing else remains of him—neither his religious beliefs nor the political system under which he lived and died. Faiths expire; political systems collapse; the elaborate structures planned by science and philosophy are reduced to picturesque ruins. Then, among the ruins, appears some broken artifact that reveals the imprint of human desires and feelings—an Egyptian statuette: a strip of tarnished metal that shows a procession of stout Sumerian dignitaries advancing to the sound of music: a fragment of an early Greek vase, with charioteers, wrestlers and a frieze of helmeted warriors bearing huge heraldic shields: an Athenian koré whose smile still warms the heart: a grim-visaged Maya seer or the scowling features of an Aztec priest.

From an ethical point of view, the Maya and Aztec worlds now seem particularly remote and strange; for the Maya priesthood were obsessed by Time—an obsession with which I can vaguely sympathise, since in my childhood I was troubled by hideous dreams about unending Time and illimitable Space—and devoted their genius to the composition of extraordinarily detailed and extensive calendars, afterwards engraved upon monumental blocks of stone; while the Aztecs imagined that their ferocious gods were constantly meditating the destruction of mankind, and that at any season the rains might cease to gather and the maize crop wither in the dusty fields, unless the divine tyrants who ruled their fate received a gigantic daily tribute of blood and suffering. Fear dominated the Aztec world; and fear and its concomitant cruelty, are reflected in all the manifestations of their art. Now and then, the creative spirit is obscured by a coarse and ugly realism; and we are confronted by the statue of a dancing priest who carries around with him the flayed-off skin of the human victim he has sacrificed, peeps through the eyeholes of the scooped-out mask and wears the flaccid hide of the dead man's torso tightly strapped about his body. There is not a smile in the Aztec pantheon, though sometimes a broad sadistic grin; and equally cold and unsmiling were the human types that the Mexican sculptor chose. The Aztecs, in their curious view of life, although they cultivated pleasure and recognised beauty, found little room for hope or joy; but again and again we encounter a statue, hewn out of dusky porous rock, to which the frowning brows and the close-shut mouth lend an air of tragic human dignty. The illusory terrors that haunted the Mexican craftsman have now been superseded by very different fears—we dread, not the vengeance of heaven, so much as a mushroom-shaped cloud arising from the earth. Yet Fear, in one of its many disguises, still overshadows the twentieth century mind; and it was the Aztec's staunch acceptance of an almost intolerable fate that gave his masterpieces their darkly impressive character.

If art is a universal language, as Ruskin—at war with his contemporaries' view that works of art were a mere decorative addition to life—never tired of pointing out, the artist himself is none the less deeply involved in the transitory problems of his own existence. The writer who fulfils his mission—which is to justify the ways of Man to men, and to produce an aesthetic harmony from the savage disorder of the world we know—would appear as a rule to have originally shouldered it for reasons that concern his own life, his own fears, his own anxieties, his own aspirations towards security and peace. His work may benefit mankind; but he is a supremely undeliberate benefactor, like the alchemist who adds to the wealth of nations during his laborious attempts at self-enrichment. In his life-time, he frequently forfeits the respect of saner and solider human beings, when they observe how small his rewards are, how disastrous his private losses, and how surely every increase of knowledge seems to be counterbalanced by some increase of doubt. Oddly enough, though, doubt is a condition that generally stimulates the creative intelligence. Thus Keats discouraged his fellow poets from seeking to arrive at definite conclusions: "the only means [he wrote] of strengthening one's intellect is to make up one's mind about nothing—to let the mind be a thoroughfare for all thoughts, not a select party"; for it is to his doubts, his self-confessed ignorance, that the creative artist owes his independence. "I doubt; therefore I am" is his emended version of Descartes' famous phrase.

In a society where to be able to make up one's mind is commonly accounted an important virtue, the artist, with his lack of fixed opinions, often cuts a somewhat unheroic figure. Keats himself, a fiercely proud young man, who had a particularly exalted view of the grandeur of the poet's task, was obliged to admit that the poet was "the most unpoetical of anything in existence . . . he has no Identity—he is continually filling some other body. The Sun, the Moon, the Sea, and men and women, who are creatures of impulse, are poetical and have about them an unchangeable attribute; the poet has none . . ." For his awareness of himself, being especially vivid, is apt to reveal him his own character in all its native incoherence; while the gift of sympathy, that becomes his greatest asset—his power of feeling with and re-living the lives of others—entails a constant loss of identity and little by little may blur the Self's outline, just as an actor's real face is slowly obliterated by the impress of the multiple parts he has played. Oscar Wilde summed up the writer's predicament in an unexpected flash of insight . . . "He who lives more lives than one [declares the prisoner of Reading Gaol] more deaths than one must die"; and, although it was Wilde's hybristic conceit, not his modest share of creative talent, that presently accomplished his personal downfall, he is speaking here for every imaginative artist who has allowed his imagination to range too widely, whose nervous system is linked at too many points to the sufferings of a world that he both loves and loathes.

From *The Sign of the Fish*, Collins, London, 1960

Aldous Huxley

The Best Picture

Borgo San Sepolcro is not very easy to get at. There is a small low-comedy railway across the hills from Arezzo. Or you can approach it up the Tiber valley from Perugia. Or, if you happen to be at Urbino, there is a motor bus which takes you to San Sepolcro, up and down through the Apennines, in something over seven hours. No joke, that journey, as I know by experience. But it is worth doing, though preferably in some other vehicle than the bus, for the sake of the Bocca Trabaria, the most beautiful of Apennine passes, between the Tiber valley and the upper valley of the Metauro. It was in the early spring that we crossed it. Our omnibus groaned and rattled slowly up a bleak northern slope, among bald rocks, withered grass and still unbudded trees. It crossed the col and suddenly, as though by a miracle, the ground was yellow with innumerable primroses, each flower a little emblem of the sun that had called it into being.

When at last one has arrived at San Sepolcro, what is there to be seen? A little town surrounded by walls, set in a broad flat valley between hills; some fine renaissance palaces with pretty balconies of wrought iron; a not very interesting church; and finally the best picture in the world.

The best picture in the world is painted in fresco on the wall of a room in the town hall. Some unwittingly beneficent vandal had it covered, some time after it was painted, with a thick layer of plaster, under which it lay hidden for a century or two, to be revealed at last in a state of preservation remarkably perfect for a fresco of its date. Thanks to the vandal, the visitor who now enters the Palazzo dei

Conservatori at Borgo San Sepolcro finds the stupendous Resurrection almost as Pierro della Francesca left it. Its clear, yet subtly sober colours shine out from the wall with scarcely impaired freshness. Damp has blotted out nothing of the design, nor dirt obscured it. We need no imagination to help us figure forth its beauty; it stands there before us in entire and actual splendour, the greatest picture in the world.

The greatest picture in the world. . . . You smile. The expression is ludicrous, of course. Nothing is more futile than the occupation of those connoisseurs who spend their time compiling first and second elevens of the world's best painters, eights and fours of musicians, fifteens of poets, all-star troupes of architects and so on. Nothing is so futile because there are a great many kinds of merit and an infinite variety of human beings. Is Fra Angelico a better artist than Rubens? Such questions, you insist, are meaningless. It is all a matter of personal taste. And up to a point this is true. But there does exist, none the less, an absolute standard of artistic merit. And it is a standard which is in the last resort a moral one. Whether a work of art is good or bad depends entirely on the quality of the character which expresses itself in the work. Not that all virtuous men are good artists, nor all artists conventionally virtuous. Longfellow was a bad poet, while Beethoven's dealings with his publishers were frankly dishonourable. But one can be dishonourable towards one's publishers and yet preserve the kind of virtue that is necessary to a good artist. That virtue is the virtue of integrity, of honesty towards oneself. Bad art is of two sorts: that which is merely dull, stupid and incompetent, the negatively bad; and the positively bad, which is a lie and a sham. Very often the lie is so well told that almost everyone is taken in by it—for a time. In the end, however, lies are always found out. Fashion changes, the public learns to look with a different focus and where a little while ago it saw an admirable work which actually moved its emotions, it now sees a sham. In the history of the arts we find innumerable shams of this kind, once taken as genuine, now seen to be false. The very names of most of them are now forgotten. Still, a dim rumour that Ossian once was read, that Bulwer was thought a great novelist and "Festus" Bailey a mighty poet still faintly reverberates. Their counterparts are busily earning praise and money at the present day. I often wonder if I am one of them. It is impossible to know. For one can be an artistic swindler without meaning to cheat and in the teeth of the most ardent desire to be honest.

Sometimes the charlatan is also a first-rate man of genius and then you have such strange artists as Wagner and Bernini, who can turn what is false and theatrical into something almost sublime.

That it is difficult to tell the genuine from the sham is proved by the fact that enormous numbers of people have made mistakes and continue to make them. Genuineness, as I have said, always triumphs in the long run. But at any given moment the majority of people, if they do not actually prefer the sham to the real, at least like it as much, paying an indiscriminate homage to both.

And now, after this little digression we can return to san Sepolcro and the greatest picture in the world. Great it is, absolutely great, because the man who painted it was genuinely noble as well as talented. And to me personally the most moving of pictures, because its author possessed almost more than any other painter those qualities of character which I most admire and because his purely aesthetic preoccupations are of a kind which I am by nature best fitted to understand. A natural, spontaneous, and unpretentious grandeur—this is the leading quality of all Piero's work. He is majestic without being at all strained, theatrical or hysterical—as Handel is majestic, not as Wagner. He achieves grandeur naturally with every gesture he makes, never consciously strains after it. Like Alberti, with whose architecture, as I hope to show, his painting has certain affinities, Piero seems to have been inspired by what I may call the religion of Plutarch's *Lives*—which is not Christianity, but a worship of what is admirable in man. Even his technically religious pictures are paeans in praise of human dignity. And he is everywhere intellectual.

With the drama of life and religion he is very little concerned. His battle pictures at Arezzo are not dramatic compositions in spite of the many dramatic incidents they contain. All the turmoil, all the emotions of the scenes have been digested by the mind into a grave intellectual whole. It is as though Bach had written the 1812 Overture. Nor are the two superb pictures in the National Gallery—the Nativity and the Baptism—distinguished for any particular sympathy with the religious or emotional significance of the events portrayed. In the extraordinary Flagellation at Urbino, the nominal subject of the picture recedes into the background on the left hand side of the panel, where it serves to balance the three mysterious figures standing aloof in the right foreground. We seem to have nothing here but an experiment in composition, but an experiment so strange and so startlingly successful that we do not regret the absence of dramatic significance and are entirely satisfied. The Resurrection at San Sepolcro is more dramatic. Piero has made the simple triangular composition symbolic of the subject. The base of the triangle is formed by the sepulchre; and the soldiers sleeping round it are made to indicate by their position the upward jet of the two sides, which meet at the apex in the face of the risen Christ, who is standing, a banner in his right hand, his left foot already raised and planted on the brim of the sepulchre, preparing to set out into the world. No geometrical arrangement could have been more simple or more apt. But the being who rises before our eyes from the tomb is more like a Plutarchian hero than the Christ of conventional religion. The body is perfectly developed, like that of a Greek athlete; so formidably strong that the wound in its muscular flank seems somehow an irrelevance. The face is stern and pensive, the eyes cold. The whole figure is expressive of physical and intellectual power. It is the resurrection of the classical ideal, incredibly much grander and more beautiful than the classical reality, from the tomb where it had lain so many hundred years.

Aesthetically, Piero's work has this resemblance to Alberti's: that it too is essentially an affair of masses. What Alberti is to Bruneleschi, Piero della Francesca is to his contemporary, Botticelli. Botticelli was fundamentally a draughtsman, a maker of supple and resilient lines, thinking in terms of arabesques inscribed on the flat. Piero, on the contrary, has a passion for solidity as such. There is something in all his work that reminds one constantly of Egyptian sculpture. Piero has that Egyptian love of the smooth rounded surface that is the external symbol and expression of a mass. The faces of his personages look as though they were carved out of some very hard rock into which it had been impossible to engrave the details of a human physiognomy—the hollows, the lines and wrinkles of real life. They are ideal, like the faces of Egyptian gods and princes, surface meeting and marrying with curved unbroken surface in an almost geometrical fashion. Look for example, at the faces of the women in Piero's fresco at Arezzo: "The Queen of Sheba recognising the Holy Tree". They are all of one peculiar cast: the foreheads are high, rounded and smooth; the necks are like cylinders of polished ivory; from the midst of the concave sockets the eyelids swell out in one uninterrupted curve into convexity; the cheeks are unbrokenly smooth and the subtle curvature of their surfaces is indicated by a very delicate chiaroscuro which suggests more powerfully the solidity and mass of the flesh than the most spectacular Caravaggioesque light and shade could do.

Piero's passion for solidity betrays itself no less strikingly in his handling of the dresses and drapery of his figures. It is noticeable, for example, that wherever the subject permits, he makes his personages appear in curious headdresses that remind one by their solid geometrical qualities of those oddly-shaped ceremonial hats or tiaras worn by the statues of Egyptian kings. Among the frescoes at Arezzo are several which illustrate this peculiarity. In that representing Heraclius restoring the True Cross to Jerusalem, all the ecclesiastical dignitaries are wearing enormously high head-dresses, conical, trumpet-shaped, even rectangular. They are painted very smoothly with, it is obvious, a profound relish for their solidity. One or two similar headdresses, with many varieties of wonderfully rounded helmets, are lovingly represented in the battle-pieces in the same place. The Duke of Urbino, in the well known portrait at the Uffizi, is wearing a red cloth cap whose shape somewhat like that of the "Brodrick" of the modern English soldier, but without the peak—a cylinder fitting round the head, topped by a projecting disc as the crown. Its smoothness and the roundness of its surfaces are emphasised in the picture. Nor does Piero neglect the veils of his female figures. Though transparent and of lawn, they hang round the heads of his women in stiff folds, as though they were made of steel. Among clothes he has a special fondness for pleated bodices and tunics. The bulge and recession of the pleated stuff fascinates him and he likes the way in which the fluted folds follow the curve of the body beneath. To drapery he gives, as we might expect, a particular weight and richness. Perhaps his most exquisite handling of drapery is to be seen in the altar-piece of the Madonna della Misericordia, which now hangs near the Resurrection in the town hall at San Sepolcro. The central figure in this picture, which is one of the earliest of Piero's extant works, represents the Virgin, standing and stretching out her arms, so as to cover two groups of suppliants on either side with the folds of her heavy blue mantle. The mantle and the Virgin's dress hang in simple perpendicular folds, like the flutings on the robe of the archaic bronze charioteer at the Louvre. Piero has painted these alternately convex and concave surfaces with a peculiar gusto.

It is not my intention to write a treatise on Piero della Francesca; that has been done sufficiently often and sufficiently badly to make it unnecessary for me to bury that consummate artist any deeper under layers of muddy comment. All I have meant to do in this place is to give the reasons why I like his works and my justifications for calling the Resurrection the greatest picture in the world. I am attracted to his character by his intellectual power; by his capacity for unaffectedly making the grand and noble gesture; by his pride in whatever is splendid in humanity. And in the artist I find peculiarly sympathetic the lover of solidity, the painter of smooth curving surfaces, the composer who builds with masses. For myself I prefer him to Botticelli, so much so indeed, that if it was necessary to sacrifice all Botticelli's works in order to save the Resurrection, the Nativity, the Madonna della Misericordia and the Arezzo frescoes, I should unhesitatingly commit the Primavera and all the rest of them to the flames. It is unfortunate for Piero's reputation that his works should be comparatively few and in most cases rather difficult of access. With the exception of the Nativity and Baptism at the National Gallery, all the really important works of Piero are at Arezzo, San Sepolcro and Urbino. The portraits of the Duke and Duchess of Urbino with their respective triumphs in the Uffizi, are charming and exceedingly "amusing"; but they do not represent Piero at his best. The altar piece at Perugia and the Madonna with saints and donor at Milan are neither of them first-rate; the St. Jerome at Venice is goodish; so too is the damaged fresco of the Malatesta, at Rimini. The Louvre possesses nothing and Germany can only boast of a study of architecture, inferior to that at Urbino. Anybody, therefore, who wants to know Piero, must go to Arezzo, San Sepolcro and Urbino.

From *Along the Road*, Harper, New York, 1925, 1953

Kaleidoscope

Charles Morgan

The Enduring Italy

Everyone, I suppose, has a few books that he reads and dips into continually and has come to think of as parts of his personal life. Other books, however much they are admired or loved, have their place in a different compartment of the mind; when they have been read, they are put back on their shelf with no certain assurance that they will be taken down again; I do not know, for example, whether I shall read again either Madame Bovary or The Charterhouse of Parma, though each is a book that I could not be without; but I do know that, as long as I live, Trelawny's Recollections of the Last Days of Shelley and Byron will come to hand again and again, sometimes for five minutes at random, sometimes for an evening, sometimes for a journey, and never will there be any sense of finality in the encounter.

The best proof that a book has become, in this sense, "personal" is that thousands of seemingly irrelevant impulses may send one to it. Lately, Trelawny came down from my shelf for no better reason than that I had been thinking about the Italian fleet in the Mediterranean—and how, since my last meeting with him, Trelawny seems to have changed! Always before, he was telling of a civilisation which, though greatly altered in a hundred years, had evident links with our own—which, if I may put it so, had surviving offspring—and it was possible, while reading, to think happily that the debt of English writers to Italy was still being increased. Now, suddenly, Trelawny appears to be writing of another world than ours, and that this should be so defines with terrible clearness the nature of the Italian tragedy.

The question that presents itself is whether the tragedy is final or whether the essential values of Trelawny's Italy may survive in another form. Nothing is ever restored; it is now more than ever certain that, of outward things, "nothing can ever be the same again"; but it did not need a second world war to make this true; the outward forms of the Italy of Shelley and Byron were gone long ago. The essential values nevertheless survived. English artists of succeeding generations found happiness or inspiration or both under Italian skies. What was it, in this strange country, which, at such different times, could draw to it such differing human beings as the Shelleys and the Brownings, and could continue, down to our own day, to give to English poets and painters renewal and freedom? What is this Italian essence that seems to have so extraordinary a power to survive political and social change?

We receive a hint of its nature very early in Trelawny's narrative. "Our icy islanders", he says, "thaw rapidly when they have drifted into warmer latitudes: broken loose from its anti-social system, mystic castes, coteries, sets and sects, they lay aside their purse-proud, tuft-hunting, and toadying ways, and are very apt to run riot in the enjoyment of all their senses. Besides we are compelled to talk in strange company, if not from good breeding, to prove our breed. . . ." This is typical of Trelawny's generalisations—rash, hasty, often trucu-lent, but always alive. A dozen holes can be picked in it by anyone who remembers how often English travellers are more purse-proud and tuft-hunting abroad than at home, but it remains true that Englishmen who live in Italy or stay there long enough to enter into Italian life do undergo an experience of release—a release not of the senses only, nor particularly of the intellect, which appears sometimes to slacken, but of the imagination. The reason is not so much that they venerate the Italian past; moonlight and ruins are seldom a vital stimulus. The effective and enduring influence is something at once childlike and expressive in the Italians, something spontaneously dramatic in them, which, though it may not be greatly productive in itself, strikes on the English box and liberates English artists from their domestic tendency to respect—or, what is worse, to resent—rules and aspects of life which, however appropriate to the "coteries, sets and sects", have nothing to do with art. The first of Italy's virtues is, then, that she enables men to stop dressing their souls for dinner and teaches them how to recognise the irrelevant and cast it off.

In this she differs from France in her attitude towards artists. I have never found that modern Italians, apart from those who were themselves artists, have been deeply interested in art, as nearly all cultivated Frenchmen are interested in it. The English, when they do not practise it, regard it, if they are frivolous, as a pastime, or, if they are solemn, as an educative or moral force; the French consider it as a human activity valuable in itself that has no need of external justification; the Italians think of it—or thought of it—quite simply in a spirit of *laissez-faire*, with the consequence that, among them, an English writer has always been, in a sense, even freer than in France—freer to discover and develop himself without feeling, as English artists are liable to feel within the artistic intellectualism of Paris, that they have somehow become enrolled in a gigantic university —though the lecture-room be not the Sorbonne but a table at the Deux Magots or the Nouvelle Athenes. Paris is a delight because no one there considers it a waste of time to discuss for a couple of hours the texture of a paragraph, the form of a verse or the balance of a scene; a student will learn more there than anywhere else in the world; but a mature artist like Byron or a passionately creative one like Shelley may well prefer the Italian freedom which, being less well-informed, is less instructive, less insistent, and intellectually looser.

And it is by no means impossible that this Italian quality may survive, just because it is passive rather than active and has its root in the character of the people—their instinct to tolerate whatever is not a disturbance of their personal life—rather than a positive energy that may be perverted. It is easier to believe that Germany may persuade France to invent—what the Germans have been unable to invent for themselves—a totalitarian philosophy of art, than to suppose that Fascism will ever be able to lash the inhabitants of Pisa and Lucca into an active hatred of artists. I will confess that, among my dreams of the future, none, except the imagining of a France reconstituted in her individualism, is dearer or more persistent than the dream of an Italy again feminine in her virtues and her faults. I have suggested that there is, in her life, something spontaneously dramatic, and I would go further in saying that her role, in its nobility as well as in its charm, is a feminine one. The success of the Fascist Revolution, and its difference from the dreary, systematised oppression of the Nazis, has consisted in Mussolini's quickness to perceive, and his power to turn to account, the dramatic characteristic of his countrymen. He has provided stage and limelight such as they had not enjoyed for many years before his coming, and they have responded with a childlike, and now a tragic, enthusiasm to the energy of this spectacular *regisseur*. But he has cast Italy for a masculine part in which, to foreign observers, she has always appeared a little ridiculous. Long before the present war, one would encounter in trains and at street-corners harmless men who, before the Revolution, would have been laughing bright-eyed and free in all the gestures of limb and mind, but who, under Fascism, seemed to have swaddled themselves in a costumier's toga, whose shoulders were set, whose mouth was clipped, and whose eyes were somehow persuaded to bulge and stare like the Duce's own.

This is by no means the impression that one received in Germany. There, men were transformed not by the putting-on of a mental fancy-dress but by a mental disease evidently incurable. In Italy, the toga would nearly always come off. The fiercest Duce of the railway train would, if addressed in tolerable Italian, unfold his arms and turn into the goldsmith of Lucca—a man so proud of his native city that he had no imperial dreams beyond its ramparts, and so delighted in his own craft and his own children that his eyes would dazzle at talk of Cellini, and he would never be so happy as when, in his little shop, he was being artificer and nursemaid at the same time. The memory of him encourages me in my dream that his country is not lost to civilisation and that the time will come again when creative artists, and not antiquarians only, will go there, as they have in the past, to find—what? Not, indeed, Trelawny's Italy, nor Browning's, nor, in outward form, the Italy of the immediate past, but still an Italy playing in the world a part natural to her, a receptive and a giving Italy where men of genius, and men less than they, may discover a renaissance of themselves.

From *Modern Essays*, Macmillan, London, 1940

D. H. Lawrence

Flowery Tuscany

Each country has its own flowers, that shine out specially there. In England it is daisies and buttercups, hawthorn and cowslips. In America, it is golden-rod, stargrass, June daisies, Mayapple and asters, that we call Michaelmas daisies. In India, hibiscus and datura and champac flowers, and in Australia, mimosa, that they call wattle, and sharp-tongued strange heath flowers. In Mexico, it is cactus flowers, that they call roses of the desert, lovely and crystalline among many thorns; and also the dangling yard-long clusters of the cream bells of the yucca, like dropping froth.

But by the Mediterranean, now as in the days of the argosy, and, we hope, for ever, it is narcissus and anemone, asphodel and myrtle. Narcissus and anemone, asphodel, crocus, myrtle and parsley, they leave their sheer significance only by the Mediterranean. There are daisies in Italy too: at Paestum there are white little carpets of daisies, in March, and Tuscany is spangled with celandine. But for all that, the daisy and the celandine are English flowers, their best significance is for us and for the north.

The Mediterranean has narcissus and anemone, myrtle and asphodel, and grape hyacinth. These are the flowers that speak and are understood in the sun round the Middle Sea.

Tuscany is especially flowery, being wetter than Sicily and more homely than the Roman hills. Tuscany manages to remain so remote, and secretly smiling to itself in its many sleeves. There are so many hills popping up, and they take no notice of one another. There are so many little deep valleys with streams that seem to go their own little way entirely, regardless of river or sea. There are thousands, millions, of utterly secluded little nooks, though the land has been under cultivation these thousands of years. But the intensive culture of vine and olive and wheat, by the ceaseless industry of naked human hands and winter-shod feet, and slow-stepping, soft-eyed oxen, does not devastate a country, does not denude it, does not lay it bare, does not uncover its nakedness, does not drive away either Pan or his children. The streams run and rattle over wild rocks of secret places, and murmur through blackthorn thickets where the nightingales sing all together, unruffled and undaunted.

It is queer that a country so perfectly cultivated as Tuscany, where half the produce of five acres of land will have to support ten human mouths, still has so much room for the wild flowers and the nightingale. When little hills heave themselves suddenly up, and shake themselves free of neighbours, man has to build his garden and his vineyard and sculp his landscape. Talk of hanging gardens of Babylon, all Italy apart from the plains is a hanging garden. For centuries upon centuries man has been patiently modelling the surface of the Mediterranean countries, gently rounding the hills, and graduating the big slopes and the little slopes into the almost invisible levels of terraces. Thousands of square miles of Italy have been lifted in human hands piled and laid back in tiny little flats, held up by the drystone walls, whose stones came from the lifted earth. It is a work of many, many centuries. It is the gentle sensitive sculpture of all the landscape. And it is the achieving of the peculiar Italian beauty which is so exquisitely natural, because man, feeling his way sensitively to the fruitfulness of the earth has moulded the earth to his necessity without violating it.

Which shows that it *can* be done. Man *can* live on the earth and by the earth without disfiguring the earth. It has been done here, on all these sculptured hills and softly, sensitively terraced slopes.

But, of course, you can't drive a steam plough on terraces four yards wide, terraces that dwindle and broaden and sink and rise a little, all according to the pitch and the breaking outline of the mother hill. Corn has got to grow on these little shelves of earth, where already the grey olive stands semi-invisible, and the grape-vine twists upon its own scars. If oxen can step with that lovely pause at every little stride, they can plough the narrow field. But they will have to leave a tiny fringe, a grassy lip over the drystone wall below. And if the terraces are too narrow to plough, the peasant digging them will still leave the grassy lip, because it helps to hold the surface in the rains.

And here the flowers take refuge. Over and over and over and over has this soil been turned, twice a year, sometimes three times a year, for several thousands of years. Yet the flowers have never been driven out. There is a very rigorous digging and sifting, the little bulbs and tubers are flung away into perdition, not a weed shall remain.

Yet spring returns, and on the terrace lips, and in the stony nooks between terraces, up rise the aconites, the crocuses, the narcissus and the asphodel, the inextinguishable wild tulips. There they are, for ever hanging on the precarious brink of an existence, but for ever triumphant, never quite losing their footing. In England, in America, the flowers get rooted out, driven back. They become fugitive. But in the intensive cultivation of ancient Italian terraces, they dance round and hold their own.

Spring begins with the first narcissus, rather cold and shy and wintry. They are the little bunchy, creamy narcissus with the yellow cup like the yolk of the flower. The natives call these flowers *tazzette*, little cups. They grow on the grassy banks rather sparse, or push up among thorns.

To me they are winter flowers, and their scent is winter. Spring starts in February, with the winter aconite. Some icy day, when the wind is down from the snow of the mountains, early in February, you will notice on a bit of fallow land, under the olive-trees, tight, pale gold little balls, clenched tight as nuts, and resting on round ruffs of green near the ground. It is the winter aconite suddenly come.

The winter aconite is one of the most charming flowers. Like all the early blossoms, once her little flower emerges it is quite naked. No shutting a little green sheath over herself, like the daisy or the dandelion. Her bubble of frail, pale, pure gold rests on the round frill of her green collar, with the snowy wind trying to blow it away.

But without success. The *tramontana* ceases, comes a day of wild February sunshine. The clenched little nuggets of the aconite puff out, they become light bubbles, like small balloons, on a green base. The sun blazes on, with February splendour. And by noon, all under the olives are wide-open little suns, the aconites spreading all their rays; and there is an exquisitely sweet scent, honey-sweet, not narcissus-frosty; and there is a February humming of little brown bees.

Till afternoon, when the sun slopes, and the touch of snow comes back into the air.

But at evening, under the lamp on the table, the aconites are wide and excited, and there is a perfume of sweet spring that makes one almost start humming and trying to be a bee.

Aconites don't last very long. But they turn up in all odd places—on clods of dug earth, and in land where the broad beans are thrusting up and along the lips of terraces. But they like best land left fallow for one winter. There they throng, showing how quick they are to seize an opportunity to live and shine forth.

In a fortnight, before February is over, the yellow bubbles of the aconite are crumpling to nothingness. But already in a cosy nook the violets are dark purple, and there is a new little perfume in the air.

Like the debris of winter stand the hellebores, in all the wild places, and the butcher's broom is flaunting its last bright red berry. Hellebore is Christmas roses, but in Tuscany the flowers never come white. They emerge out of the grass towards the end of December, flowers wintry of winter and they are delicately pale green, and of a lovely shape, with yellowish stamens. They have a peculiar wintry quality of invisibility, so lonely rising from the sere grass, and pallid green, held up like a little hand-mirror that reflects nothing. At first they are single upon a stem, short and lovely, and very wintry-beautiful, with a will not to be touched, not to be noticed. One instinctively leaves them alone. But as January draws towards February, these hellebores, these greenish Christmas roses become more assertive. Their pallid water-green becomes yellower, pale sulphur-yellow green, and they rise up, they are in tufts, in throngs, in veritable bushes of greenish open flowers, assertive, bowing their faces with a hellebore assertiveness. In some places they throng among the bushes and above the water of the stream, giving the peculiar pale glimmer almost of primroses, as you walk among them. Almost of primroses, yet with a coarse hellebore leaf and an uprearing hellebore assertiveness, like snakes in winter.

And as one walks among them, one brushes the last scarlet off the butcher's broom. This low little shrub is the Christmas holly of Tuscany, only a foot or so high, with a vivid red berry stuck on in the middle of its sharp hard leaf. In February the last red ball rolls off the prickly plume, and winter rolls with it. The violets already are emerging from the moisture.

But before the violets make any show, there are the crocuses. If you walk up through the pine wood, that lifts its umbrellas of pine so high, up till you come to the brow of the hill at the top, you can look south, due south, and see snow on the Apennines, and on a blue afternoon, seven layers of blue-hilled distance.

Then you sit down on that southern slope, out of the wind, and there it is warm, whether it be January or February, *tramontana* or not. There the earth has been baked by innumerable suns, baked and baked again; moistened by many rains, but never wetted for long. Because it is rocky, and full to the south, and sheering steep in the slope.

And there, in February, in the sunny baked desert of that crumbly slope, you will find the first crocuses. On the sheer aridity of crumbled stone you see a queer, alert little star, very sharp and quite small. It has opened out rather flat, and looks like a tiny freesia flower, creamy, with a smear of yellow yolk. It has no stem, seems to have been just lightly dropped on the crumbled, baked rock. It is the first hill crocus.

North of the Alps, the everlasting winter is interrupted by summers that struggle and soon yield; south of the Alps, the everlasting summer is interrupted by spasmodic and spiteful winters that never get a real hold, but that are mean and dogged. North of the Alps, you may have a pure winter's day in June. South of the Alps, you may have a midsummer day in December or January or even February. The in-between, in either case, is just as it may be. But the lands of the sun are south of the Alps for ever.

Yet things, the flowers especially, that belong to both sides of the Alps, are not much earlier south than north of the mountains. Through all the winter there are roses in the garden, lovely creamy roses, more pure and mysterious than those of summer, leaning perfect from the stem. And the narcissus in the garden are out by the end of January, and the little simple hyacinths early in February.

But out in the fields, the flowers are hardly any sooner than English flowers. It is mid-February before the first violets, the first crocus, the first primrose. And in mid-February one may find a violet, a primrose a crocus in England, in the hedgerows and the garden corner.

And still there is a difference. There are several kinds of wild crocus in this region of Tuscany: little spiky mauve ones, and spiky little creamy ones, that grow among the pine trees of the bare slopes. But the beautiful ones are those of a meadow in the corner of the woods, the low hollow meadow below the steep, shadowy pine slopes, the secretive grassy dip where the water seeps through the turf all winter, where the stream runs between thick bushes, where the nightingale sings his mightiest in May, and where the wild thyme is rosy and full of bees, in summer.

Here the lavender crocuses are most at home—here sticking out of the deep grass, in a hollow like a cup, a bowl of grass, come the lilac-coloured crocuses, like an innummerable encampment. You may see them at twilight, with all the buds shut, in the mysterious stillness of the grassy underworld, palely glimmering like myriad folded tents. So the Apaches still camp, and close their tepees, in the hollows of the great hills of the west, at night.

But in the morning it is quite different. Then the sun shines strong on the horizontal green cloud-puffs of the pines, the sky is clear and full of life, the water runs hastily, still browned by the last juice of crushed olives. And there the earth's bowl of crocuses is amazing. You cannot believe that the flowers are really still. They open with such delight, and their pistil-thrust is so red-orange, and they are so many, all reaching out wide and marvellous, that it suggests a perfect ecstasy of radiant, thronging movement, lit up violet and orange, and surging in some invisible rhythm of concerted, delightful movement. You cannot believe they do not move, and make some sort of crystalline sound of delight. If you sit still and watch, you begin to move with them, like moving with the stars and you feel the sound of their radiance. All the little cells of the flowers must be leaping with flowery life and utterance.

And the small brown honey bees hop from flower to flower, dive down, try, and off again. The flowers have been already rifled, most of them. Only sometimes a bee stands on his head, kicking slowly inside the flower, for some time. He has found something. And all the bees have little loaves of pollen, beebread, in their elbow joints.

The crocuses last in their beauty for a week or so, and as they begin to lower their tents and abandon camp, the violets begin to thicken. It is already March. The violets have been showing like tiny dark hounds for some weeks. But now the whole pack comes forth, among the grass and the tangle of wild thyme, till the air all sways subtly scented with violets, and the banks above where the crocuses had their tents are now swarming brilliant purple with violets. They are the sweet violets of early spring, but numbers have made them bold, for they flaunt and ruffle till the slopes are a bright blue-purple blaze of them, full in the sun, with an odd late crocus still standing wondering and erect amongst them.

And now that it is March, there is a rush of flowers. Down by the other stream, which turns sideways to the sun, and has tangles of brier and bramble, down where the hellebore has stood so wan and dignified all winter, there are now white tufts of primroses, suddenly come. Among the tangle and near the water-lip, tufts and bunches of primroses, in abundance. Yet they look more wan, more pallid, more flimsy than English primroses. They lack something of the full wonder of the northern flowers. One tends to overlook them, to turn to the great, solemn-faced purple violets that rear up from the bank, and above all, to the wonderful little towers of the grape hyacinth.

I know no flower that is more fascinating, when it first appears than the blue grape hyacinth. And yet, because it lasts so long, and keeps on coming so repeatedly, for at least two months, one tends later on to ignore it, even to despise it a little. Yet that is very unjust.

The first grape hyacinths are flowers of blue, thick and rich and meaningful, above the unrenewed grass. The upper buds are pure blue shut tight; round balls of perfect warm blue, blue, blue; while the lower bells are darkish blue-purple, with the spark of white at the mouth. As yet, none of the lower bells has withered, to leave the greenish, separate sparseness of fruiting that spoils the grape hyacinth later on, and makes it seem naked and functional. All hyacinths are like that in the seeding.

But, at first, you have only a compact tower of nightblue clearing to dawn, and extremely beautiful. If we were tiny as fairies, and lived only a summer, how lovely these great trees of bells would be to us, towers of night and dawn-blue globes. They would rise above us thick and succulent, and the purple globes would push the blue ones up, with white sparks of ripples, and we should see a god in them.

As a matter of fact, someone once told me they were the flowers of the many-breasted Artemis; and it is true, the Cybele of Ephesus, with her clustered breasts, was like the grape hyacinth at the bosom. .

This is the time, in March, when the sloe is white and misty in the hedge-tangle by the stream and on the slope of the land the peach-tree stands pink and alone. The almond blossom, silvery pink, is passing, but the peach, deep-toned, bluey, not at all ethereal, this reveals itself like the flesh, and the trees are like isolated individuals, the peach and the apricot.

A man said this spring: "Oh, I *don't* care for peach blossom! It is such a vulgar pink!" One wonders what anybody means by a "vulgar" pink. I think pink flannelette is rather vulgar. But probably it's the flannelette's fault, not the pink. And peach blossom has a beautiful sensual pink, far from vulgar, most rare and private. And pink is so beautiful in a landscape, pink houses, pink almond, pink peach and purply apricot, pink asphodels.

It is so conspicuous and so individual, that pink among the coming green of spring, because the first flowers that emerge from winter seem always white or yellow or purple. Now the celandines are out, and along the edges of the *podere,* the big, sturdy, black-purple anemones, with the black hearts.

They are curious, these great, dark-violet anemones. You may pass them on a grey day, or at evening or early morning, and never see them. But as you come along in the full sunshine, they seem to be baying at you with all their throats, baying deep purple into the air. It is because they are hot and wide open now, gulping the sun whereas, when they are shut, they have a silkiness and a curved head, like the curve of an umbrella handle, and a peculiar outward colourlessness, that makes them quite invisible. They may be under your feet, and you will not see them.

Altogether anemones are odd flowers. On these last hills above the plain, we have only the big black-purple ones, in tufts here and there, not many. But two hills away, the young green corn is blue with the lilac-blue kind, still the broad-petalled sort with the darker heart. But these flowers are smaller than our dark-purple, and frailer, more silky. Ours are substantial, thickly vegetable flowers, and not abundant. The others are lovely and silky-delicate, and the whole corn is blue with them. And they have a sweet, sweet scent when they are warm.

Then on the priest's *podere* there are the scarlet, Adonis-blood anemones: only in one place, in one long fringe under a terrace, and there by a path below. These flowers above all you will never find unless you look for them in the sun. Their silver silk outside makes them quite invisible, when they are shut up.

Yet, if you are passing in the sun, a sudden scarlet faces on to the air, one of the loveliest scarlet apparitions in the world. The inner surface of the Adonis-blood anemone is as fine as velvet, and yet there is no suggestion of pile, not as much as on a velvet rose. And from this inner smoothness issues the red colour, perfectly pure and unknown of earth, no earthiness, and yet solid, not transparent. How a colour manages to be perfectly strong and impervious, yet of a purity that suggests condensed light, yet not luminous, at least not transparent, is a problem. The poppy in her radiance is translucent, and the tulip in her utter redness has a touch of opaque earth. But the Adonis-blood anemone is neither translucent nor opaque. It is just pure condensed red, of a velvetiness without velvet, and a scarlet without glow.

This red seems to me the perfect premonition of summer—like the red on the outside of apple blossom—and later, the red of the apple. It is the premonition in redness of summer and of autumn.

The red flowers are coming now. The wild tulips are in bud, hanging their grey leaves like flags. They come up in myriads, wherever they get a chance. But they are holding back their redness till the last days of March, the early days of April.

Still, the year is warming up. By the high ditch the common magenta anemone is hanging its silky tassels or opening its great magenta daisy-shape to the hot sun. It is much nearer to red than the big-petalled anemones are; except the Adonis-blood. They say these anemones sprang from the tears of Venus, which fell as she went looking for Adonis. At that rate, how the poor lady must have wept, for the anemones by the Mediterranean are common as daisies in England.

The daisies are out here too, in sheets, and they too are red-mouthed. The first ones are big and handsome. But as March goes on, they dwindle to bright little things, like tiny buttons, clouds of them together. That means summer is nearly here.

The red tulips open in the corn like poppies, only with a heavier red. And they pass quickly, without repeating themselves. There is little lingering in a tulip.

In some places there are odd yellow tulips, slender, spiky, and Chinese-looking. They are very lovely, pricking out their dulled yellow in slim spikes. But they too soon lean, expand beyond themselves, and are gone like an illusion.

And when the tulips are gone, there is a moment's pause, before summer. Summer is the next move.

From *Phoenix: The Posthumous Papers of D. H. Lawrence,* Viking, New York, 1936

E. M. Forster

The Solitary Place

Delicate, yet august, the country that stretches westward from the expiring waters of Lake Mariout is not easy to describe. Though it contains accredited oriental ingredients, such as camels, a mirage, and Bedouins, and though it remounts to a high antiquity, yet I cannot imagine our powerful professional novelists getting to work at it, and entreating from its quiet recesses hot tales about mummies and sin. Its basis is a soft limestone, which rises on the seaward side into two well defined and parallel ridges, and swells inland into gentle hills where outline and colouring often suggest a Scotch moor; the whole district has a marked tendency to go purple, especially in its hollows—into that sombre brownish purple that may be caused by moorland growths. Many of the bushes are like flowerless heather. In the lower ground barley is cultivated, and depends for its success upon an occasional violent thunderstorm which shall swell a sudden torrent off the hills. The ancients cultivated vines and olives here too, as the remains of their presses prove, and Cleopatra has a garden here, but from such luxuries the soil has desisted. It has beat a general retreat from civilisation, and the spirit of the place, without being savage, is singularly austere. Its chief episode is the great temple of Abousir, which with its attending beacon-tower stands so magnificently upon the coastal ridge. And inland lie the marble basilicas of St. Menas and its holy well. But these apart, there is nothing to catch the attention. The tents of the Bedouins, so Mongolian in outline, seldom cut the lines of the sky, but blend in colour with the stone, against which they crouch. The quarries, vast and romantic, lie hidden in the flanks of the limestone. They do not play the part a chalk-pit does in the landscape of the Sussex downs. The place is not a wilderness, it is a working concern. But it is essentially solitary, and only once a year does it, for a brief space, put its solitude away, and blossom.

There is nothing there of the ordered progress of the English spring, with its slow extension from wood anemones through primroses to the buttercups of June. The flowers come all of a rush. One week there is nothing but spikes and buds, then the temperature rises and the wind drops, and whole tracts turn lilac or scarlet. They scarcely wait for their leaves, they are in such a hurry, and many of them blossom like little footstools, close to the ground. They do not keep their times. They scarcely keep their places, and you may look in vain for them this season where you found them last. There is a certain tract of yellow marigolds which I suspect of migration. One year it was in a quarry, the next by the railway lines, now it has flown a distance of five and a half miles and unfolded its carpet on the slopes beneath Abusir. All is confusion and hurry. The white tassels of garlic that wave in the shadow of the temple may be fallen to-morrow, the blue buds of the borage never have time to unfold. The pageant passes like the waving of a handkerchief, but in compensation without the lumber that attends the passing of an English spring, no stalks and reluctant exits of half dead leaves. As it came, so it goes. It has been more like a ray of coloured light playing on the earth than the work of the earth herself, and if one had not picked a few of the flowers and entombed them in vases upon an Alexandrian mantelpiece, they could seem afterwards like the growth of a dream.

It would require a botanist to do justice to these flowers, but fortunately there is no occasion to do justice to flowers. They are not Government officials. Let their titles and duties remain for the most part unknown. The most permanent of them are, oddly enough, the asphodels, whose coarse stems and turbid venous blossoms have disappointed many who dreamt of the Elysian Fields. How came the Greeks to plant so buxom a bulb in the solitary place they imagined beyond the grave—that place which, though full of philosophers and charioteers remains for ever empty? The asphodel is built to resist rough winds and to stand on slopes of an earthly hill. It is too heavy for the hands of ghosts, too harsh for their feet. But perhaps ours were not the asphodels the Greeks planted, and their ghosts may have walked upon what we call Stars of Bethlehem. The marigolds are solid too, but for the most part the flora are very delicate, and their colours aerial. There is a tiny vetch that hesitates between terra cotta and claret. There is a scented yellow flower the size of flax which is only found in one part of the district and which closes in the evening when the irises unfold. Two of these irises are dwarf, and coloured purple and a deep blue; a third is larger and china blue. There are tracts of nightscented stock. Down in the quarries grows a rock plant with a dull red spire and a fleshy leaf that almost adheres to the stone. As for the shrubs some have transparent joints that look filled with wine; while from the woolly fibre of others jut buttons like blue scabious. Other blue plants wave their heads in the barley. Mignonette, purple and white anemones, scarlet and yellow ranunculus, scarlet poppies, coltsfoot and dwarf orange marigolds, nettles genuine and false, henbane, mallows, celandine, hen and chicken, lords and ladies, convulvulus. English daisies I do not remember, and many of these flowers are not the varieties we know in England. The lords and ladies, for instance, are smaller and thrust up their pale green spoons in the open ground. While, to compensate, there is a larger kind—an arm of great rise with a coal black sheath and clapper—a positively Satanic plant such as Des Esseintes could have commanded for his conservatory. In this way, just here and there, the tropic note is struck, and reminds us that these familiar and semi-familiar flowers are after all growing in Africa and that those swelling hills stretch southward towards the heart of the dark continent.

But what impresses one most in the scene is the quiet persistence of the earth. There is so little soil about and she does so much with it. Year after year she has given this extraordinary show for a few Bedouins, has covered the Mareotic civilisation with dust and raised flowers from its shards. Will she do the same to our tins and barbed wire? Probably not, for man has now got so far ahead of other forms of life that he will scarcely permit the flowers to grow over his works again. His old tins will be buried under new tins. This is the triumph of civilisation, I suppose, the final imprint of the human upon this devoted planet, which should exhibit in its apotheosis a solid crust of machinery and graves. In cities one sees this sort of development coming, but in solitary places, however austere, the primaeval softness persists, the vegetation still flowers and seeds unchecked, and the air still blows untainted hot from the land or cold from the sea. I have tried to describe this Mariout country as it is at the beginning of March, when the earth makes her great effort. In a few days the wind may scratch and tear the blossoms, in a few weeks the sun will scorch the leaves. The spontaneous red growth of the ice-plant will dry up and the bones of the limestone reappear. Then all will be quiet till the first winter rain, when the camels will be driven out to surface-plough. A rectangle is outlined on the soil and scattered with seed barley. Then the camel will shuffle up and down dragging after him a wooden plough that looks like a half-open penknife, and the Bedouin, guiding it, will sing tunes to the camel that he can only sing to the camel, because in his mind the tune and the camel are the same thing.

From *Pharos and Pharillon,* Hogarth, London, 1923 (written in 1918)

The Pagan Gown

There is a pleasant pagan atmosphere about the countryside of my Italian home. Trees here and there, hornbeam or mulberry, are twisted in a canopy of boughs; and an oleograph of St. Anthony, or of the Madonna and Child, is plaited in the leafy frame. The growing shrine stands usually in a hedge or beside a gate, to guard the crops behind it; and the older peasants, moving with a slow swing and muddy boots beside their creaking oxen, may be heard even to-day to mutter ejaculations to Bacchus or Diana or, possibly, in one breath, to Hercules and the Virgin together.

Who does not feel pagan in the spring? That languor, when first the grassblade is folded so that it can hold a shadow; when lakes are soft, the colour of mist and light; when the streams run transparent with liquid notes, their wavelets cold as snowdrops. Cats lie in the sun with the five toes of each paw stretched out and sleep, like a slow serpent, moves up and down their spine. The notes of birds at evening drop like water falling in water; and the buds, especially beech, have a sharp and bitter smell. The earth is damp, sucking dead leaves down into the furnace of her year, working at growth in warmth and darkness. I hope old age will not deprive me of this repeated visitation of delight in which, with the whole of our planet, we turn ourselves in space towards the sun. While this is happening, the puritan dies in us; there is a soul in inanimate things. Our Monsignor with his little procession walks about, blessing the fields or sprinkling holy water in the houses. His choir boys follow him, with white cassocks and tidy hair, and muddy boots from the paths round their homes. They carry their brass bowl and the olive bough for sprinkling with a nonchalant air, for they too are distracted by the many voices. Their ceremony is part of a ritual far older than anything our civilisation can remember; and the church, like a great ship under sail, carries as its ballast, hidden far below the water-line, the whole pagan history of men.

One wonders when the puritan first began. This cleavage of poly- and mono-theist, of hedonist and ascetic, of Epicurean and Stoic, of Catholic and Protestant, seems to be one of the genuine divisions of human kind. What first made the creature dissatisfied with that which for all the rest of creation appears to be sufficient? Perhaps it was the desert, where "the barren earth entwines few tentacles about the heart; it stretches away dark and empty beneath our feet, a mere footstool for meditation".*

This is tiresome about the puritan. Why must things be gaunt and bare for people to meditate upon them?

Whatever the ultimate origins, the book of Genesis gives a summary of the repeated story: delight in external things, and then human hunger for truth beyond. Eve, Psyche, Pandora, they would look, not, like the Lady of Shalot, *away* from the mirror, but *through* it, to see what is hidden behind the moving show: until the face of things becomes an impediment to them and a torment, a barrier to the simplicity of truth.

One of the more charming of the Muhammedan saints walked always barefoot out of respect for earth, the carpet of God. Indeed the kindlier among saints have all found the same answer, seeing the divine unity in all its variegated vestments of fugitive beauty and transitory life. But ordinary sons of men quarrel to this day, unable to walk the tightrope betwen worship of creatures on the one hand and on the other a blindness towards the presence of what is divine. A fair Protestant, I am yet inclined to think the pagan in less danger: to kiss the hem of a garment in reverence is better than to have it fluttering unrecognized about one. The windows of hill towns that shine in dawn or sunset are but paltry glass that tell of the hidden sun: yet the inexperienced eye that thinks it fire, may be pardoned for not realizing how far beyond the horizon are its origins. So, indirectly, in our everyday life we see the presence of God. The eagle-sighted alone can witness it unhooded, or

*George Santayana, "Soliloquies in England".

those whose wings are feathered for great space. Yet the reflection is indeed originally sunlight, and if sometimes we forget the interval and distance of its journey and worship—that is surely more venial than to forget altogether that its glitter is divine.

For this reason I have no quarrel with superstition, unless cruelty comes to darken and corrupt.

In southern India, where one lives in a happy muddle of familiarity with gods, and even the little chipmunk has a place in temples—since Rama stroked him with his fingers and left three streaks down its back—I was surprised to find how natural paganism appears.

What else but those crowded pyramids of deity would one expect above the seething tanks whose steps are alive all day with naked limbs below the white and red-striped temple walls? Sea-waves beat the shore of this land with the strength of a bull's neck; one can feel their pull in a few inches of water, for they have the whole emptiness westward from Australia in which to gather themselves together. In the forests that clothe the mountain horizon thin-flanked flat-headed tigers roam, and cobras sway with glazed eyes in the sun. How can man, living in this coconut strip of land, in a sort of under-water atmosphere, dim green beneath the unending aisles and fronds, think of himself as more than a part of it all?

Once a year the gods leave their temples and, escorted by king, court, cabinet and army, bathe themselves in the sunset and the sea; and pass, with their elephants and drums, between the soldiers in smart uniforms of Europe who line a sanded path where all walk barefoot, attending the smiling gods borne on their stands. In the evening, after this has happened, they walk abroad. In the mute streets, in rich darkness, scented and heavy with flowers, the people come to look. Their king must shoot an arrow in their defence, and no sound warns the enemy till all is over. The enemy's head is a coconut hidden in a little hut of leaves at a crossroads; and here, under the stars, the whole town gathers; their white gowns are visible dimly; the sound of their brown feet is smothered in the sand; and they wait, thousands of them, in silence.

Presently, still soundless, with torches in clusters, and shields and bows, the procession comes to the temple. The gods in their wreaths and flowers are placed to see. And, humbly, in a plain toga, with bare shoulders, a lamp and a bow in his hands, the king advances. He places the lamp on the ground and fits his arrow and, standing alone in front of the hidden malignity, shoots fair and true. So small and humble, he seems the epitome of man fighting with the courage created by the presence of his gods; and as the arrow finds its mark, the people shout, the drums and trumpets make all the noise they can; and city and temple are safe for another year.

I have watched the same sort of ceremony in the Alps, at the yearly blessing of the Monte Rosa glacier. A small procession gathers in the last village beyond Macugnaga, and walks behind the cross and the priest in yellow cope with swinging incense, across the meadows where the harvest hay and the fountains of wild roses are breathing out a summer incense of their own. The glacier pours down into the head of the valley, threatening the pastures beyond its drift of boulder-strewn moraine. At its edge the flowers have thinned away to *soldanella* or *ranunculus glacialis;* all else is only the makings of earth out of chaos, the oozing clay and sobbing patches where ice-water breaks through, and steep torrents, white and green, that swell in the afternoons with the melting snowfields, and shrink again at night.

Facing all this, on the cushiony grass of pastures, the little ceremony is performed: the cross is lifted, and the prayer spoken that is to hold the slow-moving giant in its bond; and he, overhanging with glittering height, and icy caverns and pinnacles against the burning sky, declares, with the contrast of his hugeness, the glory and audacity of man.

Religion is all an adventure in courage, and superstition a print of adventuring footsteps in the past, though it is apt to become more coercive than a footprint and to freeze, if it can, the exploring spirit from which itself was born. That, I imagine, is why the mystic is inclined to retreat from the habitations of man; to seek a world where every object he sees is not wound in a cocoon of thought and images created by others. He needs to get away from all these voices, he needs a footstool for meditation, and to watch, in the silence of his own heart, for the trail which so many wayfarers have confused. The true call of the desert, of the mountains, or the sea, is their silence—free of the network of dead speech. This silence without which no enduring progress can be built must enter into all education that is worthy of the name: it is the reason why climbing or walking or sailing should come, if possible, into the life of every child:

> *The thought of death sits easy on the man*
> *Who has been born and dies among the mountains.* *

*W. Wordsworth, "The Brothers".

Some people, out of strength or weakness, come to love such solitude as the breath of life. Many, strangers to their own souls, shun it with fear. But the well-strung creature finds in it a tonic, a pause from which he comes refreshed. With the mountain lightness still in his eyes and feet, he is happy to return from the wilderness and to find himself again among the paths and dwellings and habits, the rites and symbols which in their long trail of history have made him what he is.

From *Perseus in the Wind*, J. Murray, London, 1948

John Galsworthy

Burning Leaves

When autumn comes, and leaves are gathered into little heaps and slow fire set to them, all who have passed the meridian of life are moved by the acrid odour and the trailing blue of the smoke, as if they saw and scented the leafage of their own pasts burning—leafage, which was green and smelled of lemons when it burst from the bud. A townscent—this of burning leaves, whose nearest parallel in the country is the scent of rotting leaves; not so strong or provocative of melancholy, perhaps because the uncleared leaves are going naturally back to the mould from which the trees have drawn their life; or perhaps—a less literary reason—because the scent from rotting leaves is so much milder in the nostril. All primitive inevitability—birth, coupling, death—takes a larger place, and yet is less poignant and startling in the country than in towns. Out in the open we are framed in the unceasing process of Nature, among plants and birds and animals; in town bound in mechanical conspiracy to conceal that process, we burn our leaves, and remove the sight of their long decay; we compress slow emotion into swift feeling.

Curious, by the way, that we should have a prayer against sudden death; and if our Litany were to be revised, suffrage would convert it. Most of us would now prefer to have our lives blown out as a man blows out a candle; choose to burn steadily to a swift last, instead of with a flickering, sorrowful dwindling of our flames into darkness that we can see creeping round us. "To sudden death, not premature, O Fate, deliver us! " would run our prayer. There has ever been something mean, too, about a preparation for dying, with its calculated confession of wrong living, and its squirming effort to square accounts at the last; as if a man, having comfortably cheated his neighbours all his life, sought the odour of honesty only when mortal sickness deprives him of the power of cheating them any more. A singular cynicism or a strange lack of charity in estimating the Divine character attends the notion of a "deathbed repentance".

But when we smell burning leaves we do not remember our murky thoughts and actions; the smouldering heaps are golden, the smoke therefrom the colour of happiness, its scent sharp-sweet. Relish in past experience spent and absent now, is what moves him or her who watches and sniffs that smoke.

A pity that we cannot see, slow-forming before our eyes, the ghost trees of our past lives, their trunks and spine branches of development, with all our sensations budding, living, fluttering upon them, see our every action, thought and feeling spread in the pattern of their growth towards the top where leaves are already few. Self-growth is hard to comprehend in its slow and imperceptible transformations. The children we were are frankly unrecognisable by ourselves at fifty. Our spiritual and bodily metabolism, so probably one and the same thing, is beyond our powers of tracing out; but scenting the trailed smoke of burning leaves we come perhaps nearer than at any other time to appreciation of how we stretch back year on year to innocence in a holland suit.

"Oh! the long days in the distance enchanted! " Piled in that heap, they exhale their burnt incense, no flame visible; it trails away thin and blue towards where the sunset is preparing. Lives! What invisible runners they are!

From *Castles in Spain and Other Screeds,* Heinemann, London, 1927

Llewelyn Powys

The First Fall of Snow

There is not one of us, I suppose, who does not experience a curious sensation of romantic interest at seeing each winter the first fall of snow. There is something about the appearance of these delicately congealed, feathery morsels descending so uncertainly, so lightly, from the sky that is ever provocative of attention. The most stolid citizen upon noticing the white flakes on his sleeve is disposed to raise his eyes and for a moment at least to contemplate with a vague, uneasy interest the clouds above his head.

So must our ancestors have regarded the same phenomenon when, leaving the languid security of warmer regions, they wandered forth in the direction of the poles. For snow has ever about it a suggestion of those chilled, flattened acres where for centuries upon centuries black waters have been enclosed by measureless layers of ice.

Is it, after all, but an old race-memory astir in us still that causes us so inevitably, when we hear that it is snowing, to cross our fire-lit rooms and glance between the curtains out of the window? Do we retain in our round skulls, in our square skulls, in our narrow hatchet-shaped skulls certain subconscious recollections of the appalling struggles of our race in far-off glacial periods? Do we to this day, when these dainty fragments of frozen moisture float downwards between the high walls of our houses, become aware of an ancient menace?

Walter Pater used to mark with pleasure the faint reflected light that snow-covered lawns cast on the white ceiling of an interior; and which of us can not remember our own amazement at waking up after a storm to find the familiar landscape outside completely transformed? What elation to walk along strange, muffled roads, under trees whose gaunt, naked branches are illuminate to their topmost twig in the bright winter sunshine! On such occasions, if one wanders for a few steps into a forest, what a strange initiation one undergoes into the secrets of nature, into its faculty of negation, for complete rest! Mutely, patiently, the boughs of the green firs bear their burdens. A kind of majestic audience would seem to be in attendance. It is as though every upright piece of sentinel-timber were waiting, waiting for a voice to speak. How dare the irreverent squirrels emerge from their clefts even for a moment; how dare those sharp-eyed, thick furred creatures mark with delicate filigree the crisp, unruffled surface of the forest floor? Even to pray were a desecration in such a place, a place articulate of timeless eternity, of ineffable, sublime cessation. Small wonder the tiny shoots that survive against all reason, still quick under fallen autumn leaves beneath the snow—small wonder they hesitate to disturb by the slightest pressure that august stillness.

The influence of snow has in it a magical quality that cannot be gainsaid; an influence entirely different from that of rain. In the tropics I have known what it is to see a parched and thirsty land awake to life at the beginning of the wet season. I have seen the buck come gambolling down to the valleys to nibble impatiently at the few first blades of green grass, have heard the winged fantastics that in Africa are called birds, fly screaming through the forest branches whose flat leaves are dripping with round drops of lukewarm moisture. I have felt the earth, our ancient mother earth, beneath my feet, tremble and quiver in an ecstasy of childbirth under the sweet persuasion of those torrential downpourings; but never once did she attain to such mysterious power as when, at rest under a covering of snow, she lies with the appearance and potency of a sculptured goddess who is in truth dead and yet retains that upon her ivory forehead which is equivalent to immortality.

How strangely children understand the enchantment of snow; watching with shining, excited eyes the dun clouds gathering about the distant horizons while the weather-vanes on housetop or shed-roof resolutely predict colder weather; realizing the latent power in those clouds so grim and solid, a power that can confound the best-laid plans of their elders, can choke the progress of enormous iron locomotives and set every township agog with spade, shovel and steam-plough! And afterwards, from the nursery window, how delightful to watch it falling—like bees, we used to say—falling, falling, falling this way and that, wavering and uncertain as life itself!

Each winter what delight to snuff up through our nostrils the unexpected, unmistakable odour of snow! There is a fine privilege in that. For snow does smell. It is indeed odorific of the empyrean, of the actual tract of space across which we speed at the heels of the sun. Not only does it smell, but it can take to itself also a thousand incredible colours. It is a mistake to imagine that snow is always white. I have seen fields of it in the high Alps of the colour of a red-rose petal; and in the dark northern forests where the wolves howl under the pines, its shadowy levels towards evening resemble stretches of charcoal. Thrust a stick deep into a snow-bank and one discovers to one's amazement that the interior of the aperture made is blue, is, in fact the precise colour of the inside of a wave as it stands, for a single second, motionless and curled before its final breaking into lineal froth against the wild sea-banks of pebble or sand.

But just as freshly fallen snow gives one the impression of absolute virginal purity more than anything in the world, so, after contact with the base matter of the earth does it seem to typify that which has been degraded. There are few things more depressing to look upon than a heap of soiled snow, several weeks old, banked up against the sidewalk. It is then, when one's eyes light upon scraps of human refuse projecting from the soiled mass, that one's imagination conceives with a shock the vision of the planet so radiant in itself being rapidly disfigured by the presence of an importunate, restless animal, who, for all its upright stature and brave brainpan, is unseemly in its habits and continues with appalling thoroughness to litter the surface of its winged prison-house.

Small wonder that the great English poet in contemplating the birth of God upon our planet conceived it as having occurred when the wilful, ungenerate land was concealed as with a winding-sheet. It is with Christmas that most of us associate the curious, evasive beauty of this strange white substance. Nobody wishes the ground to be green at that hallowed time of the year. A uniform whiteness seems more in accord with that most daring of human fancies which represents to our reason the assumption that, in very fact, a divine messenger from the other side of the flaming ramparts did actually in the latter days become incarnate.

From *A Selection of His Writings*, Macdonald, London, 1952 (written in 1930)

Ronald Duncan

Three Peach Stones

Observe a child; any one will do. You will see that not a day passes in which he does not find something or other to make him happy, though he may be in tears the next moment. Then look at a man; any one of us will do. You will notice that weeks and months can pass in which every day is greeted with nothing more than resignation, and endured with polite indifference. Indeed, most men are as miserable as sinners, though they are too bored to sin—perhaps their sin is their indifference. But it is true that they so seldom smile that when they do we do not recognise their face, so distorted is it from the fixed mask we take for granted. And even then a man can not smile like a child, for a child smiles with his eyes, whereas a man smiles with his lips alone. It is not a smile; but a grin; something to do with humour, but little to do with happiness. And then, as anyone can see, there is a point (but who can define that point?) when a man becomes an old man, and then he will smile again.

It would seem that happiness is something to do with simplicity, and that it is the ability to extract pleasure from the simplest things—such as a peach stone, for instance.

It is obvious that it is nothing to do with success. For Sir Henry Stewart was certainly successful. It is twenty years ago since he came down to our village from London, and bought a couple of old cottages, which he had knocked into one. He used his house as a weekend refuge. He was a barrister. And the village followed his brilliant career with something almost amounting to paternal pride.

I remember some ten years ago when he was made a King's Counsel,

Amos and I, seeing him get off the London train, went to congratulate him. We grinned with pleasure; he merely looked as miserable as though he'd received a penal sentence. It was the same when he was knighted; he never smiled a bit, he didn't even bother to celebrate with a round of drinks at the "Blue Fox". He took his success as a child does his medicine. And not one of his achievements brought even a ghost of a smile to his tired eyes.

I asked him one day, soon after he'd retired to potter about his garden, what it was like to achieve all one's ambitions. He looked down at his roses and went on watering them. Then he said "The only value in achieving one's ambition is that you then realise that they are not worth achieving". Quickly he moved the conversation on to a more practical level, and within a moment we were back to a safe discussion on the weather. That was two years ago.

I recall this incident, for yesterday, I was passing his house, and had drawn up my cart just outside his garden wall. I had pulled in from the road for no other reason than to let a bus pass me. As I set there filling my pipe, I suddenly heard a shout of sheer joy come from the other side of the wall.

I peered over. There stood Sir Henry doing nothing less than a tribal war dance of sheer unashamed ecstasy. Even when he observed my bewildered face staring over the wall he did not seem put out or embarrassed, but shouted for me to climb over.

"Come and see, Jan. Look! I have done it at last! I have done it at last! "

There he was, holding a small box of earth in his hand. I observed three tiny shoots out of it.

"And there *were* only three! " he said, his eyes laughing to heaven.

"Three what? " I asked.

"Peach stones", he replied. "I've always wanted to make peach stones grow, ever since I was a child, when I used to take them home after a party, or as a man after a banquet. And I used to plant them, and then forgot where I planted them. But now at last I have done it, and, what's more, I had only three stones, and there you are, one, two, three shoots", he counted.

And Sir Henry ran off, calling for his wife to come and see his achievement—his achievement of simplicity.

From *The Blue Fox*, Museum P., London, 1951

Joseph Conrad

A Preface to
A Handbook of Cookery,
by Jessie Conrad

Of all the books produced since the most remote ages by human talents and industry those only that treat of cooking are, from a moral point of view above suspicion. The intention of every other piece of prose may be discussed and even mistrusted; but the purpose of a cookery book is one and unmistakable. Its objects can conceivably be no other than to increase the happiness of mankind.

This general consideration, and also a feeling of affectionate interest with which I am accustomed to view all the actions of the writer prompt me to set down these few words of introduction for her book. Without making myself responsible for her teaching (I own that I find it impossible to read through a cookery book), I come forward modestly but gratefully as a Living Example of her practice. That practice I dare pronounce most successful. It has been for many priceless years adding to the sun of my daily happiness.

Good cooking is a moral agent. By good cooking I mean the conscientious preparation of the simple food of everyday life, not the more or less skilful concoction of idle feasts and rare dishes. Conscientious cookery is an enemy to gluttony. The trained delicacy of the palate, like a cultivated delicacy of sentiment, stands in the way of unseemly excesses. The decency of our life is for a great part a matter of good taste, of the correct appreciation of what is fine in simplicity. The intimate influence of conscientious cooking by rendering easy the process of digestion promotes the serenity of mind, the graciousness of thought, and that indulgent view of our neighbour's failings which is the only genuine form of optimism. Those are the titles to our reverence.

A great authority upon North American Indians accounted for the sombre and excessive ferocity characteristic of these savages by the theory that as a race they suffered from perpetual indigestion. The noble Red Man was a mighty hunter, but his wives had not mastered the art of conscientious cookery. And the consequences were deplorable. The Seven Nations around the Great Lakes and the Horse Tribes of the Plains were one vast prey to raging dispepsia. The noble Red Men were great warriors, great orators, great masters of outdoor pursuits; but the domestic life of their wigwams was clouded by the morose irritability which follows the consumption of ill-cooked food. The gluttony of their indigestible feasts was a direct incentive to councels of unreasonable violence. Victims of gloomy imaginings, they lived in abject submission to the wiles of a multitude of fraudulent medicine men—quacks—who haunted their existence with vain promises and false nostrums from the cradle to the grave.

It is to be remarked, that the quack of modern civilisation, the vendor of patent medicine, preys mainly upon the races of Anglo-Saxon stock who are also great warriors, great orators, mighty hunters, great masters of outdoor pursuits. No virtues will avail for happiness if the righteous art of cooking is neglected by the national conscience. We owe much to the fruitful meditations of our sages, but a sane view of life is, after all, elaborated mainly in the kitchen—the kitchen of the small house, the abode of the preponderant majority of the people. And a sane view of life excludes the belief in patent medicine. The conscientious cook is the natural enemy of the quack without a conscience; and then his labours make for the honesty and favour the amenity, of our existence. For a sane view of life can be no other than kindly and joyous, but a believer in patent medicine is steeped in the gloom of vague fears, the sombre attendants of disordered digestion.

Strong in this conviction, I introduce this little book to the inhabitants of the little houses who are the arbiters of the nation's destiny. Ignorant of the value of its methods, I have no doubt whatever as to its intention. It is highly moral. There can not be the slightest question as to that; for is it not a cookery book? —the only product of the human mind altogether above suspicion.

In that respect no more need, or indeed can, be said. As regards the practical intention, I gather that no more than the clear and concise exposition of elementary principles has been the author's aim. And this too, is laudable, because modesty is a becoming virtue in an artist. It remains for me only to express the hope that by correctness of practice and soundness of precept this little book will be able to add to the cheerfulness of nations.

From *Last Essays*, Dent, London, 1926

A. A. Milne

Love and Marriage

Is love necessary to a happy married life? It depends what you mean by "love". My answer to the question would be that what I mean by "love" is only experienced by the happily married. I do not mean "married" in the technical sense. No formula of Church or State makes two people one. But it is not until a man and a woman have lived together for years in utter contentment of each other that they know what love is; as distinct from passion, as distinct from affection, as distinct from friendliness, community of interest, good-comradeship; as distinct from everything else which this world has to offer. Is love necessary for a happy married life? Well, then, it depends on what you mean by "happy".

Married life, of course, is difficult. It would hardly offer such complete happiness if it were not. The Victorians found it more easy. The wife said "Yes, John" and "No, John", and went on having children. Was the husband happy? At least he was comfortable; and part of his comfort was derived from one fact that his marriage was a success. Never a disagreement between them? "Yes, John", "No, John". Was the wife happy? I know of Victorian women who spent the first five years of their married lives in an agony of fear: fear that they were going to have children, fear of the children whom they knew they were going to have. No doubt the husband had often said at the club, cigar in mouth: "My wife has no secrets from me". Yet I think she had this one secret. Otherwise, surely, he could not have been so comfortable.

To-day, women have no secrets from us. It makes life more difficult.

That is why we dislike beggars in the street; not because they pester us, but because we are reminded of their shameful secret; their poverty. How easy marriage would be if we could go on saying, "*my* house", "*my* children", "*my* money", and the woman went on saying "Yes, John", and kept her secrets to herself; just as the fox keeps his secret to himself, and enables us to assure him that he enjoys being hunted. But Women talk to us now as man to man, and Man is suddenly in the horrible position of realising that a "happy marriage" in some ridiculous way has got to mean happiness for the women also. Is it any wonder that there is this rush of unhappy marriages? What would happen to all the happy shooting-parties each autumn, if they had suddenly to include happiness for a vocal pheasant?

But are we then, to renounce the real happy marriage as too difficult of attainment? Those who are content with what is called the "French marriage" have already done so. If marriage in France is truly regarded as a means to an end only, the founding of a family, no doubt a "safe" marriage—in which little of value, as between husband and wife, is given and asked—is the best form of marriage possible. But I confess (and I am aware that it may be a personal idiosyncrasy of mine) that mere propagation has never seemed to me an overwhelming achievement in itself. To provide the next generation seems to me less praiseworthy than to provide *for* the next generation, and even this is less important than that the present generation should do something of value with its own lives. One really happy marriage to-day is a greater achievement than the provision of human material for a thousand loveless marriages in the future. To miss the most beautiful thing in life in order that there shall be a next generation to miss it too, is a poor way of expressing one's personality. Not for a moment do I deny that there is a beauty in childhood, beauty in motherhood, beauty in the relation of parent to child. If any man or woman says: "I love children; I have not the temperament for a happy marriage, but I could make a child happy. And I want to experience the joys of fatherhood or motherhood", then let him or her make a "safe" marriage, convenient for the purpose. But if he says: "I must marry so as to keep up the birthrate", then honestly I do not know what he is talking about. Is he trying to help God—or the British Empire? Probably he makes no distinction.

How can the happy marriage be achieved? I think it is less a matter of choice and more a matter of temperament than is supposed. The assumption of every unhappy husband is that if he had only met Mary before he met Jane, all would have been well, and that, as soon as Jane has divorced him he and Mary will at last have a chance of being happy together. I fancy that it is a small chance. He did not choose the wrong woman; he was, and will always be, the wrong man. I shall never win the Mixed Doubles at Wimbledon however carefully I choose my partner. My form is hopeless for Wimbledon anyhow. There are thousands of men and women whose form is hopeless for Dunmow.

What, then, is the correct form? I should say it was found in an eagerness, all day and every day, to see things from the point of view of the other. It is difficult; particularly for the man, who can never quite forget that his wife promised to obey him ... and never quite remember that he has endowed her with all his goods. It is always difficult to see the other person's point of view; always lamentably easy to say: "Oh, but that's different". However, one gets better with practice.

And is this, you ask, what I mean by love—just seeing things from each other's point of view, making allowances for each other? Of course not. This is merely the top-dressing which gives the ache, the longing, the glory, the misery, all that you first felt when you pledged yourselves to each other, a chance to grow into real love. Love, as I mean it, can only be experienced by the happily married, but I doubt if the happily married will ever experience it unless they were "in love" at some time first. So perhaps that is the answer to the question.

From *By Way of Introduction,* Methuen, London, 1929

C. E. Montague

The Blessings of Adam

A man with some darling craft of his own must scratch his head in wonder when he hears some of the things that are daily said about work. One day he finds labour put down as a curse that came on Adam at the Fall—as if Adam had never done a day's digging before his eviction. Another day we are bidden to hope that if the invention of tricks to save labour can only go on as fast as it is going now, we may yet have no need to work more than two hours a day, or possibly one. Even sages as fully accredited as Mr. Bertrand Russell propose that we should knock off presently for all but four hours a day. He would turn us out for the rest of our time, to get what good we could out of a set of fine abstract nouns—science and art, friendship and love, the contemplation of natural beauty and of the immensity of the universe. Husks, mere husks, unless you peg away at them so hard that this, too, becomes work, and so gives you back the delicious fatigue you have lost.

As if we could not see for ourselves that one of the saddest men on earth is he who has made his pile in some business early in life and who looks in at the office for only one or two hours a day to bully the clerks and then return to his Old Masters and roses, the wife of his bosom and the spectacle of the firmament. As if we had never seen children or artists or scientific researchers! A normal child has no spite against work until you have drilled one into him by some form of dis-education. You put him out in a sunny garden to play: he has about him everything that Mr. Bertrand Russell rates highest—sand for engineering science, a paint-box for art, dolls for his affections, a foreground of agreeable landscape and the whole dome of the heavens to contemplate. No good; in half an hour he is plaguing you to let him do some "real work"; he wants to sweep up dead leaves or to help with the mowing. He will not tire of doing it, either, except in the bodily way, and then he will come again, thirsting for toil, the next morning. So powerful is this innate craving for labour that it may take all the massed resources of a great public school and of a famous and ancient university to make a boy believe that real work is a thing to flee from, like want or disease, and that doing it and "having a good time" are states naturally and immutably opposed to each other.

Or look at the man of science, the mighty hunter of knowledge, some time when his nose is well down on a hot scent. Offer him a release from all but two hours' work in the day. He will hoot at you. Why, when he goes to bed of a night he probably thinks greedily, "Only just the few hours that I'm asleep—and those don't really count—and then time for dressing and breakfast, and then I can get at it again. Hurrah! "

Consider, above all, the artist. Some years ago the leagued artists of Italy, bitten by the spirit of the age, proclaimed a one-day strike—to "draw attention", as the phrase is, to the scurvy mutilation of a portrait by a noble lord who had sat for it and then did not like it. Whether this bolt from blue Southern skies blasted the impious peer is not certain, but every feeling heart knew that it must, at any rate, have inflicted a pretty smart pang on its projectors. For strikes are deeply different things when the work you lay down is a job that suffers from some relative poverty in charm, such as totting up endless small sums at a desk or feeding coal in at the door of a furnace, and when it is one that keeps you full of a pleasant presentiment that before long you will set the Thames or the Tiber on fire with the enormous sparks that are constantly being given off by your genius. Any sound moralist will tell you that your sense of the dignity of labour, and of the moral beauty of sweeping a room as by divine law, ought to make stoking or dusting a task as amusing as that of turning out masterpieces in marble or paint. Yet those of us who do neither of these good things have a rooted notion that it must be some of the best fun in the world to paint as Reynolds did it, and quite poor fun, in a comparative sense, to dust out railway carriages. The cleaner can, as a rule, control for long time his passion for the act of cleaning for cleaning's sake. But an inspired painter would pretend in vain that he did not mind downing brushes at all, and that football and a little racing were quite good enough to pass the time for him. We pretty well know that, to this grade of labour, work is what alcohol is to the dipsomaniac.

It shows once more the ineradicable goodness of human nature that, knowing this, we pay the artist any wages at all. Tactically we others have him in a cleft stick. A miner who will labour gratis in his vocation is, as Dugald Dalgetty said of the refusal of coined money, a sight seldom seen in a Christian land. But if the world firmly refused to give the artist a farthing for his wares, the passionate creature would still go on painting. He could not give up, and, however rich he might be to the end of the stoppage, the misery of a long strike might be the death of him.

If it came to a grand economic dispute, no doubt the artist might try to dissemble this congenital disinclination for striking, in hopes of loosening this fine hold that we of the general public would have upon him. And sometimes the thought is apt to arise—must not a certain amount of this prudent dissimulation be practised by others? Or can it really be that a skilful plumber, or Mr. Bertrand Russell himself, would sincerely like to work at plumbing or at advanced mathematics and political philosophy for only two hours a day? At every congress of organized workmen there seems to run through almost every speech an implication that bodily work is nothing but an evil to be born only for the sake of the pay that it brings, and that the few poor devils who do not work but try to while away their shabby days with expensive attempts at self-amusement have got hold of an undue share of happiness, to the exclusion of everybody who is busy. Is it possible that none of the speakers has ever known the kind of pervasive benediction that seems to descend on body and mind after the first hour or two of a day's digging, house-decorating or reaping? Or that delicious satisfaction in every tissue of yourself when you have completed the new hen-house, and stump off at the end of the day to sleep in Elysium, stiff, slow and full of a contentment and serenity passing all understanding?

Of course they have, all of them. There is no kind of work which is not loved passionately by some of those who do it—loved sometimes to the point of selfishness, so that a man will sooner let wife and children go short of food and teaching than give up the work of his choice for some other work on which the family could live better. And yet this kind of true love seems, in our time, to have no more than others of the knack of running smoothly. Like Viola, a good trade unionist will never tell his love. Something keeps the barrister earning his hundred pounds a day from letting out that even if every client were able to bilk him, and did it, still he would stick to his gladiatorial work for the joy and thrill of it, as so many shepherds who piped in Thessaly would manifestly have remained in the business, even if rural labour in those parts had become wholly unremunerative. On all sides the happy toiler's lips are apparently sealed by the real or supposed necessity of taking thought for the possibly evil effect of descants of joy and praise upon the mind of some human paymaster who comes into the affair.

Besides, there is the mischief that so much of our work has been bedevilled by unavoidable changes of circumstance. Childish as it is to think of going back, on any large scale, to archaic hand-work and petty production of all sorts, still the sentimentalists of hand-spinning, hand-weaving and hand-sewing have got hold of one truth—that there is more joy in a person who has slowly and clumsily made a whole piece of cloth single-handed than in ten persons who have made a thousand pieces of cloth between them in the same time, by the aid of several cunning machines which they only half understand. To make the whole of a boat or wheelbarrow or vase with your own hands is to live again through a heartwarming triumph of early mankind's; you become a more or less conscious creator, a chuckling dominator of intractable elements and resistant forces. Little of the glee may be left if your part in making the vase be only to sift or wet the clay for somebody else to throw on the wheel. But it cannot be helped. We can no more go back, at this point in the life of our world, to be like the solitary master-potter of Omar Khayyám wetting his clay for himself in the market-place, than middle-aged men can return to the use of their first teeth or the vocabulary of the nursery. The caravan has to go on; to loiter at any distance behind is to court extinction sooner than it need come. Machinery and mass-production are our fate, and if they have taken the natural delightfulness of work out of a great deal of it, that was when the real Fall came and not when Jehovah told Adam that there was a great deal of perspiration before him.

If a Fall it has been, then all the more reason to treasure those species of work which have not been deported from Eden. They may at least keep alive in the minds of the fallen some idea of what life was like in the garden. Even Genesis does not explicitly say, though it allows us to see, what the prime joy of it was—that Adam and Eve were creators as well as creatures—God's fellow-workmen as well as pieces of his handiwork. And that joy of theirs goes on to this day wherever a painter, a writer, or any sort of artist is plying his trade at the top of his form.

In current talk about such activities, and even in the theorizing of learned men, it is commonly taken for granted that before a Shakespeare or a Leonardo begins to write or paint a Hamlet or a "Last Supper" he has already before his mind the whole thing which we now see—indeed a good deal more than we are now able to see of the unfortunate "Last Supper". The actual painting or writing is taken to be a mere transcribing of this pre-existent vision into paint or words. In one of the smallest and wisest of books about art, Professor Alexander's *Art and Material,* this grand mistake is put right. Few artists of any sort can and will tell how they do their fine things. But Mr. Alexander has divined it.

That pre-existent vision does not pre-exist at all. It comes into existence only while the technical and physical work of painting or writing goes on. To what may end by being a masterpiece an artist may come at first with a mind empty and stone-cold. It may be that "Another commonplace model to paint! " was all Raphael thought as he began the Sistine Madonna. Suppose it is so. Well, he gets his tackle out and starts. In a little while the mere feel of the brush in his hand begins to excite him; the cold engine of his mind is warmed a little; it inclines to move; there kindles in him a faint spark of curiosity about the being who is before him; the quickened mind enlivens the hand, and the brush moves more featly; eagerness is growing in all the employed faculties of the man; images, thoughts, memories, sympathies crowd in upon him till he wonders at himself, with a kind of alarm mixed in his delight—will he ever be able to keep himself up to this pitch, he is now so much above par, so strangely endowed, for while it may last, with spiritual insight and also an unwonted dexterity of hand?

With an ease and confidence that amaze him he sees, infers, conjectures new things behind the fleshen mask of the familiar model's face. A wonderful creature, this sitter! Wonderful creature, a nursing mother! A marvel, all motherhood, all humanity. "What a piece of work is a man! " So it goes on, and if he can hold long enough of the pitch of this exaltation, this mutual stimulation of spiritual and technical power, a masterpiece may come of it, a Sistine Madonna, a Hamlet, or a Giaconda, a thing absolutely new and surpassing, where nothing like it had been before—just what Adam was when first made. For we are to remember that before that exultant supernormal interaction of imaginative and technical energies began in the man, there was, of all that came afterwards, nothing existent even as a vision in the man's mind—merely the commonplace Hamlet of some old melodrama, or some average middle-class lady or well-built laundress walking about like others in Florence. As Mr. Alexander says, "The portrait proceeds, not from imaginative anticipation of the portrait that is to be executed, but from a lively and intelligent excitement, using the skilled brush-hand as its instructive organ".

Art is only work utterly unspoilt, and drudgery is only art gone utterly wrong. But there was no necessary curse on Adam in this matter of work. He went out of Eden with Rome and Athens, Venice and Constantinople to build, and with all the rest of the world to turn, if he chose, into gardens where people could knit in the sun, and workshops where they could whistle over the making of delectable implements, weapons and playthings. That was all blessing, as far as it went, whatever mess the poor fellow may have since made of his chance.

From *A Writer's Notes on His Trade*, Chatto & Windus, London, 1930 (written in 1925)

Alice Meynell

The Foot

Time was when no good news made a journey, and no friend came near, but a welcome was uttered, or at least thought, for the travelling feet of the wayfarer or the herald. The feet, the feet were beautiful on the mountains; their toil was the price of all communication, and their reward the first service and refreshment. They were blessed and bathed; they suffered, but they were friends with the earth; dews in grass at morning, shallow rivers at noon, gave them coolness. They must have grown hard upon their mountain paths, yet never so hard but they needed and had the first pity and the readiest succour. It was never easy for the feet of man to travel this earth, shod or unshod, and his feet are delicate, like his colour.

If they suffered hardship once, they suffer privation now. Yet the feet should have more of the acquaintance of earth, and know more of flowers, freshness, cool brooks, wild thyme, and salt sand than does anything else about us. It is their calling; and the hands might be glad to be stroked for a day by grass and struck by buttercups, as the feet are of those who go barefoot; and the nostrils might be flattered to be, like them, so long near moss. The face has only now and then, for a resting-while, their privilege.

If our feet are now so severed from the natural ground, they have inevitably lost life and strength by the separation. It is only the entirely unshod that have lively feet. Watch a peasant who never wears shoes, except for a few unkind hours once a week, and you may see the play of his talk in his mobile feet; they become as dramatic as his hands. Fresh as the air, brown with the light, and healthy from the field, not used to darkness, not grown in prison, the foot of the contadino is not abashed. It is the foot of high life that is prim, and never lifts a heel against its dull conditions, for it has forgotten liberty. It is more active now than it lately was—certainly the foot of woman is more active; but whether on the pedal or in the stirrup, or clad for a walk, or armed for a game, or decked for the waltz, it is in bonds. It is, at any rate, inarticulate.

It has no longer a distinct and divided life, or any that is visible and sensible. Whereas the whole living body has naturally such infinite distinctness that the sense of touch differs, as it were, with every nerve, and the fingers are so separate that it was believed of them of old that each one had its angel, yet the modern foot is, as much as possible, deprived of all that delicate distinction: undone, unspecialized, sent back to lower forms of indiscriminate life. It is as though a landscape with separate sweetness in every tree should be rudely painted with the blank—blank, not simple—generalities of a vulgar hand. Or as though one should take the pleasures of a day of happiness in a wholesale fashion, not "turning the hours to moments", which joy can do to the full as perfectly as pain.

The foot, with its articulations, is suppressed, and its language confused. When Lovelace likens the hand of Amarantha to a violin, and her glove to the case, he has at any rate a glove to deal with, not a boot. Yet Amarantha's foot is as lovely as her hand. It, too, has a "tender inward"; no wayfaring would ever make it look anything but delicate; its arch seems too slight to carry her through a night of dances; it does, in fact, but balance her. It is fit to cling to the ground, but rather for springing than for rest.

And, doubtless, for man, woman, and child the tender, irregular, sensitive, living foot, which does not even stand with all its little surface on the ground, and which makes no base to satisfy an architectural eye, is, as it were, the unexpected thing. It is a part of vital design and has a history; and man does not go erect but at a price of weariness and pain. How weak it is may be seen from a footprint; for nothing makes a more helpless and unsymmetrical sign than does a naked foot.

Tender, too, is the silence of human feet. You have but to pass a season amongst the barefooted to find that man, who, shod, makes so much ado, is naturally as silent as snow. Woman, who not only makes her armed heel heard, but also goes rustling like a shower, is naturally silent as snow. The vintager is not heard among the vines, nor the harvester on his threshing-floor of stone. There is a kind of simple stealth in their coming and going, and they show sudden smiles and dark eyes in and out of the rows of harvest when you thought yourself alone. The lack of noise in their movement sets free the sound of their voices, and their laughter floats.

But we shall not praise the "simple, sweet" and "earth-confiding feet" enough without thanks for the rule of verse and for the time of song. If Poetry was first divided by the march, and next varied by the dance, then to the rule of the foot are to be ascribed the thought, the instruction, and the dream that could not speak by prose. Out of that little physical law, then, grew a spiritual law which is one of the greatest things we know; and from the test of the foot came the ultimate test of the thinker: "Is it accepted of Song? "

The monastery, in like manner, holds its sons to little trivial rules of time and exactitude, not to be broken, laws that are made secure against the restlessness of the heart fretting for insignificant liberties— trivial laws to restrain from a trivial freedom. And within the gate of these laws which seem so small, lies the world of mystic virtue. They enclose, they imply, they lock, they answer for it. Lesser virtues may flower in daily liberty and may flourish in prose; but infinite virtues and greatness are compelled to the measure of poetry, and obey the constraint of an hourly convent bell.

It is no wonder that every poet worthy the name
has had a passion for metre, for the very
verse. To him the difficult fetter is
the condition of an interior
range immeasurable.

From *Essays*, Burns, O., London, 1921 (written in 1918)

W. Somerset Maugham

The Fragment

When you travel in China I think nothing amazes you more than the passion for decoration which possesses the Chinese. It is not astonishing that you should find decoration in memorial arches or in temples; here the occasion for it is obvious; and it is natural enough to find it in furniture; nor does it surprise, though it delights you, to discover it on the commoner objects of household use. The pewter pot is enriched with a graceful design; the coolie's rice bowl has its rough but not inelegant adornment. You may fancy that the Chinese craftsman does not look upon an article as complete till by line or colour he has broken the plainness of a surface. He will even print an arabesque on the paper he uses for wrapping. But it is more unexpected when you see the elaborate embellishment of a shop-front, the splendid carving, gilt or relieved with gold, of its counter, and the intricate sculpture of the signboard. It may be that this magnificence serves as an advertisement; but it does so only because the passer-by, the possible customer, takes pleasure in elegance; and you are apt to think that the tradesman who owns the shop takes pleasure in it too. When he sits at his door, smoking his water-pipe and through his great horn spectacles reading a newspaper, his eyes must rest with good humour sometimes on the fantastic ornamentation. On the counter, in a long-necked pot, stands a solitary carnation.

You will find the same delight in the ornate in the poorest villages where the severity of a door is mitigated by a charming piece of carving, and where the trellis of the windows forms a complicated and graceful pattern. You can seldom cross a bridge, in however unfrequented a district, without seeing in it the hand of an artist. The stones are so laid as to make an intricate decoration, and it seems as though these singular people judged with a careful eye whether a flat bridge or an arched one would fit in best with the surrounding scene. The balustrade is ornamented with lions or with dragons. I remember a bridge that must have been placed just where it was for the pure delight of its beauty rather than for any useful purpose, since, though broad enough for a carriage and pair to pass over it, it served only to connect a narrow path that led from one ragged village to another. The nearest town was thirty miles away. The broad river, narrowing at this point, flowed between two green hills, and nut trees grew on the bank. The bridge had no balustrade. It was constructed of immense slabs of granite and rested on five piers; the middle pier consisted of a huge and fantastic dragon with a long and scaly tail. On the sides of the outer slabs, running the whole length of the bridge, was cut in very low relief a pattern of an unimaginable lightness, delicacy and grace.

But though the Chinese take such careful pains to avoid fatiguing your eye, with sure taste making the elaborateness of a decoration endurable by contrasting it with a plain surface, in the end weariness overcomes you. Their exuberance bewilders. You cannot refuse your admiration to the ingenuity with which they so diversify the ideas that occupy them as to give you an impression of changing fantasy, but the fact is plain that the ideas are few. The Chinese artist is like a fiddler who with infinite skill should play infinite variations upon a single tune.

Now, I happened upon a French doctor who had been in practice for many years in the city in which I then found myself; and he was a collector of porcelain, bronze, and embroidery. He took me to see his things. They were beautiful, but they were a trifle monotonous. I admired perfunctorily. Suddenly I came upon the fragment of a bust.

'But that is Greek', I said, in surprise.

'Do you think so? I am glad to hear you say it'.

Head and arms were gone, and the statue, for such it had been, was broken off just above the waist, but there was a breastplate, with a sun in the middle of it, and in relief Perseus killing the dragon. It was a fragment of no great importance, but it was Greek, and perhaps because I was surfeited with Chinese beauty it affected me strangely. It spoke in a tongue with which I was familiar. It rested my heart. I passed my hands over its age-worn surface with a delight I was myself surprised at. I was like a sailor who, wandering in a tropic sea, has known the lazy loveliness of coral islands and the splendours of the cities of the East, but finds himself once more in the dingy alleys of a Channel port. It is cold and grey and sordid, but it is England.

The doctor—he was a little bald man, with gleaming eyes and an excitable manner—rubbed his hands.

'Do you know it was found within thirty miles of here, on this side of the Tibetan frontier? '

'Found', I exclaimed. 'Found where? '

'*Mon Dieu,* in the ground. It had been buried for two thousand years. They found this and several fragments more, one or two complete statues, I believe, but they were broken up and only this remained'.

It was incredible that Greek statues should have been discovered in so remote a spot.

'But what is your explanation? ' I asked.

'I think this was a statue of Alexander', he said.

'By George! '

It was a thrill. Was it possible that one of the commanders of the Macedonian, after the expedition into India, had found his way into this mysterious corner of China under the shadow of the mountains of Tibet? The doctor wanted to show me Manchu dresses, but I could not give them my attention. What bold adventurer was he who had penetrated so far towards the East to found a kingdom? There he had built a temple to Aphrodite, and a temple to Dionysus, and in the theatre actors had sung the Antigone and in his halls at night bards had recited the Odyssey. And he and his men listening may have felt themselves the peers of the old seaman and his followers. What magnificence did that stained fragment of marble call up and what fabulous adventures! How long had the kingdom lasted and what tragedy marked its fall? Ah, just then I could not look at Tibetan banners or celadon cups; for I saw the Parthenon, severe and lovely, and beyond, serene, the blue Aegean.

From *On a Chinese Screen,* Heinemann, London, 1922

J. B. Priestley

Youth in Disguise

The ending of Tchekhov's masterpiece, *The Cherry Orchard,* seems to me, as apparently it does to many people, rather a mistake. The play should really end when you are left with the empty stage after all the people have driven away, and you watch shutter after shutter being closed from the outside, so that you feel you are actually inside the vacant darkening house, hearing the thud of the axe in the cherry orchard. There is no more to be said and done, and the final introduction of old Firs, who has been left behind, forgotten, is an unnecessary stroke. But there is one line spoken then so poignant, so strangely significant, that for its sake alone you are perhaps ready to forgive the author his blunder and the character, that poor old crazed ghost of humanity, its intrusion. "Life", says the old man as he totters through the vacant shuttered rooms, "Life has slipped by as though I hadn't lived". Is there such a moment waiting for all of us, not when we realise that we are on the point of death, that the last page has been turned and the unseen hand is curving to write Finis, but simply when there comes crushing down upon us the knowledge that we are old, that life has slipped by? Is there such a moment lying in wait for us, inevitably springing out at last, next year, ten years hence, or whenever it may be? The question is neither Socratic nor merely rhetorical: I really wish to know; for as yet no such conviction has forced itself upon me. That may be because I am still comparatively young, yet I do not feel to be drawing any nearer to such thoughts the older I become, for as the years pass there seems more and more life stirring about me. Nothing, I feel, has slipped by so far. I take hold of the new while still refusing to loosen my grasp upon the old.

So far as my own experience goes—and I stand here willing to be corrected by those of an ampler experience—we never really feel old, not even when we say we do. The company of the very young, who happen to be callow, unduly optimistic, cocksure and so forth, may irritate us into declaring that we feel a thousand years old, but always in such instances, it will, I think, be discovered that what we really feel is a temporary advantage or disadvantage. We feel that we know more, have passed through certain stages that are still enchanting the more youthful person in our company; or we feel a temporary and accidental physical disadvantage, being shorter in the wind, less elastic, heavier and slower, but nevertheless are convinced that this is merely because we have not had much time to devote to exercise of late, and are less interested in violent exertion than we used to be; but all our former powers are there if we should really want to make use of them. I do not say that they actually are there, but only that we feel they are there. Putting it shortly, then, we can say that the situation seems to be this, that we never really feel older than other people but only different, to our advantage or disadvantage, in some particular; whereas we always do feel definitely younger than other people. The smallest boy cannot make me feel an old man, but even an moderately elderly man can make me feel a mere boy.

Indeed, now that I come to think of it, I never really feel grown up at all. Perhaps this is because childhood, catching our imagination when it is fresh and tender, never lets go of us. This was brought home to me the other night, when I had my friend the Poet staying with me. We had sat up very late, being engaged in one of those enormous rambling talks in which, as Stevenson so finely observed, "you can pass days in an enchanted country of the mind", and we suddenly found ourselves in the small hours and very hungry. So we both stole off to the pantry and stealthily plundered it. "Don't you still feel guilty", the Poet whispered through a mouthful of meat pie, "even when it is your own pantry you are raiding? " And of course, I did. Both of us had guilt written all over us. Yet it was my very own pantry, to do what I liked with, and there was nobody in the house with either the power or the inclination to say me nay. (Though even if there had been, I would not have been deterred. Only the other week-end, staying with some friends in a country house—a very hungry kind of place, not because my hosts were not bountiful but because the local air was sharpening—and finding myself still awake very late, I stole down and raided their pantry after a long and exciting search for it.) But the old habit of mind, the result of boyhood's marauding, occasional discovery and punishment, still persisted under all my new trappings. Nor shall I be glad to see it go, if it ever does go.

So, too, many a time when I am in company, I find myself suddenly still in childhood and look about me, wondering, amazed. The talk will be tremendously adult, of politics and economics and legal reform and all manner of grand affairs, and suddenly one of the greybeards present will turn to me and say: "What's your opinion Mr. Priestley? " or "Don't you agree with me, sir? " and for a second or so I will be astonished, flattered beyond belief, at being so addressed. "Great Heavens" I cry to myself, "he thinks I'm grown-up. I'm taking them in". And then, of course, I am particularly solemn and pompous in my replies, ecstatic at the sight of their sober interest, amazed that the more facetious of my elders does not wink at the rest, or that the more severe do not order me to bed. To this day there are times when, as my host passes the cedarwood box, there returns to me, even though only faintly, that thrill I had years ago when my father first handed me a cigar—a fine symbolic act this, celebrating my first article in print (I was only 18, and it was a London paper too, and paid me a guinea for it), and declaring my emancipation at one fragrant stroke. This is to be foolish, no doubt, but I wonder how many of the others who dip into the box enjoy their cigars as I do, who see so many pictures, humorous and tender, through the slow, sweet drift of the smoke? Who would condemn that boy who is almost bursting inside because he is sitting up with the adults, hearing Father and Old Johnsen settling the Balkans or putting Russia in its place; or that blushing awkward hobbledehoy who, at a kind word or a gesture, delightedly finds the title-deed of man's estate placed in his hands; who would wave them back to limbo? Not I, for one. Let them live for ever.

Perhaps they do live for ever, merely donning white wigs and painting-in wrinkles as the years pass. You may catch this everlasting child in yourself, as we have seen, and sometimes you can catch it in others, and particularly in those very near and dear to you. The sexes have an odd trick of being able to spy the child in one another. I remember that, some time ago, I was lunching in a restaurant with a friend of mine, a woman with humour and imagination, and we chanced to see four men who, having lunched, were making their way to the door, perhaps a little boisterously. They were, however, all elderly men, solid City fellows, grey and bearded. "Look at them! " my companion whispered, "aren't they just like little boys?" Perhaps I was able to see them for a moment through her eyes, her imagination capturing mine, but certainly they did look like little boys, the same attitudes, gestures, eyes, but like little boys, who were playing an elaborate game of make-believe, and had even gone to the length of whitening their hair, wearing false whiskers, and putting cushions up their waistcoats. All the marks of age were clearly there, but somehow they did not seem quite real, only something temporarily imposed or assumed through which there shone the essential boyishness. What were they feeling, I wonder, in their heart of hearts? Were there somewhere behind those ample suits of fine broadcloth, those whiskers and gold watches and bald pates and cheque-books and wrinkles, four stout lads who had just finished plundering an apple orchard or were stealing upstairs from the moonlit pantry with a ruin of pastry behind them? The whole matter is, of course, of no importance, except that if we could settle it all to our satisfaction, if we could know why one state seems real and another unreal, perhaps we should come near to uncovering the heart of this, our mystery.

From *All About Ourselves and Other Essays,* Heinemann, London, 1956

Rose Macaulay

Flower Shop in the Night

How it glows, golden lit, empty of people, mysterious and dumb, behind curved glass that is as space bending unseen, that melts into the still, thin air, guarding what seems to the deceived eye unguarded and free to the touch. Still and bright and strange, like a deserted fairyland, like Eden after its erred denizens had been ousted, like a palace garden whence queens have fled, gleams that ordered and enchanted space, blossoming like a greenhouse in the dead of night. Golden baskets are piled high with pink roses; crimson roses riot in curious jars; hydrangeas make massed rainbows beneath many-coloured lights; tall lilies form a frieze behind, like liveried, guarding angels. Among the flowers are piled exotic fruits, pears and pines and medlars, little round fruitlets from China; clusters of purple grapes, asparagus in close formation, pressed together like sardines reared on end.

It is all very lovely, this gleaming vision of the night, so still, remote and bright, entranced behind its unseen glass, as if it were a water garden deep planted in green seas, lit by the phosphorescent illumination of a thousand fish. And look, it has glass tanks of fish, coral and sea horses, softly shining in each corner, sending faint light over the flower garden from below, while brighter lights illustrate it from the high walls.

It is a scene so exquisite and so strange that it might be a mirage, to melt away before the wondering gaze. We will leave it, while it is still clear and brilliant; turn away and walk down the cold, empty and echoing street, looking not back lest that bright garden be darkened and fled like a dream before dawn.

From *Personal Pleasures,* Gollancz, London, 1935

About the Authors

BELLOC, HILAIRE, 1870-1953

Historian, poet, essayist, biographer. Born Joseph Hilaire Pierre Belloc, son of a French barrister and an English mother. Schooling in England (Birmingham); first studied mathematics at the Sorbonne, later history at Oxford. After finishing his studies he turned first to journalism but started soon to publish his first books, which, owing to his wide interests, touched almost every aspect of literature. In 1903 he became a naturalised British subject. From 1906 to 1910 Liberal Member of Parliament, and from 1911 to 1913 Head of the English Department of East London College. Together with G. K. Chesterton (q.v.) he founded *The New Witness*, a weekly in which both authors aired their views and disclosed political irregularities. "Until the death of Chesterton these two writers associated with unusual closeness in ideas, so that Mr. Bernard Shaw christened them "The Chesterbelloc" (*TCA*). Belloc has also written children's books which have become classics.

CARDUS, NEVILLE, 1889-

Music critic and writer on cricket. Born in Manchester, where he attended elementary school until the age of thirteen (see his excellent autobiography). From 1904 to 1912 he worked as messenger boy and clerk in an insurance office and continued his education by reading and studying in his spare time after work. He began to write, and his first articles appeared in 1912. He became music critic to the *Daily Citizen*, Manchester, in 1913, joined the staff of the *Manchester Guardian* in

1917, and wrote for most parts of the paper, from descriptive articles to leaders. He was assistant to Samuel Langford, the paper's music critic, and after his death became the *Guardian's* chief music critic. He has also contributed articles on cricket to the *Guardian* since 1919 and was unique in the way he reported on this English national sport. Many of these articles are considered classics and have been collected in book form. Since 1951 he has been the London music critic of the *Guardian*. He was knighted in 1967.

CHESTERTON, GILBERT KEITH, 1874-1936

Essayist, novelist, poet, critic, and journalist. Educated at St. Paul's School, London. Studied at the Slade School of Art (he later illustrated the novels of his friend H. Belloc). Worked first at reviewing books in *The Bookman*. To his work as a journalist we owe many remarkable essays, which appeared weekly and were later collected in book form. During the First World War he founded and edited (together with H. Belloc) *The New Witness* (1916-1923) and from 1925-1936 *G. K.'s Weekly*. In 1922 he was received into the Catholic Church by his friend Father O'Connor, the original of "Father Brown" the detective. During the remainder of his life he wrote mainly on religious subjects. "Stout, untidy, absent-minded, good-natured, with a tremendous sense of fun and a genius for illuminating paradox, Chesterton was one of the most popular writers of his time" (*TCA*).

CHURCH, RICHARD THOMAS, 1893-

Poet, novelist, and literary critic. Born in London, educated at Dulwich Hamlet School. Entered the Civil Service at the age of sixteen and remained a civil servant until he was forty. Apart from a book on Mary Shelley he published only poetry up to 1930. After that he published many novels and a beautiful autobiography in two volumes entitled *Over the Bridge* and *The Golden Sovereign,* which made him known to a wider public.

CHURCHILL, WINSTON LEONARD SPENCER, 1874-1965

Statesman, soldier, historian, and biographer. Son of Lord Randolph

Churchill and Jenny Jerome, an American. Educated at Harrow and Sandhurst, from where he went into the Army. He combined soldiering with journalism, took part in the Spanish campaign in Cuba and on the North West Frontier of India while on leave from his regiment. He also served under Kitchener at Omdurman. During the Boer War he was a special correspondent for the *London Morning Post,* was taken prisoner and successfully made a famous escape. He was elected a Member of Parliament in 1900 and soon rose to ministerial rank. He became successively Under-Secretary for the Colonies (1906), President of the Board of Trade (1908), Home Secretary (1910), and First Lord of the Admiralty (1911). He served in Flanders in 1916, was made Minister for Munitions in 1917, Secretary for War in 1918, and went to the Colonial Office once more in 1921. Having been defeated at the polls in 1922 and so being out of politics, he wrote a history of the First World War, *The World Crisis 1914-1918.* Elected again into Parliament in 1924, he became Chancellor of the Exchequer. After 1929, when the Labour party was in power, he devoted all his time to writing, producing among others the four volume *Life of Marlborough,* his famous ancestor. On the outbreak of the Second World War in 1939 he was again made First Lord of the Admiralty and Prime Minister the year after, in which post he remained during the whole of the war. As a result of the Labour victory in 1945 he was out of office again, but was elected Prime Minister once more in 1951, in which post he remained until his retirement in 1955. His history of the Second World War in six volumes was published from 1948 to 1950, and he was awarded the Nobel Prize for Literature mainly for this work. "It may well be that Winston Churchill's lasting reputation in letters, as well as politics, will finally rest on his magnificent, moving wartime orations. . . . That these are 'literature' in the most ancient and epic sense of the word, few who have heard or read them will deny" (*TCA*).

CONNOLLY, CYRIL VERNON, 1903-

Essayist and journalist. Educated at Eton and Balliol College, Oxford. He has written for the *New Statesman* and other journals. Founded and edited the journal *Horizon* together with Stephan Spender from 1930-1950. A member of the staff of the *Sunday Times* since 1951. An Officer of the Legion of Honour.

CONRAD, JOSEPH, 1857-1924

Master mariner and novelist. His original name was Joseph Conrad Korzeniowski. He was the son of a Polish patriot who was exiled to northern Russia with his family. The father was a poet, critic, and translator of Shakespeare. After being orphaned, Conrad was brought up by an uncle in Cracow. At the age of sixteen he went to Marseilles and to sea as a registered seaman in the French merchant navy. After gaining experience at sea he joined with three companions in using the vessel *Tremolino* for smuggling, until she was deliberately wrecked. (Some of this is recounted in *The Mirror of the Sea* and *The Arrow of Gold.*) He visited England for the first time in 1878 and sailed in various British ships in the Indian Ocean, the scene of many of his later novels (*The Nigger of the Narcissus, Shadow Line, Lord Jim, The Rescue*). He obtained his Master Mariner's certificate in 1886, the year he became a naturalised British subject. When, four years later, he commanded a river steamer in the Belgian Congo, one of his childhood ambitions was fulfilled (*Heart of Darkness*). "A passionate lover of geography, who earned the derision of his playmates by pointing to the blank 'unknown' space on the map of Africa and announcing, 'When I grow up, I shall go *there*' " (*TCA*). On one of his travels he met John Galsworthy (q.v.), who encouraged him to leave the sea in order to become a full time writer (1894). In 1896 he married an English-woman, Jessie George, and settled down in England. "Probably no stranger life-story exists than that of this man, who, a native of an inland country, spent all his youth at sea, and who, utterly ignorant of English at twenty, became not only a great novelist in that tongue, but also a supreme English stylist" (*DNB*).

DUNCAN, RONALD, 1914-

Poet and playwright. Born in Rhodesia, he was educated in Switzerland and Cambridge, England. He has farmed in Cornwall since 1947. He founded the "Devon Festival of Arts" (1953) and the "English State Company" (1955). He cooperated with Benjamin Britten and wrote some of the librettos to his operas. He edited the letters of Alexander Pope and published a selection of Gandhi's writings. Known to the wider public by his essays, which appeared first as "Diary of a Countryman" in the *Evening Standard* (London) and were later published in book form. He wrote an autobiography in two volumes entitled *All Men are Islands* and *How to Make Enemies*.

ELIOT, THOMAS STEARNS, 1888-1965

Poet, essayist, and playwright. Born in St. Louis, Missouri. Educated at Smith Academy (of Washington University), Harvard, the Sorbonne, and Merton College, Oxford. Worked first as a schoolmaster (Highgate School, London), then in Lloyd's Bank. From 1917 to 1919 he was assistant editor of the *Egoist*. In 1922 he founded his own journal, *The Criterion,* of which he was the editor until 1939 when the journal ceased. In 1927 he became a naturalised British subject and joined the Anglo-Catholic Church in the same year. Eliot paid his first visit to the United States after 18 years in 1932, where he held the post of Professor of Poetry at Harvard. It was not until 1935 that he emerged as a playwright with "Murder in the Cathedral". Many more plays followed. He was awarded the Nobel Prize for literature in 1948. His critical work includes essays on Dryden, Milton, Marvell, and Dante. He claimed that he was "an Anglo-Catholic in religion, a classicist in literature, and a royalist in politics". He also was a director of Faber & Faber, publishers.

FORD, FORD MADOX 1873-1939

Novelist and essayist. Son of the music critic Francis Hueffer. Educated at University College school, London. Collaborated with Joseph Conrad on two novels (*The Inheritors,* 1901, and *Romance,* 1903) and independently wrote two other novels. In 1908 he founded the *English Revue.* He served in the First World War and published *The Good Soldier* (1915). After the war, having changed his name to Ford, he published a series of war novels. From 1924 onward he edited the *Transatlantic Review* in Paris, to which James Joyce and Ernest Hemingway contributed. The last years of his life were spent in France and the United States.

FORSTER, EDWARD MORGAN, 1879-1970

Novelist and essayist. Educated Tonbridge School and King's College, Cambridge. Published four novels up to 1914 and then none for ten years. He visited India in 1910. During the First World War he was stationed in Alexandria, doing civilian war work. While there he contributed to the *Egyptian Mail* a number of studies which in 1923 were published as *Pharos and Pharillon.* Returning to England, he wrote criticism and *feuilletons* for different weeklies (*New Statesman, Spectator*) and also was for a short time editor of the literary part of the *Daily Herald.* Following a second visit to India in 1921 he wrote his best known novel, *A Passage to India* (1924). In 1927 he delivered the Clark Lecture at Cambridge on "Aspects of the Novel" and published a study of Virginia Woolf in 1942. He lived as a fellow in King's College, Cambridge but demonstrated "an utter freedom from stuffiness, an enviable assurance in dealing with the English literary tradition, a readiness to converse with the reader on terms of intellectual equality, and a shy humility—that famous minor tone—which is immensely pleasing and, in this assertive age, frequently moving" (Irving Howe). Forster also wrote the libretto for Benjamin Britten's opera *Billy Budd.* He received an Hon. Litt. D. from Hamilton College (U.S.A.) and was an Honorary Corresponding Member of the American Academy of Arts and Letters.

GALSWORTHY, JOHN, 1867-1933

Novelist and playwright. Educated at Harrow School and New College, Oxford. Studied law, was called to the Bar in 1890 but never practised. Instead he travelled in the Far East, mainly in merchant ships. "Journeying by sailing ship from Adelaide to South Africa, he made friends with a Polish officer who showed him a half-written novel, with which Galsworthy encouraged him to proceed. The officer's name was Joseph Conrad, the book was *Almayer's Folly,* and the meeting was the beginning of an affectionate friendship which lasted until Conrad's death" (*TCA*). Galsworthy himself started to write only in 1897, his models being the Russian novelists, especially Turgenev. He also had extensively read Dickens, Maupassant, Anatole France, and Tolstoy. The first volume of his group of novels, later called *The Forsyte Saga, The Man of Property* appeared in 1906. Galsworthy is the one English writer who has strongly influenced the opinion of foreign readers about the English character and the English way of life, in spite of the fact that the well-to-do commercial Edwardian society he portrayed has practically ceased to exist after two wars and their consequences. *The*

Forsyte Saga occupied Galsworthy for 26 years. He also wrote plays which were outspokenly critical of the existing social order. Conrad described him as a "humanitarian moralist". Having refused a knighthood, he was awarded the Order of Merit in 1929 and the Nobel Prize in 1932.

GOOCH, GEORGE PEABODY, 1873-1968

Historian. Educated at Eton. Studied in London, Cambridge, Berlin, and Paris. Liberal Member of Parliament from 1906 to 1910. President of the Historical Association and of the English Goethe Society. President of the National Peace Council 1933-1936. Editor of the *Contemporary Review* and joint editor of the *Cambridge History of British Foreign Policy* and *British Documents on the Origins of the War, 1898-1914*.

GOULD, GERALD, 1885-1936

Poet and journalist. Educated at University College, London and Oxford. Lecturer in English and Fellow of Merton College from 1909 to 1916. Taking up journalism, he was on the staff of the *Daily Herald* from 1915-1922 and of the *Saturday Review* from 1922-1926. He also wrote literary criticism, poetry, and essays.

GREENE, GRAHAM, 1904-

Novelist and essayist. Educated at his father's school and Balliol College, Oxford. From 1926 to 1930 he was a sub-editor on the *London Times*. He converted to Catholicism in 1927. He was literary editor of the *Spectator,* 1940-1941, on the staff of the Foreign Office from 1941 to 1944, and was sent on a special mission to West Africa, 1942-1943. He has travelled in the United States and Mexico—the background of some of his novels. He himself first called attention to the split character of his work—the "entertainments" and the works of serious, sombre, moral, and religious reflection. Two important influences on his writings he ascribes to the late John Buchan (Baron Tweedsmuir, 1875-1940), who was master of the spy novel, and the French novelist François Mauriac. He has been an Honorary Associate of the American Institute of Arts and Letters since 1961.

HUXLEY, ALDOUS, 1894-1963

Novelist and essayist, the grandson of the biologist T. H. Huxley. Educated at Eton and Balliol College, Oxford. He started to study medicine but had to give it up owing to an affliction of the eyes (Keratitis) which at times rendered him almost blind. This illness decisively influenced his attitude to life because, as he himself has said, it forced him back on his own resources and isolated him during his early manhood from his fellowmen. When his illness subsided he took a course in English at Oxford. In 1919 he joined the staff of the *Antheneum,* a London weekly, for which he wrote literary and musical criticism. From 1923 to 1930 he lived in Italy where many of his novels, essays, and short stories were written. Here he associated with D. H. Lawrence, and they formed a friendship which lasted until Lawrence's death in 1930. In 1934 he travelled in Central America and in 1937 settled permanently in California. "His real genius is as an essayist. . . . His novels are either a series of character sketches, or a group of essays, or simple facts, or tracts. His essays, however, are always brilliantly executed" (David Daiches).

LAWRENCE, DAVID HERBERT, 1885-1930

Novelist, essayist, and poet. Father a coal-miner, mother a school-teacher, as described in his autobiographical novel *Sons and Lovers* 1913. Educated at the High School and University College, Nottingham. Until 1911 he was a schoolmaster in a London suburb. He published his first poetry in 1909, his first novel in 1911. Some of his novels were banned on publication both in Britain and the United States. Lawrence was suffering from tuberculosis and travelled for his health in Italy, Australia, and Mexico. He returned for a short time to England but died in 1930 at Vence near Nice. "In one sense, all his stories and many of his poems are studies of the least articulate and most decisive movements of sympathy and antipathy between people . . . . He has enriched our literature with a fresh idiom of human relationships, a new way of discerning and evaluating experience . . . . He was a great lover of the visible world; and particularly a lover of flowers. . . . 'Flowery Tuscany' is surely unsurpassed, of its kind, by any writer in this century". (Desmond Hawkins)

LEHMANN, JOHN, 1907-

Poet and essayist, son of a well-known journalist and an American mother. Educated at Eton and Trinity College, Cambridge. Lived in Vienna for some years where he was a member of the Anglo-American Press Association. After his return to England, he went into publishing, first as co-worker of Leonard and Virginia Woolf (q.v.) and subsequently as their partner in the Hogarth Press. Later on he founded his own publishing firm, was founder and editor of the periodical *New Writing*, 1936-1950, and also of the literary monthly *The London Magazine*, 1954. He actively supports young poetic talents and is a member of the Council for Poetry of the British Arts Council.

LYND, ROBERT, 1879-1949

Essayist, literary critic, and journalist. Son of an Irish clergyman. Educated at the Royal Academical Institution and at Queens College, Belfast. Soon after his graduation he went to London and entered journalism. Early in his career he specialised in literary criticism. He also became literary editor of the *News Chronicle* and wrote weekly articles for the *New Statesman* over the signature "Y. Y." He was a true essayist who wrote only in this form. "If an omnibus collection could be made of the very best of the essays in his many volumes, American readers would readily understand why his reputation is so great in England" (*TCA*).

MACAULAY, ROSE, 1881-1958

Novelist, essayist, and poetess. Father a lecturer in English literature in Cambridge. Educated in Italy and Oxford. She wrote and published her first novel when still a student, and first came into prominence when she published her satirical novel *Potterism* (1920), which was in a way a precursor of Sinclair Lewis's *Babbit.* She also published three volumes of poetry, as well as studies of Milton and E. M. Forster. She belonged to the "Bloomsbury Group" of authors. One critic applied to her her own description of one of her characters in her novel *Staying with Relations*—"ironic, amused, passionless, detached, elegantly celibate . . . travelled European, a bland mocker, a rather mincing young gentlewoman".

MAUGHAM, WILLIAM SOMERSET, 1874-1965

Novelist and playwright. As his father was solicitor to the British Embassy in Paris, he spoke French before he spoke English. Educated at King's School, Canterbury, Heidelberg University, and London. He studied medicine for six years but never practised except for his year in the Lambeth slums as an intern—an experience which produced his first novel, *Liza of Lambeth.* During the First World War he served with the Red Cross and later with the Intelligence Department, out of which experience grew his spy novel *Ashenden.* After the war he travelled in the Far East and settled finally in southern France. At the outbreak of the Second World War, he was assigned to special work at the British Ministry of Information in Paris. The Nazi advance overtook him there, but he managed to reach England. In October 1940 he went to the United States, ostensibly on a visit but in all probability on a government mission. His last years were spent in the south of France.

MEYNELL, ALICE THOMPSON, 1847-1922

Poetess, essayist, and journalist. Born in London but spent most of her childhood in Italy. A convert to Catholicism, she is best known through her poems which, in England, are likened to those of Christiana Rosetti. Her prose was nearly all journalism, but her journalism was always literature. She was on intimate terms with the great poets and writers of her time: Tennyson, Browning, Ruskin, Rosetti, George Eliot, Patmore and Meredith. She and her husband rescued and cared for the poet Francis Thomson until he died. She edited various anthologies.

MILNE, ALAN ALEXANDER, 1882-1956

Novelist, journalist, and playwright. Son of a London schoolmaster. Educated Westminster School, London, and Trinity College, Cambridge. From 1903 freelance journalist and from 1906 to 1914 assistant editor of *Punch.* For his son—Christopher Robin—he wrote a series of books which have become children's classics. In 1934 he published a passionate plea against war, *Peace with Honour.* He wrote a highly successful detective story *The Red House Mystery* in 1921, and four plays of which the most successful was *The Perfect Alibi* (1932).

"Milne remains one of the best loved of contemporary English authors—for his warm and engaging verse, for his 'bland and agile' prose and for his literate and thoroughly entertaining plays. But essentially, and perhaps ironically, it is his writing for children for which readers know and love him best" (*TCA*).

MONTAGUE, CHARLES EDWARD, 1876-1928

Journalist and novelist. Son of an Irish, former Catholic priest. Educated at City of London School and Balliol College, Oxford. He joined the staff of the *Manchester Guardian* in 1890 and became chief assistant to the editor and proprietor, C. P. Scott; he also was chief editorial writer and dramatic critic for this paper for 35 years. Montague retired in 1925 to apply himself solely to writing. "As a stylist he sought for the inevitable word and was never guilty of 'journalese' or of a cliché " (*TCA*).

MORGAN, CHARLES, 1894-1957

Novelist, son of Sir Charles Morgan, an eminent civil engineer. Educated and studied at the Naval Colleges of Osborne and Dartmouth. Served from 1907 to 1913 and from 1914 to 1918 in the Atlantic Fleet and in marine stations in China. Left the service in 1913 in order to study but reenlisted at the beginning of the First World War. He was made a prisoner of war during the retreat from Antwerp and interned in Holland on parole until 1917. He later used his experiences and knowledge of the country in his novel *The Fountain* (1932). After the war he studied in Oxford and later on (1921) joined the staff of the *London Times* as assistant to A. B. Walhely, the noted dramatic critic, whom he succeeded in 1926 as the chief dramatic critic on that paper, a position he held until 1939. *Reflections in a Mirror*, the collection in book form of a series of critical essays he contributed to the *Times Literary Supplement*, were described (by Donald Stauffer) as "reflecting the sweetness, the tolerance, the freedom, the tentative judgements, the consciousness of large and spiritual issues that have made the great democracies . . . enduring". In France he was one of the most popular of English novelists; he was a Member of the French Academie and an Officer of the Legion of Honour.

NICOLSON, HAROLD, 1886-1968

Diplomat, biographer, and journalist. He grew up as his father's posts changed (Baron Carnock, chargé d'affaires in the British Embassy) in Persia, Bulgaria, Morocco, and Teheran, thereby becoming a cosmopolitan almost from birth. Educated at Wellington College and Balliol College, Oxford. He entered the diplomatic service in 1909 (Madrid, Istanbul, Teheran, and Berlin), resigned in 1929, and turned to journalism, joining the staff of the *Evening Standard*, and was later the literary editor of the *Daily Express*. He was a member of Parliament from 1935 to 1945 (National Labour) and was part of the time Parliamentary Secretary to the Ministry of Information. From 1941 to 1946 he was one of the directors of the B.B.C. The main book reviews in the *London Observer* were written by him until shortly before his death.

PHILLPOTTS, EDEN, 1862-1960

Novelist, poet, and playwright. Born in India where his father was a political agent. Educated in England (Plymouth) and studied at a dramatic school in London, which he however soon left. He then entered the offices of the Sun Fire Insurance Co. and served there from 1880 to 1890, working during daytime in the office and writing by night. Afterwards he lived by writing alone and lived in Exeter. He wrote many novels, some good mystery stories, and several successful plays.

POWYS, LLEWELYN, 1884-1939

Essayist and novelist. Son of a parson, educated at Sherborne School and Cambridge. Two of his brothers, John Cowper Powys and Theodore Francis Powys, were also well known English novelists. He lectured in America in 1909 but fell ill of consumption, and for health reasons spent the years 1914 to 1919 in Kenya as manager of a ranch. From 1920 to 1925 he worked as a journalist in New York, where he married Alyse Gregory, an American who had been managing editor of *The Dial*. From then on he lived in England but had to go to Switzerland because of his recrudescent consumption. He died there in 1939. His works include many stories and sketches with an African background.

PRIESTLEY, JOHN BOYNTON, 1894-

Novelist, dramatist, essayist. Son of a schoolmaster. Educated at Bradford and Trinity Hall, Cambridge (English literature) but had been writing since he was sixteen. Indeed, he helped to keep himself at Cambridge by his writings—mainly essays. He worked in London as reviewer and critic. His first and greatest literary success was his novel *The Good Companions* (1929). Apart from novels, he wrote plays and comedies, also the biographies of George Meredith and Thomas Love Peacock as well as *The English Comic Characters, A Short History of the English Novel,* and *Literature and Western Man.* During the Second World War he was, next to Churchill, the most popular speaker on the B.B.C. "He was often called the unofficial voice of the common people of Britain" (*TCA*).

QUENNELL, PETER COURTNEY, 1905-

Critic, poet, biographer. Educated at Berkhamstead Grammar School and Balliol College, Oxford. Wrote critical essays for various periodicals like the *New Statesman, Life and Letters, Criterion,* and others. In 1930 he was appointed Professor of English Literature at Tokyo University. Returning to London, he edited the *Cornhill Magazine* from 1944 to 1951. He is best known for his biographies of *Byron, Caroline of England, John Ruskin* and a critical volume on *Baudelaire and the Symbolists.* "He is that rare thing among contemporary writers, a conscious stylist" (*TCA*).

ROWSE, A. L., 1903-

Historian. Born and educated in Cornwall and Christ Church, Oxford. Fellow of All Soul's, Oxford. He was the Trevelyan Lecturer in Cambridge for 1958. *The Elizabethans and America* was one of his most successful publications.

SACKVILLE-WEST, EDWARD CHARLES, 1901-1965

Novelist and literary and musical critic. Educated at Eton and Christ Church, Oxford. He was an expert pianist and studied during his school years with Irene Sharrer, the wife of his tutor in Eton. Musical critic of the *Spectator* in 1924 and on the staff of the *New Statesman,*

1926-1927 under the then literary editor Desmond MacCarthy. Lived long in Germany and France and translated Rilke's *Duineser Elegien* into English.

SAMPSON, GEORGE, 1873-1950

Scholar, elementary school teacher, headmaster, and inspector of schools. Could not attend any school owing to illness up to the age of eleven. Had to leave school for the same reason when he was sixteen. Trained to be a teacher. He was appointed headmaster and also inspector of schools for the London County Council at the age of thirty-seven. In 1921 he published *English for the English,* a book in which he advocated and pleaded for improved teaching of the English language. This work has been very influential and has been reprinted many times. Sampson combined his teaching activities with the writing of criticism. He also edited the works of Berkeley, Burke, Newman, Thomas More, George Herbert, Emerson, Keats, Coleridge and Hazlitt. His main work was the one-volume condensation of the *Cambridge History of English Literature* (1941).

SAYERS, DOROTHY, 1893-1959

Writer of detective stories, playwright, and translator, an expert on the literature of the Middle Ages. Educated at Somerville College, Oxford, she was one of the first women to receive an Oxford degree. She worked for some time as a copy writer in a London advertising agency and utilised the experience she gained there in one of her first detective stories, *Murder Must Advertise.* She also wrote a number of religious plays. "The Christian faith", she has said, "is the most exciting drama that ever staggered the imagination of man—and the dogma *is* the drama". She also translated the whole of Dante's *Divina Comedia* into English.

SCOTT, CHARLES PRESTWICH, 1846-1932

Journalist. Educated at Manchester and Corpus Christi College, Oxford. Joined the staff of the *Manchester Guardian,* was made its editor at the age of 25, and was editor-in-chief of the paper from 1872 to 1929 when his son succeeded him. The way he dealt in his paper with the important problems of the times (the struggles of the dockers in 1889, those of the miners in 1893 and the engineers in 1897) prepared the public for the great constructive reforms of the two liberal regimes of the twentieth century in England. During the Boer War the paper stood by its unpopular opposition to the war—incurring heavy financial losses—with the courage and integrity which were (and are) typical of the way highly controversial subjects are treated in this paper. Scott was a liberal Member of Parliament from 1895-1905. During the First World War he supported Churchill and Lloyd George. He also influenced considerably the discussions leading to the treaty with Ireland in 1921. In order to guarantee the quality and independence of the paper, he paid himself only a modest salary and used accruing money to accumulate a reserve for that purpose. He paid democracy the compliment of assuming that it was open to reason. "He raised a honorable but unknown newspaper to a leading position and made it a moral force in world politics" (*TCA*).

SHAW, GEORGE BERNARD, 1856-1950

Dramatist and journalist. Educated at Wesley College, Dublin. His real education, however, came from a thorough grounding in music and painting, gained at home through his mother and by omnivorous reading. From 1871 to 1876 he worked as a cashier in a Dublin land agency, but threw up his job, joined his mother in London, and tried to make a living by writing. He produced five novels, every one of which was promptly rejected. In 1885 he made use of his musical knowledge by working as a music critic under the pseudonym of Corno di Bassetto for the *Star* and further wrote book reviews for the *Pall Mall Gazette* (1885-1888). He was also dramatic critic for the *Saturday Review* (editor Frank Harris). In 1882 he became a socialist and joined the Fabian Society in 1884. His first play was published in 1892 but was not performed until 1904. The long prefaces introducing many of his plays are virtually tracts driving home the message the plays are intended to convey. He was awarded the Nobel Prize for Literature in 1925 and used the money to found the "Anglo-Swedish Literary Foundation" for the translation of Swedish literature into English. He left the residue of his estate for the institution of a British alphabet of at least forty letters. He wrote of himself: "I have had no heroic adventures. Things have not happened to me: on the contrary it is I who have happened to them; and all my happenings have taken the form of books and plays. Read them, or spectate them; and you have my whole story".

SPENDER, JOHN ALFRED, 1862-1942

Journalist. Educated at Bath and Balliol College, Oxford. He worked first as a journalist and became editor of the *Morning News* in 1886. In 1892 he joined the influential *Westminster Gazette* (liberal) of which he was editor-in-chief until 1922. His political influence was considerable.

STARK, FREYA, 1893-

Travel writer. Born in Paris, educated privately in Italy, at Bedford College, and the London School of Oriental Studies. "An imaginative aunt who, for my 9th birthday, sent a copy of the *Arabian Nights,* was, I suppose, the original cause of the trouble" she writes in the preface of *The Valleys of the Assassins.* She is an accomplished linguist. Visited Syria in 1927 and later explored the interior of Arabia and out of the way parts of Persia. In England she is called "the little Gertrude Bell". During the Second World War she did propaganda work among the Arabs for the British government and founded the "Brotherhood of Freedom" which was meant to prepare the Arabs for independence. She lives in Treviso in Italy.

STRACHEY, GILES LYTTON, 1880-1932

Biographer, essayist, and critic. Educated at Liverpool and Trinity College, Cambridge. He worked for the *Spectator,* for which he wrote reviews and articles. Together with E. M. Forster, J. M. Kaynes, Virginia Woolf, and Roger Frey he belonged to the so-called "Bloomsbury Group". He soon started to write historical biographies in a form which has been called "the agnostic biography" (Clifford Bower-Shore). Virginia Woolf maintained that he had turned to biography because he was in doubt about his own creative abilities.

TREVELYAN, GEORGE MACAULAY, 1872-1962

Historian. Son of the well-known historian Sir G. O. Trevelyan and grand-nephew of Macaulay. Educated at Harrow School and Trinity College, Cambridge. Was Professor for Modern History at Cambridge from 1927 to 1940 and Master of Trinity College from 1940 until his death. He was convinced that history should be interesting as well as sound. "The best that can be said of me", he said in an autobiographical essay, "is that I tried to keep up to date a family tradition as to the relation of history to literature, in a period when the current was running strongly in the other direction towards history exclusively 'scientific', a period therefore when my old fashioned ideas and practice have had, perhaps, a certain value as counterpoise" (*Clio, a Muse*). His books have always had many interested readers in England.

WOOLF, LEONARD SIDNEY, 1880-1969

Historian, political essayist. Son of a barrister. Educated at St. Paul's School and Trinity College, Cambridge (*Classics*). He passed the Civil Service examination in 1904 and went into the Ceylon Civil Service— part of the time in charge of a district (1904-1911). Returning to England, he joined the Fabian Society and the Labour Party. He published two reports on international government. In 1918 he began writing for the *New Statesman* and was literary editor of *The Nation* from 1923 to 1930. Together with his wife, Virginia Woolf, he started the Hogarth Press, an amateur publishing business, and published modern authors (K. Mansfield, T. S. Eliot, E. M. Forster) in small editions printed on hand presses. Hogarth Press became one of the most distinguished publishing firms in England. (John Lehmann was at one time a partner in the firm.) Woolf's main writings were on international politics and foreign policy. He also published an excellent and very human autobiography.

WOOLF, ADELINE VIRGINIA, 1882-1941

Novelist, critic, and essayist. Daughter of Leslie Stephen, the well known writer. Educated at home. In 1912 she married Leonard Woolf (q.v.) with whom she founded the Hogarth Press in 1917. Their home was the centre for a group of writers and artists, the so-called Bloomsbury Group, of which E. M. Forster has said: "The atmosphere of her home is saturated with all that is finest and mellowest in English culture and letters—all the wealth of thirty generations of humour and thought and splendid leisurely living". Her writings were influenced by Joyce and Proust; the theories of William James, Bergson, and Freud also helped to shape her work. Her critical essays covered almost the entire range of English literature. She was also one of the most eloquent champions of women's rights in England (*A Room of One's Own, Three Guineas*). She committed suicide during the Second World War.